Heating

RSES

# Electric Heating

The HVACR Training Authority

ISBN-13: 978-1-61607-047-2
ISBN-10: 1-61607-047-1

## TABLE OF CONTENTS

**Lesson 1**
Heating with Electricity . . . . . . . . . . . . . . . . . . . . . . . . . . . . . . . . . . . . . . . . . . . . . . . . . . . . . . . . . . . . . . . 1

**Lesson 2**
Resistance Heating . . . . . . . . . . . . . . . . . . . . . . . . . . . . . . . . . . . . . . . . . . . . . . . . . . . . . . . . . . . . . . . . . . 25

**Lesson 3**
Heat Pumps . . . . . . . . . . . . . . . . . . . . . . . . . . . . . . . . . . . . . . . . . . . . . . . . . . . . . . . . . . . . . . . . . . . . . . . 45

**Lesson 4**
Radiant Heating Systems . . . . . . . . . . . . . . . . . . . . . . . . . . . . . . . . . . . . . . . . . . . . . . . . . . . . . . . . . . . . . 63

**Lesson 5**
Duct Heaters and Furnaces . . . . . . . . . . . . . . . . . . . . . . . . . . . . . . . . . . . . . . . . . . . . . . . . . . . . . . . . . . 103

**Lesson 6**
Baseboard and Unit Heaters . . . . . . . . . . . . . . . . . . . . . . . . . . . . . . . . . . . . . . . . . . . . . . . . . . . . . . . . . 137

**Lesson 7**
Radiant Heat Installation . . . . . . . . . . . . . . . . . . . . . . . . . . . . . . . . . . . . . . . . . . . . . . . . . . . . . . . . . . . . 157

**Lesson 8**
System Control Devices . . . . . . . . . . . . . . . . . . . . . . . . . . . . . . . . . . . . . . . . . . . . . . . . . . . . . . . . . . . . . 175

**Lesson 9**
Electric Furnaces . . . . . . . . . . . . . . . . . . . . . . . . . . . . . . . . . . . . . . . . . . . . . . . . . . . . . . . . . . . . . . . . . . 203

**Lesson 10**
Duct Heaters. . . . . . . . . . . . . . . . . . . . . . . . . . . . . . . . . . . . . . . . . . . . . . . . . . . . . . . . . . . . . . . . . . . . . . 211

**Lesson 11**
Multi-Step Controllers (Part 1) . . . . . . . . . . . . . . . . . . . . . . . . . . . . . . . . . . . . . . . . . . . . . . . . . . . . . . . . 233

**Lesson 12**
Multi-Step Controllers (Part 2) . . . . . . . . . . . . . . . . . . . . . . . . . . . . . . . . . . . . . . . . . . . . . . . . . . . . . . . . 249

**Lesson 13**
Electronic Sequencing Control. . . . . . . . . . . . . . . . . . . . . . . . . . . . . . . . . . . . . . . . . . . . . . . . . . . . . . . . 255

**Lesson 14**
Decentralized Electric Heating Systems . . . . . . . . . . . . . . . . . . . . . . . . . . . . . . . . . . . . . . . . . . . . . . . . 263

**Lesson 15**
Electric Boilers . . . . . . . . . . . . . . . . . . . . . . . . . . . . . . . . . . . . . . . . . . . . . . . . . . . . . . . . . . . . . . . . . . . . 289

**Appendix**
Student Supplement

## INTRODUCTION

Congratulations on your decision to further your education and career by participating in an RSES training course!

This book belongs to you. It is your primary learning tool, and should serve you well as a source of reference in the future. Feel free to write in your book, and make notes as needed in the page margins. Note that the information contained in RSES training courses reflects "standard" trade practices in the U.S. Some infomation may not be in compliance with regulatory codes in your area. Be aware that *local codes always take precedence.*

RSES comprehensive training courses cover all aspects of the HVACR service industry, beginning with basic theory and extending to complex troubleshooting. Training courses can be conducted by local Chapters, corporate training facilities, or through self-study. RSES training course series include refrigeration and air conditioning, electricity, controls, heating, heat pump, and the RSES Technical Institute Training Manuals.

Continuing education units (CEUs) are issued only to those students who participate in an instructor-led course. Some courses have been recognized by North American Technician Excellence (NATE). Technicians who successfully complete one or more of these instructor-led courses may receive credit toward renewing their NATE certification.

In addition to its renowned training course manuals, RSES offers a selection of CD-ROMs, DVDs, and other materials intended to assist technicians enhance their skills and knowledge of the HVACR industry. Membership in RSES offers a wide variety of benefits. For membership information and to find out more about RSES, please visit the RSES Web site at www.rses.org.

## OBJECTIVES

**Lesson 1**
**Heating with Electricity**
- Explain the difference between conventional combustion heating and electric heating.
- Define the following terms: *power, resistance, current, voltage*.
- State Ohm's Law.
- Solve mathematical equations that contain the following units of measurement: *volts, amperes, ohms, watts, Btuh*.
- Describe the characteristics of a good resistor.
- Explain the difference between direct thermostat control and relay control.
- Explain the difference between direct current and alternating current.
- Explain the difference between single-phase power and three-phase power.
- Explain the difference between line voltage and low voltage.

**Lesson 2**
**Resistance Heating**
- Identify different types of electric heating elements.
- List and describe the different types of electric heaters.
- Explain the different approaches to central electric heating systems.
- Identify the different types of electric heaters used for space heating in commercial and industrial applications.
- Demonstrate how to size a makeup air unit.
- Explain how insulated cable and wire are used for melting snow and ice.

**Lesson 3**
**Heat Pumps**
- Describe the basic operation of a heat pump.
- Name the different types of heat pumps, as classified by the source of heat and the medium to which heat is dispersed.
- Explain the difference between packaged units and split-system units.
- Demonstrate how to calculate the coefficient of performance for a heat pump.
- Explain how heat pumps are rated for efficiency.
- Describe how, when, and why auxiliary heat is used with heat pumps.

**Lesson 4**
**Radiant Heating Systems**
- Explain how various types of electric radiant heaters operate.
- Describe infrared snow-melting systems.
- Select high-intensity electric infrared heaters to fit given applications.
- Size electric infrared heaters to heat buildings.
- Design spot heating systems using electric infrared heaters.

## Lesson 5
### Duct Heaters and Furnaces
- Explain the proper installation of electric duct heaters and furnaces.
- Define the key technical terms used in electric heating.
- Install ductwork for electric duct heater and furnace systems.
- Explain electrical wiring applications.
- Describe the safety controls required for electric duct heaters and furnaces.

## Lesson 6
### Baseboard and Unit Heaters
- Install electric baseboard, floor, ceiling, and unit heaters properly.
- Demonstrate proper wiring techniques.
- Perform start-up and pre-operational inspections and routine maintenance for electric unit heaters.

## Lesson 7
### Radiant Heat Installation
- Install electric infrared heaters.
- Install natural convection heaters.
- Install radiant ceiling panels.
- Lay out an in-floor radiant heating system.
- Describe how floor coverings affect performance.
- Determine cable spacing.
- Wire an in-floor electric heating system, and correctly install the thermostat.

## Lesson 8
### System Control Devices
- Adjust the heat anticipator on a thermostat.
- Calibrate different kinds of thermostats.
- Check out and troubleshoot control systems.

## Lesson 9
### Electric Furnaces
- Explain the general characteristics of electric furnaces.
- Describe sequencer operation.
- Start up, operate, and adjust electric furnaces.
- Check electric heater operation.

## Lesson 10
### Duct Heaters
- Install duct heaters.
- Explain contactor power circuitry.
- Install and maintain air flow switches for duct heaters.

## Lesson 11
### Multi-Step Controllers (Part 1)
- Explain the function and operation of cam-operated electric heat multi-step controllers.
- Explain the function and operation of pneumatic electric heat multi-step controllers.
- Explain the function and operation of solid-state electric heat multi-step controllers.

**Lesson 12**
**Multi-Step Controllers (Part 2)**
- Describe the operation of multi-stage electronic heat thermostats and controls.
- Describe the operation of electronic electric heat multi-step controls.

**Lesson 13**
**Electronic Sequencing Control**
- Describe the function and operation of multistage electronic heat sequencing control systems.
- Explain the difference between single-zone and multizone control systems.

**Lesson 14**
**Decentralized Electric Heating Systems**
- Describe different types of decentralized heating systems.
- Explain common methods used to control baseboard heaters.
- Define cross control.
- Discuss the advantages and disadvantages of ceiling cables.
- Devise a spacing arrangement of infrared heaters to radiate a required space.
- Explain common methods used to control infrared heaters.

**Lesson 15**
**Electric Boilers**
- Explain the functions of electric boilers used for space heating.
- Explain the functions of electric boilers used for steam humidification.

# Heating with Electricity

## ENERGY FOR HEATING

There are at least two methods used to heat buildings with electricity. This Lesson is concerned primarily with the method called *electric resistance heating*. The other method, the *heat pump*, is discussed in another Lesson. Before we examine the process of converting electrical energy into heat, let's compare electric heating with the more traditional method of combustion heating with fossil fuels.

### Combustion heating

In combustion heating, "packaged" energy in the form of fuel is brought to the house and released during burning, as shown in Figure 1-1 on the next page. Coal is stored in a bin. Oil is kept in a tank. Gas may be stored on the premises in a tank under pressure, but usually comes from underground mains. Whatever the form, burning fuel produces wastes. They must be removed from the premises. Coal and coke, for example, contain non-combustible minerals that form ashes. All fuels, when burned, yield gases that must be vented to the outside.

The "packaged" energy that is stored in fuel is converted into heat when the fuel burns. Burning is the simple process of rapid oxidation that begins when the fuel is heated to its ignition temperature in the presence of air (which contains oxygen). Various means of heating fuel to its ignition point are used, depending on the fuel and the type of heater or burner. The heat of the fire is transferred by convection and radiation to the walls of the combustion chamber and flue passages, and then to the air or water that carries the heat in ducts or pipes to various parts of the house. In room heaters, the heat often is delivered directly to the room air from the heated surfaces of the combustion chamber.

The heat output of any fired heating unit depends on how much fuel it burns. Each heating fuel produces a well-defined measure of heat for each measure of fuel. For example, burning one cubic foot of natural gas provides about 1,000 Btu. A gallon of oil or a pound of coal also gives a certain amount of heat, depending on the type and grade.

Combustion heating equipment generally is rated by heat output in Btu per hour. To select the proper size of heating unit, the contractor must know how much heat, in Btu per hour, is required—that is, how much heat is needed every hour to replace that lost from the space. The heating appliance, the burner, and the associated controls, pipes, fittings, tanks, etc., are designed or sized for the amount of fuel that must be burned to meet the demand of the application.

### Electric heating

In essence, the same is true of electric heating. But the "fuel" for electric heating is not delivered in tangible quantities, such as gallons, pounds, or cubic feet. Electricity comes to the home at a certain voltage and frequency, usually 240 volts, 60 Hertz. These are factors of its heat-producing capacity. Electricity is sold by the watt-hour or kilowatt-hour. Each watt-hour of electricity produces an equal amount of heat. The size of the electric

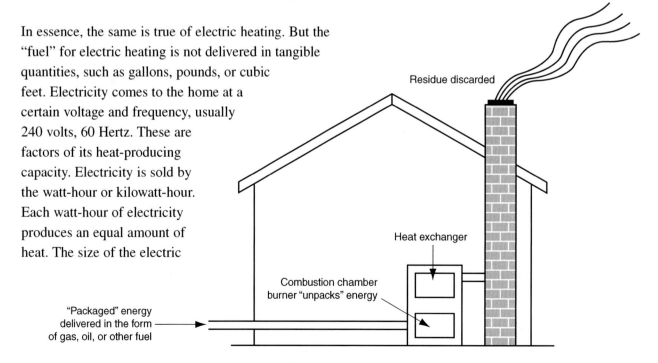

FIGURE 1-1. *"Packaged" energy is "unpacked" through combustion*

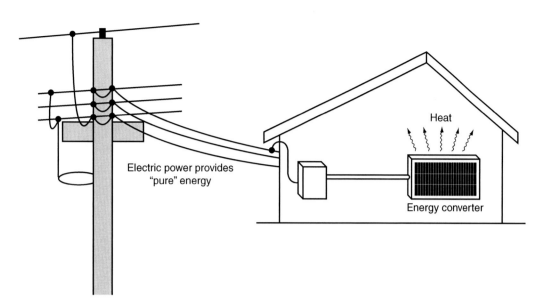

**FIGURE 1-2.** *Electric heating leaves no waste*

resistance heating unit is given in watts, which may be converted directly to
Btu per hour.

Unlike combustion heating, electric heating leaves no residue. As shown in
Figure 1-2, energy in the form of electricity flows into the house through wires.
There are no wastes. All the energy expended is converted into heat. This is why
electricity is called "pure" energy. (Combustion of fuel may take place, but the
fire is far away, in the boilers of the power plant.)

In this country, 80% of electric power is produced by steam-driven generators.
In steam electric plants, the heat from fuel combustion is converted into
electrical energy through these generators. They are driven by high-velocity
jets of steam directed against turbine blades. In hydroelectric plants, the energy
of falling water drives a turbine or some other form of water wheel. The turbine
or wheel, in turn, drives the generator, which produces electricity.

Heating an entire home requires a lot of heat—many thousand Btu per hour—
regardless of the heating method. Electrically, the load during heating season
may be a continuous 10 to 20 kilowatts. This is not an unusual or especially
large load. However, when compared with that of a typical home using only
lighting and normal appliances, there is quite a difference.

What does this mean? Several things, depending on your concern. Homeowners
new to electric heating will find their electric bills to be higher than they are
used to. More of the cost of the home is in the electrical system. There are other
economic considerations, but these should be evaluated in terms of the benefits.

To the HVACR contractor, electric heating means taking several other considerations into account, including:

- checking the available electrical service carefully before selling a job

- knowing additional building codes and regulations

- installing bigger, more complex, heavier electrical systems, and more equipment and controls.

The utility company, of course, must provide completely satisfactory electrical service. This may involve such changes as increased generating capacity, new regulations allowing higher voltages, and different electrical rates.

Surely, people need to know more about the use of electricity in heating systems. The rest of this Lesson is about the fundamentals of electricity, especially as related to making and controlling heat.

## FUNDAMENTALS OF ELECTRICITY

### Basic terminology

Voltage, current, and resistance are three basic factors to consider in understanding how heat is produced from electricity. (There is a further explanation of these forces in the "Background Information" section at the end of this Lesson.)

*Voltage* (E) is the force or electrical "pressure" that produces an electric current. The unit of voltage is the volt (V). *Current* (I) is the movement or "flow" of electrons in an electrical conductor. The measure of current is the ampere (A). To maintain a current, the conductor must be a complete circuit from one pole to the other of the voltage source. *Resistance* is the property or force within a conductor that opposes current. It is like friction. One unit of resistance is the ohm ($\Omega$). Voltage *produces* current, resistance *opposes* it.

Electric current depends on the voltage and resistance in a circuit. Varying one or both will change the current. Higher voltage results in higher current. Higher resistance results in lower current. This is, in effect, what *Ohm's Law* says. Ohm's Law is the basic law of electricity. It states that current equals the voltage divided by the resistance:

$$\text{current} = \frac{\text{voltage}}{\text{resistance}}$$

Or, in abbreviated form:

$$I = \frac{E}{R}$$

Using common values, 120 volts applied to a resistance of 10 ohms produces a current of 12 amperes:

$$\frac{120 \text{ V}}{10 \text{ }\Omega} = 12 \text{ A}$$

If you know the magnitude of two of the three elements of electricity—voltage, current, or resistance—you can calculate the third by using Ohm's Law. These equations apply:

$$E = I \times R$$

$$R = \frac{E}{I}$$

$$I = \frac{E}{R}$$

Cover symbol for unknown value...

...and remaining two are in correct relationship:

$$E = I \times R \qquad \text{or} \qquad I = \frac{E}{R} \qquad \text{or} \qquad R = \frac{E}{I}$$

**FIGURE 1-3.** *Using the basic Ohm's Law circular chart*

Figure 1-3 shows a basic Ohm's Law circular chart. Simply cover one of the values with your thumb, and the other two are shown in their correct relationship. For example, if you know voltage and current, you can solve for resistance by holding your thumb over the unknown value (*R*). What remains— the *E* over the *I*—tells you that you must divide the voltage by the current to obtain your answer.

Here's a practical example. Even the copper from which most electrical wire is made has some resistance. There is always a little voltage loss, or "drop," in the wiring to an appliance. How many volts are used to push 10 A of electric current to a heater 50 ft from the electric service, as shown in Figure 1-4? Use the equation $E = I \times R$. This job calls for 100 ft of wiring,

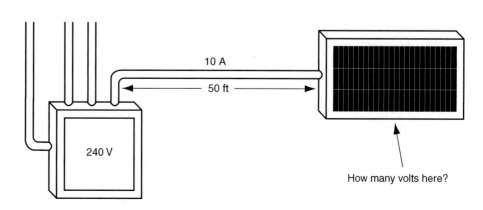

**FIGURE 1-4.** *An example of determining voltage*

since the wire must go to the heater and back. A hundred feet of AWG No. 14 copper wire has a resistance of about 0.25 Ω. The current times the resistance equals the voltage:

$$10 \text{ A} \times 0.25 \text{ } \Omega = 2.5 \text{ V}$$

In general practice, a 3% voltage drop is the maximum recommended in conductors to an appliance. The 10-A example is within the standard limits, both for 120 and 240 V. A 15-A 120-V load under the same conditions would not be. A larger wire, such as No. 12—which has a lower resistance—would have to be used. Table 1-1 shows various wire sizes and their resistances.

### Heating power

An electric current produces heat in any conductor that has resistance. If the amount of resistance in the conductor varies, the current, or the voltage causing it, will vary directly the amount of heating. Thus, in order to produce heat with electricity, we use *resistance heating elements*—conductors that have a definite, relatively high resistance. We apply a voltage to induce an electric current in the resistance element, and the element produces heat, as shown in Figure 1-5.

Heat-producing elements are placed in all sorts of fixtures and appliances. Examples include ranges, ovens, hair dryers, room heaters, furnaces, and hundreds of others. Remember that resistance elements are made to produce a specified or rated amount of heat when connected to a specified voltage. The amount of heat is usually stated in watts. The selection and some aspects of the application and installation of a heating unit are based on—among other things—the amount of heat that it produces.

| Wire size AWG No. (American Wire Gauge) | Conductor diameter, in. | Area, circular mils | Resistance, ohms per 1,000 ft at 68°F |
|---|---|---|---|
| 14 | 0.0641 | 4,110 | 2.52 |
| 13 | 0.0720 | 5,180 | 2.00 |
| 12 | 0.0808 | 6,530 | 1.59 |
| 11 | 0.0907 | 8,230 | 1.26 |
| 10 | 0.1019 | 10,380 | 1.00 |
| 9 | 0.1144 | 13,090 | 0.7925 |
| 8 | 0.1285 | 16,510 | 0.6281 |
| 7 | 0.1443 | 20,820 | 0.4981 |
| 6 | 0.1620 | 26,240 | 0.3952 |
| 5 | 0.1819 | 33,090 | 0.3134 |
| 4 | 0.2043 | 41,740 | 0.2485 |
| 3 | 0.2294 | 52,620 | 0.1971 |
| 2 | 0.2576 | 66,360 | 0.1563 |
| 1 | 0.2893 | 83,690 | 0.1239 |
| 0 | 0.3249 | 105,600 | 0.09825 |

**TABLE 1-1.** *Wire sizes and resistances*

The heat output of a resistance heating unit is stated in watts. The *watt* (W) is the product of voltage and current. It is a measure of electric *power* (P). In electrical terms, watts equal volts times amperes, or $P = E \times I$. Thus, 240 V and 10 A in a resistance element produce 2,400 W of electric power:

$240\text{ V} \times 10\text{ A} = 2{,}400\text{ W}$

100% of the electric power is converted directly into heat, with every watt producing 3.413 Btu per hour (Btuh).

To convert watts to Btuh, multiply by 3.413:

$100\text{ W} \times 3.413 = 341.3\text{ Btuh}$

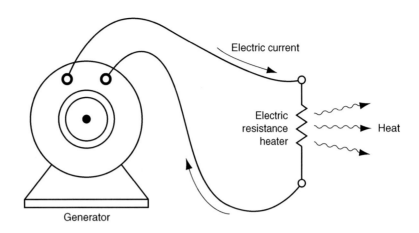

**FIGURE 1-5.** *A resistance element producing heat*

Conversely, to change Btuh to watts, multiply by 0.293:

$34.13\text{ Btuh} \times 0.293 = 10\text{ W}$

These relationships are two of the bases of sizing the heating equipment and the electrical system of an electrically heated building.

Once again, you can calculate any one of the basic elements of electricity—current, voltage, resistance, or power—if any two others are known. Find the proper equation in the "Ohm's Law wheel" in Figure 1-6.

The heating effect of a current is intended in a heating element, but in the wires that transport electricity it is both wasteful and dangerous. For instance, consider the earlier example of a 100-ft No. 14 wire to an electric heater. It wastes 25 W of power. You can calculate this by using the equation $P = I^2R$. The resistance of 100 ft of No. 14 wire is 0.25 $\Omega$, and the current draw of the heater is 10 A, so:

$10^2\text{ A} \times 0.25\ \Omega = 25\text{ W}$

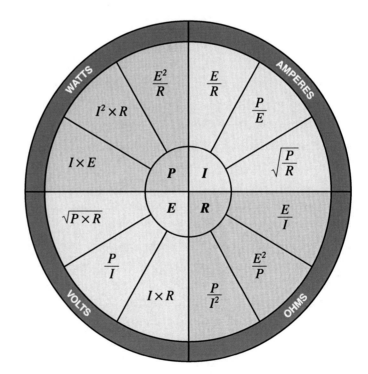

**FIGURE 1-6.** *Ohm's Law wheel*

Too much heating of this kind may occur in wiring that is too small. Resistance per foot of wire increases as the size of the wire decreases. The insulation on overheated wires deteriorates faster than it should. With extreme overheating, there is an immediate danger of fire. For these reasons, the current-carrying capacities of conductors are limited by electrical codes.

This brief review of fundamentals shows how important it is to know how to handle the relatively large amounts of electricity used in electric heating. In one form or another, these basic rules must be followed and applied if you are to select proper wiring materials, controls, and heating units.

## HEATING RESISTORS

The fact that a current through a resistance produces heat suggests a question: What are the necessary qualities of a resistance heating material?

Conductors, such as copper or aluminum, are selected purposely for their *low* resistance. They are used to conduct electricity and prevent excessive voltage drop or power loss. Heaters, on the other hand, are selected intentionally for their relatively *high* resistance. Their function is to convert electricity into heat. Efficient heating resistors have these important characteristics:

- durability at operating temperature

- high resistance per unit of length and thickness

- stable resistance with change in temperature.

To deliver heat at a useful rate, a heating element must operate at a temperature considerably above that of its surroundings. If it is primarily a radiant heating element, it may operate red or nearly white hot. If it melts, softens, or oxidizes and corrodes rapidly at operating temperature, it will soon fail and have to be replaced. *Durability* is a necessity.

A wire resistor must have the correct total resistance in a limited length to produce a specified amount of heat. You can go only so far in concentrating a large length of wire into the small space inside a heater. The cost and weight, too, may be prohibitive. Therefore, a wire with *high resistivity* (resistance per unit of length and thickness) tends to be the best heating resistor. Iron, nickel, chromium, manganese, and alloys of these metals have high resistivities. They are the ones commonly used in heater elements.

The heat output of a material can be varied in several ways. You can change its composition, which changes its resistivity. Or you can change its size and/or length. In a 4,000-W 240-V heating element, for example, the resistance must be almost 14½ Ω. To get this resistance in a No. 18 copper wire would require more than 2,000 ft of wire! A nichrome (nickel chromium alloy) wire in the same size, however, needs to be only 35 ft long. To get the same heat from double the surface area, and more length, you could use a No. 12 nichrome wire about 140 ft long. Note the wire size comparison in Figure 1-7.

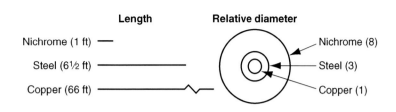

**FIGURE 1-7.** *Relative wire sizes for equal resistance*

Resistance change with temperature is a characteristic of all materials that conduct any current at all. This change in a heating resistor should be as small as possible. Remember that heat output varies directly with resistance ($P = I^2R$). Therefore, an element that exhibits *stable resistance* is desirable. One whose resistance varies widely in different temperatures could be difficult to control.

The wire resistors most commonly used are various alloys of nickel and chromium. Some of them contain a little iron and some small amounts of other elements. They have *high resistivity*, a *stable resistance* (low change) with temperature, and a *high durability*. Clay, glass, rubber, and other high-temperature materials can be filled with bits of conductive material to yield very high resistances. The are useful where the length or fine diameter of a wire would not be practical.

Any of these may be formed or fabricated to be convectors, radiant heaters, or both. The relative proportions of heat given off by convection and radiation are determined by surface temperature and area. A low-temperature radiant heater operating at 80 or 90°F requires a large area from which to radiate 1,000 W. A very hot element, such as a fused-quartz tube (infrared), can operate at 4000°F. It is less than an inch in diameter and only inches in length, but emits the same 1,000 W. A convector might operate at roughly 150°F. However, it requires fins or convolutions of some kind, which provide a much greater surface area exposed to circulating air in a confined space.

## CONTROLLING ELECTRICITY AND HEATING

As in all other types of heating systems, a thermostat is used to control temperature in an electric heating system. This is a distinct advantage to homeowners. It is convenient, automatic, efficient, and economical. Modern living has taught us to expect these things. But thermostatic control of electric heat causes certain problems that should be recognized, too.

The rate of heat input must be controlled to match the heat loss of the space or its occupants. The problem is that heat losses on the coldest days far exceed those of the warmest days. There are any number of conditions possible in between. Heating equipment must be sized to handle the coldest extremes, when it is required to provide the most heat. On all warmer days, the heat output of the system must be reduced somehow. This is one dimension of electric heating control.

The other is controlling the electricity itself. Electric power not only operates the control equipment. It also generates all the heat required to heat a house. There are large currents to control. This calls for heavy-duty control equipment, which may be cumbersome or inaccurate.

### Making heat input match loss

The voltage-current-wattage relationships reviewed earlier suggest that one of three methods may be used to achieve continuous heat input to match the steady rate of heat loss:

- varying the current

- varying the resistance of the heating element

- varying the applied voltage.

Varying the *current* with a rheostat or variable reactor is hardly practical. At 15% load, for example, a rheostat would have to dissipate about 1½ times as much heat as the heating element. This heat would have to be wasted or stored. Otherwise, it would overheat the house.

Means of varying the *resistance* of the heating element would complicate its construction. This would increase the cost by an unreasonable amount. This is particularly true for small room units, such as baseboard convectors and heating panels.

Varying the *voltage* with a variable transformer or autotransformer is possible. But such equipment in the larger sizes required for adequate capacity is relatively high in cost. None of these by itself is practical enough to be used widely today.

However, there is an approach to voltage control that is being used economically today. It is a *two-stage* system that switches from 120 to 240 V when heating demand increases by a certain amount. With this method, the 120-V supply is intermittently switched on during the lightest heating periods. It produces only up to 25% of total capacity, because half-voltage yields only a quarter of full-voltage heat output. When demand reaches 25%, the 120-V element is on continuously. In colder weather, the controller switches over from 120 to 240 V for a time, and then back to 120 V. The length of time that the 240 V operates varies with the demand. Thus, total heat output in each complete low-high-low cycle can equal the heat requirement of the space.

But even this is far short of continuous heat input exactly matching the heat loss. Actually, it is a better example of the control method that is almost universally used. That is, the power is switched on and off at intervals when less than total heating capacity is needed. This ON/OFF method of control tends to produce temperature variations, or *swings*, in the space. Assume that the heating element is fast, has very low mass, and is directly exposed to the room air and surfaces. If so, the heat input to the space increases very rapidly during the ON period. But it falls to nearly zero a few moments after the heat shuts off. There is not enough heat "stored" in the element to spread out the delivery of heat (generated during the ON period) over a significant part of the OFF period.

This is like trying to drive a car at *exactly* constant speed by alternating your foot between full throttle and the brake. Such jobs require a good controller. It must be able to respond so fast that the temperature will not have time to rise excessively during the ON period nor to fall too far in the OFF period.

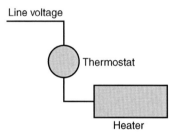

**Direct control by thermostat**

### Direct control and relay control

Switching the heater power on and off may be done *directly* by the thermostat. It can also be done through a *relay* controlled by a thermostat. Both methods are shown in Figure 1-8. In either case, the large electric current requires a heavy-duty switch. If the heavy-duty contacts are in the thermostat, it will have to be massive enough to operate them. The more massive the thermostat, the slower its response. The slower the response, the more the temperature variation in the room.

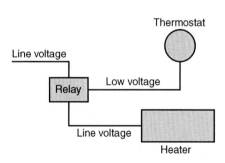

**Thermostat control using relay**

**FIGURE 1-8.** *Using thermostats for direct control and relay control*

In addition, a thermostat is sensitive to heat—wherever the heat comes from. The resistance of the switching contacts and other current-carrying parts inside the thermostat case may be small by ordinary standards. But it can be *large enough* to generate a significant amount of heat inside the thermostat when the heating element current flows through it. Such heat may make the thermostat control point *drift* (become inaccurate). Suppose, for example, that the resistance of a switch is as small as 0.004 Ω. In controlling a 4,000-W heater, it must intermittently carry 16 A. Since $P = I^2R$, the heat generated by the switch inside the thermostat—and felt by its sensing element—may be as much as *one watt*. This causes the thermostat to "feel" that the room is warmer than it really is. Such heavy-duty thermostats are not suitable for comfort control. They are fine for many other uses, however.

The most practical way to get sensitive, accurate, fast-acting control in a comfort heating system is to use a low-voltage control system. Low-voltage thermostats control the heater by operating an intermediate switching relay. Thus, the thermostat itself is not affected by the heater's electrical load.

## BACKGROUND INFORMATION

### Visualizing an electric current

The generally accepted mental picture of electricity is based on the theoretical structure of an atom. As illustrated in Figure 1-9, you can visualize an atom as a nucleus, with one or more electrons moving in orbits around it. The nucleus consists of one or more positively charged *protons* and usually one or more electrically neutral particles called *neutrons*. They contribute to the total mass of the atom. Each orbital electron is a negative charge. It is equal in magnitude and opposite to the positive charge on a nuclear proton.

An atom is electrically *neutral* if it has an equal number of positive charges and negative charges. But an electron in the outer orbit, or *valence* band, can be dislodged. It becomes a "free" electron, separated from the atom. The atom is then left with a net positive charge. A free, "vagrant" electron may attach itself to an atom. It presumably lodges in the valence band, and creates a net negative charge on the atom.

The conception of positive and negative charges on atoms is illustrated in Figure 1-10. Note the "holes" imagined to be left by the loss of electrons from the atoms along the copper wire connected to the positive (+) terminal of the cell. Also note the extra electrons that represent the negative (–) atoms in the other wire.

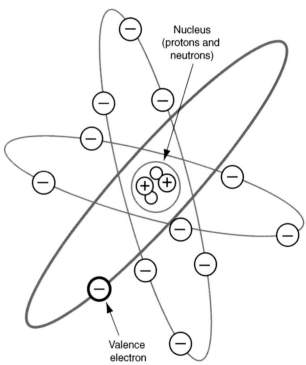

**FIGURE 1-9.** *Picturing the structure of an atom*

From these ideas, scientists derive our present notion of electron flow or electric current in a solid wire. When you try to visualize *current*, think of it as a migration of electrons through the wire from the negative to the positive terminal of the source. The transfer of electrons must take place as if by microscopic "bucket brigade." Imagine a line-up of atoms or molecules, each receiving an electron with the left hand and passing another on to the next atom with the right. More literally, imagine a moving electron penetrating the outer shell of an atom and lodging there. Another electron is

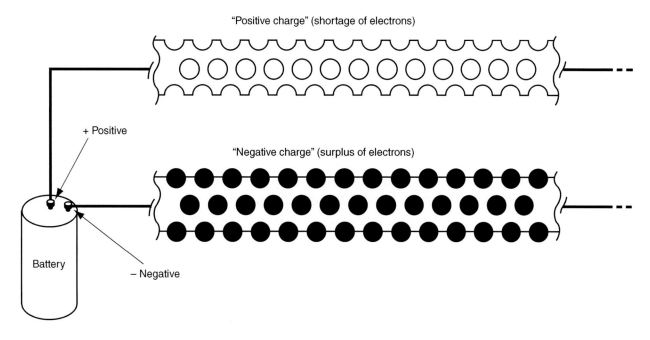

**FIGURE 1-10.** *Positive and negative charges*

dislodged as a result. It migrates to an adjacent atom, as shown in Figure 1-11. The process then repeats itself over and over again, like a chain reaction.

Water flow may seem to be a natural analogy. But the "flow" of electrons is certainly not like a flow of water rushing through a pipe. Such a misconception can be fatal, literally. What makes current flow is *voltage*. It is often called by some other name, such as *potential difference*. Think of voltage as the driving force, somewhat like *pressure* of air or water, behind the electron flow. Or think of it as the combination of a positive charge on one terminal of the source, and a negative charge on the other. Voltage in an electric circuit must be *generated*. This is done by electric generators or dynamos, or by other means such as batteries, fuel cells, and thermocouples.

Two factors contribute to the force of voltage. On the one hand, there is the mutual repulsion of electrons, which

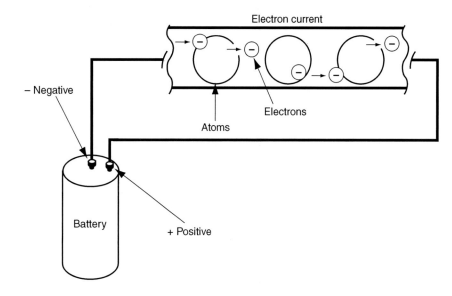

**FIGURE 1-11.** *Electron "migration" from atom to atom*

tends to make electrons rush away from each other. (Like charges repel each other, so positive charges also tend to move apart, if free to move.) On the other hand, the mutual attraction between *unlike* charges creates a kind of pull. It draws electrons toward the positively charged atoms.

There is an older notion that current flows from positive to negative. It is still used, often in textbooks and electrical diagrams, as a *convention*, a kind of accepted representation or customary code. It was a long time before the modern conception of atomic structure and electron behavior was developed. Now, it frequently seems convenient to continue using the older understanding of electron flow—and, in fact, the positive-to-negative notion fits some situations very well.

Consider an instance in which a material carrying positive charges is physically transferred. The arc stream of a direct-current arc welder is a good example. Molten rod metal, positively charged, is attracted to the negative workpiece. It is fused to it—and, in the process, neutralized.

A good mental picture of electron flow also helps to pin down our notion of flow rate. *Flow rate* is measured in amperes. Electricity flows at a constant speed, about the same as that of light. If the velocity is constant, there is only one variable left to account for differences in flow rate. It is what electrical engineers often refer to as *current density*. This factor—that is, how many free electrons are hitchhiking along from atom to atom—determines the amperes of current, the *quantity* of electricity passing through the circuit per unit of time. Quantity of electricity is usually measured in coulombs. A *coulomb* can be defined roughly as "so many electrons or positive charges." The number is unimaginably large. It is so astronomical that it is hardly worthwhile trying to remember it. (But, if you're curious, one coulomb is 6,240,000,000,000,000,000 electrons!) Nevertheless, one ampere equals one coulomb of electricity passing a point in the circuit every second.

### What resists current and produces heat?

In recent years, low-temperature research has shown that some "good" conductor metals become "super" conductors at temperatures near absolute zero (–459.6°F). But at normal temperatures, something in even the best conductor opposes the flow of electric current. We can't see it or measure it directly, but we can measure it indirectly, and give it a name: *resistance*. As you know, the unit of resistance is the *ohm*.

Here's one way to imagine resistance. Recall our mental picture of one electron being dislodged from its mother atom when another electron, looking for a home, moves in. In one metal (say, iron or nickel) the valence electrons are more reluctant to leave the family circle than they are in other metals (such as copper, a very good conductor). The tighter these babies of the family "cling to the mother's apron strings," the harder the "punch" needed to make them let go.

The apron string in the analogy represents the intra-atomic energy that holds the electron in orbit. When the electron is driven from the atom, some of this intra-atomic energy is released. This energy, evidently in the form of molecular motion, can be measured as heat. Every material offers more or less resistance to the flow of electrons. This characteristic is called its *resistivity*. Metals generally have a relatively low or moderate resistivity. Therefore, they are fair or good conductors. Non-metallic materials are usually insulators, or at least poor conductors, because they offer high resistance to electric current. High resistance, then, you may think of as "tight apron strings," or strong forces holding the outer electrons in orbit. The stronger these forces—that is, the higher the resistivity—the more energy is released as heat when current flows through the material.

The apron string image and the binding force story may not offer the best or most accurate way to visualize electrical resistance. If another kind of comparison would be more helpful, think of resistance as acting very much like mechanical friction. Consider, for instance, the effects of friction on an unlubricated bearing. Friction:

- retards rotation of the shaft

- absorbs turning force (torque)

- generates heat.

You can think of electrical resistance in much the same way. Resistance:

- limits electric current

- uses up voltage pressure

- converts the energy into heat (measured in watts).

### What's a watt?

A *watt* (W) is a unit of power (defined as the rate of delivering energy). It is the same *kind* of unit, although not the same size, as one Btu per hour (Btuh) or one horsepower (hp) and can be converted directly into either one:

1 W = 3.413 Btuh
1 Btuh = 0.293 W
1 hp = 746 W

When an electric motor is rated at 1 hp, it means that the motor can do mechanical work at a rate of 33,000 foot-pounds per minute (ft-lb/min). If it were 100% efficient, it would be *converting electric energy into mechanical work at a rate of 746 watts*. In electric heating, electricity is converted into heat rather than mechanical work. The "motor" is the resistance heating element. Furthermore, a resistance heating unit *is* 100% efficient. *All* the electrical energy passing through it is converted to heat. Figure 1-12 illustrates the difference between mechanical work and electric heating.

To compute the energy conversion rate in watts, you multiply current by voltage. There are several other ways of figuring wattage, but this one most directly answers the question: What is the rate of heat supply?

Stating the relationship in mathematical terms, you get the basic equation for power (P), or heating rate:

$$P = E \times I$$

This equation says, in effect: "The heavier the flow rate (in amperes) at a given supply pressure (in volts)—or conversely, the higher the pressure behind a given flow— the higher the rate (in watts) at which energy (heat) is being supplied and used." An electric utility company, for example, might want to know the load demand on the distribution lines in kilowatts. To find out, they might use this equation. A contractor may wish to know the rating of a thermostat or relay switch in watts. To find out, he too uses this equation. For example, a common electric heating contact rating is 22 A. At 240 V, this will handle 5,280 W, or about 5 kilowatts (kW):

$$240 \text{ V} \times 22 \text{ A} = 5,280 \text{ W}$$

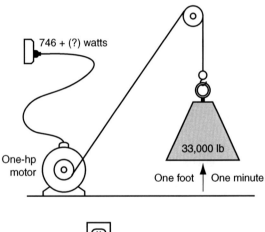

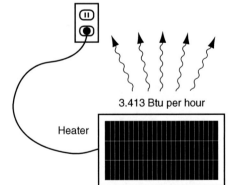

**FIGURE 1-12.** *A comparison of mechanical work and electric heating*

Here's another way to look at it. Resistivity limits current. This requires a certain voltage at the source to get a certain current at the point of use. The greater the resistance, the greater the pressure required to produce a given flow. Current and resistance together, then, imply the required voltage pressure. That is stated in Ohm's Law as $E = I \times R$ (voltage equals current times resistance).

Combining the two equations, you can write $P = E \times I$, and then substitute $I \times R$ for $E$. You then have $P = (I \times R) \times I$, or $P = I^2R$. In other words, the current squared times the resistance equals the power (in watts). This form of the basic statement is especially appropriate when determining the power loss in transmitting electricity.

A No. 14 copper wire, 100 ft long, has a resistance of about 0.25 Ω. Maintaining a current of 10 A in this conductor wastes about 25 W, which are dissipated along the wire as heat:

$$10^2 \text{ A} \times 0.25 \text{ Ω} = 25 \text{ W}$$

### Direct current and alternating current

So far, this Lesson has discussed some of the elementary aspects of electricity only as they relate to direct current. A few words should be said about alternating current. *Direct current* (dc) always flows in one direction in an electric circuit. It flows from the negative to the positive terminals of the source, if you are tracing electron movement.

*Alternating current* (ac) is a little different. The voltage and current induced in the armature of an ac generator actually reverse polarity and direction periodically. The power is fed to the terminals and the outgoing power lines directly from the armature windings. Consequently, ac voltage and current in the external circuit reverse direction and polarity periodically or cyclically. At one instant, a terminal of the generator is positive, but a fraction of a second or half-cycle later, it is negative. In a 60-Hz power supply (the most commonly used), each cycle of one complete rise and fall of the voltage in one direction and one rise and fall in the other takes place in $\frac{1}{60}$ second. Figure 1-13 at the top of the next page illustrates the difference between ac and dc. Since this Lesson considers only *resistance circuits*, you can conclude that everything in this Lesson applies to ac as well as dc. Reactances, which are factors in ac circuits with coils and capacitors, do not affect electric resistance heating circuits.

### Single-phase and three-phase supply

Most homes receive single-phase alternating current. If the single-phase supply voltage is 110 V, there is only one circuit breaker or fuse needed. This is because one side of the line is neutral or grounded. If the single-phase voltage is 208 or 240 V, two circuit breakers or fuses are needed. This is because neither side of the line is grounded. In single-phase supply circuits, both lines are 110 V above ground.

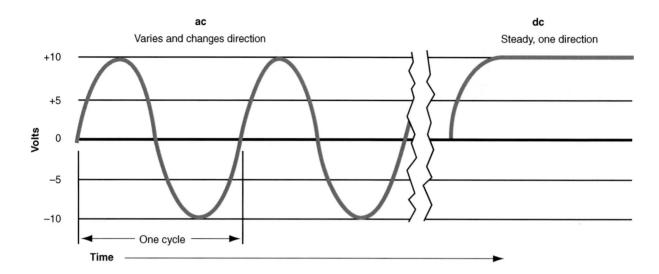

**ac**
Varies and changes direction

**dc**
Steady, one direction

**FIGURE 1-13.** *A comparison of alternating current and direct current*

Alternating current is sent over transmission and high-voltage distribution lines in three-phase mode to many large commercial and industrial users. Three-phase power is common simply because it is quite efficient to generate and use. There is nothing mystical about it, but wiring practices and appliances used with it must be more complex. As a rule, the complexities are not worthwhile unless a lot of power is involved.

Occasionally, a commercial or industrial electric resistance heating installation employs three-phase power. One or two basic points must then be kept in mind. Three-phase power is carried over three wires, connected to the source (generator or transformer) so that they make up three pairs of conductors. One conductor is always common to two pairs. The rated voltage appears between the two wires in each pair: A to B, B to C, and C to A, as shown in Figure 1-14. The generator (or transformer) has three sets of coils. They are located physically so that they act like the coils of three inter-connected generators. They are running at the same speed, but out of step with each other.

For electric resistance heating, individual heater elements are powered separately. Each is powered from one of the three phases or pairs of conductors. (This amounts to the same as having three separate single-phase power supplies). This triple system raises the following consideration. If the loads represented by individual heaters are relatively large, they should be divided among the three phases. The current demands among the three conductors should be balanced as evenly as possible. Conductor A carries the current of phase A-B and C-A, conductor

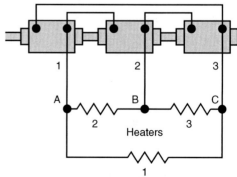

**FIGURE 1-14.** *Heater elements supplied by three-phase power*

B carries the current of B-C and A-B, etc. Total currents in individual conductors should not differ much from one to another. As a general rule, the current draw on three-phase electrical equipment should be within 10% on all three phases.

In single-phase power, the wattage is determined by multiplying the voltage times the amperage ($W = V \times A$). In three-phase power, the wattage is calculated by multiplying the voltage times the amperage times 1.732 ($W = V \times A \times 1.732$).

In 208 or 240-V three-phase supply circuits, one line is 110 V above ground and the other line may be 110 or 240 V above ground. This depends on which line is used and the type of supply circuit. In 480-V supply circuits, the lines are 277 V above ground. Since none of the three conductors in a three-phase circuit is grounded, all three must be protected by fuses or circuit breakers. Another Lesson discusses some practical problems in connection with grounding and circuit protection.

### Line voltage and low voltage

In the utility industry, *low* voltage refers to utilization as opposed to distribution voltages. More specifically, it refers to voltages from 110 up to 600 V. (For residential service, 240 V is usually the maximum.) *High* voltage is used in transmission or primary distribution lines. Also, it is sometimes used for very large motors and similar industrial loads, up to 5,000 or 6,000 V. Table 1-2 lists common service voltages.

In the temperature control industry, particularly, and sometimes in connection with other applications, the utility's *low* voltage is referred to as *line* voltage. This is the voltage of the power supply to the building. *Low* voltage in control circuits usually is defined as 30 V or less, or as 24 V nominal.

| Nominal line voltage | Probable service voltage | Nominal motor rating | Motor operating range |
|---|---|---|---|
| 120 | 114 to 126 | 115 | 103 to 126 |
| 208 | 197 to 218 | 200 | 180 to 220 |
| 240 | 228 to 252 | 230 | 207 to 253 |
| 277 | 265 to 288 | 277 | 250 to 305 |
| 480 | 456 to 504 | 460 | 437 to 506 |
| 2,300 | 2,185 to 2,415 | 2,200 | 1,980 to 2,420 |
| 4,160 | 3,950 to 4,370 | 4,000 | 3,600 to 4,400 |

**TABLE 1-2.** *Common service voltages*

Transmission and distribution voltages are stepped down to the required line voltage through transformers, as shown in Figure 1-15 on the next page. The low voltage used in temperature control circuits also is obtained from line voltage through a transformer.

There are a few points to watch in working with low-voltage temperature control circuits, especially with regard to transformers. Often, the transformer supplying a control device (a relay, for example) is built into the device. This is especially common in control relays and control center panels. However, the installer may find it necessary to mount and wire a separate transformer as part of the control system or for related purposes.

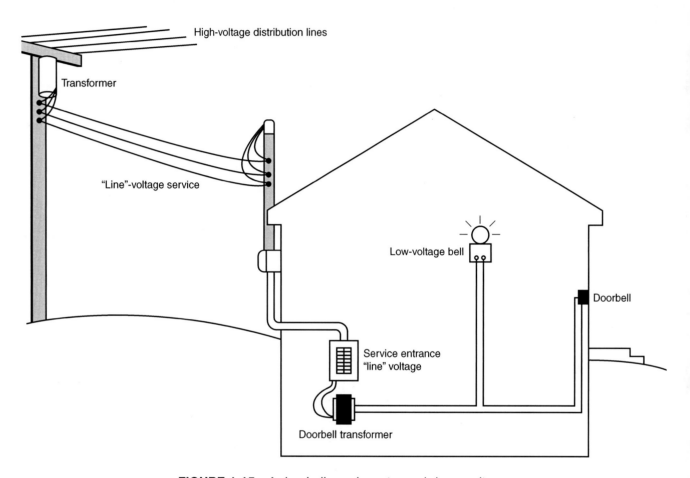

**FIGURE 1-15.** *A doorbell requires stepped-down voltage*

1.      Name two methods generally used to heat buildings with electricity.

2.      Name one advantage of heating with electricity.

3.      Is 10 to 20 kilowatts considered an unusually large load for electrically heating a home?

4.      What is *current*?

5.      What term is used for the force that opposes current in an electric circuit?

6.      What is the basic equation stated by Ohm's Law?

7.      What is the maximum recommended voltage drop between an appliance and the power source?

8.      What happens when current flows through a conductor that has resistance?

9.      What unit of measurement is used for the heat output of an electrical heating unit?

10.     What is the wattage of a 240-V circuit with a current of 20 A?

11.     What is the Btuh equivalent of one watt?

12.     What is the Btuh of a 240-V circuit with a current of 20 A?

13. What metals are most commonly used for resistors in electric heaters?

14. Name three methods of varying the heat output of a fixed circuit.

15. What is meant by a "two-stage" system?

16. How do low-voltage thermostats control heaters?

17. A neutral atom has an equal number of _____ and _____.

18. What makes current flow?

19. What happens to the current-carrying ability of an electrical conductor when its temperature drops?

20. What is the ft-lb/min rating for a 1-hp electric motor?

21. What is the resistance of an AWG No. 14 copper wire 100 ft long?

22. Do voltage and current in an alternating current circuit reverse polarity?

23. Why is it necessary in 208 or 240-V single-phase electric resistance heating to protect both lines by fuses or circuit breakers?

24. Why is three-phase power common?

25.     For electric resistance heating, individual heater elements are powered separately, each from one of _____ phases.

26.     Why is it necessary in electric resistance heating to protect all three phases by fuses or circuit breakers?

27.     What is considered "low" voltage for control circuits?

28.     Transmission and distribution lines are stepped down to the required voltages for home heating through the use of _____.

# Resistance Heating

## HEATING ELEMENTS

Any electrical conductor with a resistance produces heat when an electric current passes through it. The quantity of heat produced depends on how much resistance there is in the conductor, and on the applied voltage and current flow. Most common heating elements are metals or metal alloys, which are durable electrical conductors. They can be manufactured in the appropriate form with a predetermined resistance. Other elements are made of glass or rubber. They are combined with other materials to make them conduct electricity and produce radiant heat.

Electric heating elements in general are small in mass. They tend to heat and cool quickly unless they are encased in or attached to materials of greater mass. Heat transfer can take place by conduction, convection, and radiation. In many cases, elements are designed so that one method predominates. Thus, they are called *radiant heaters* or *convectors*, depending on how they deliver the most heat.

### Open wire and ribbon elements

Wire elements are either straight or coiled, wrapped around porcelain forms, strung in frames, or completely enclosed, as in heat lamps. Ribbon elements are usually wrapped on a flat insulating material and then used with or without a

25

covering. Figure 2-1 on the next page shows a closeup of the open wire elements in a duct heater.

### Screw base elements

Open heating elements of many shapes have been developed over the years. Among the first were the cone-shaped and straight porcelain elements with screw bases, shown in Figure 2-2. They were typically used in portable heaters.

### Fixed elements

Many variations of the open wire heating element are permanently installed in appliances. They are replaceable, but usually only by competent service technicians. Such elements are often found in bathroom wall heaters and other radiant heaters. Figure 2-3 shows a single hairpin element heater.

### Encapsulated elements

Another type of element used in electric heaters is the *encapsulated*, or completely encased element. The outer sheath is ceramic or metal. It protects the resistance wire from physical damage, corrosion, and deterioration. Electrical insulation between the resistance wire and outer sheath makes the element electrically neutral. Rigid encapsulated elements sometimes have heat-dissipating fins. The fins increase the rate of heat transfer to the surrounding medium—air, water, etc. They can be made in straight lengths or curved shapes for a wide range of applications. This type of element is used in stoves, radiant and convective heaters, and water heaters.

Another version of the encapsulated element is flexible. It is covered with a plastic insulation that will withstand heat. These are known as "low-temperature" cables, and do not exceed 2.75 watts per foot. Some have a lead sheath over the insulation. Typical applications include:

- ceiling cable

- ice-melting cable

- greenhouse bed-heating cable

**FIGURE 2-1.** *Open wire elements in a duct heater*

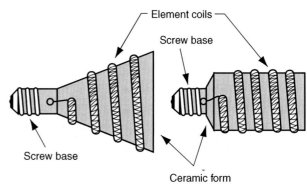

**FIGURE 2-2.** *Screw base elements*

■ wraparound frost-protection cables for water pipes.

Reflectorized infrared bulbs (commonly used in heat lamps), quartz tube elements, and other sources of infrared radiant heat find a wide range of applications for *spot* heating. Figure 2-4 shows a quartz tube radiant heater. The infrared rays are similar to visible light, so reflectors can project and focus the heat. Infrared rays can travel through air without losing much heat to the air—a characteristic that makes infrared heating desirable for certain kinds of heating applications.

Making accurate heat loss calculations is important for all types of heating and cooling installations. But accurate heat loss or load calculations are even more important for electric heating, since it generally has a higher operating cost than other kinds of heating. Obviously, a properly sized system will operate at a lower cost. This is especially true in states that have not only a commercial demand charge, but a residential demand charge as well.

## TYPES OF HEATERS

Electric heaters are made in a great variety of types and styles, and often are classified by location or installation method. Among the many types of heaters are:

■ portable heaters

■ wall-mounted heaters

■ ceiling heaters

■ baseboard heaters

■ floor-inserted heaters.

There are many other kinds of electric heating units, and new ones appear frequently. This Lesson cannot cover them all. The examples and illustrations included here are only representative.

CHROMALOX, WIEGAND INDUSTRIAL DIVISION OF EMERSON ELECTRIC CO.

**FIGURE 2-3.** *Single hairpin element heater*

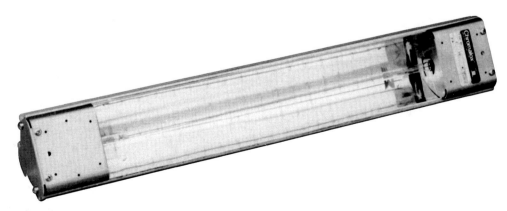

CHROMALOX, WIEGAND INDUSTRIAL DIVISION OF EMERSON ELECTRIC CO.

**FIGURE 2-4.** *Quartz tube radiant heater*

### Portable heaters

*Portable* heaters are commonly used for supplementary heating and outdoor spot heating. They can be either radiant or convective. They vary greatly in size and heat output, beginning at about 500 W. Early portable heaters had a screw-in heating unit mounted in the center of a metal reflector. The heating unit itself was an open wire coil on a ceramic core. The reflector directed most of the heat toward the subject, since radiant heat can be reflected in much the same way as light.

In more modern heaters, the element and reflector are often built into attractive cabinets. The open-wire elements still are used, but in many new arrangements. They are sometimes strung between insulators on a frame. Encapsulated elements, too, are popular in modern portable heaters.

A familiar sight in basements and recreation rooms is the portable forced-air heater. A fan or blower in the cabinet blows air over the heating element and into the room. Figure 2-5 shows an electric forced-air unit heater. Ceramic electric heaters also are used as a source of portable electric heat.

Another type of portable heater is the plug-in liquid-filled radiator with electric heating elements inside. The radiator and the liquid it contains form a relatively large mass. Thus, this type of heater does not heat up as quickly as some others, nor does it cool as fast when turned off. This tends to level the heat output. Some portable heaters are controlled by built-in thermostats. Others have manual ON/OFF switches, or no switch at all. The latter simply are plugged in or unplugged as needed. Some have a built-in safety switch that turns power off if the heater tips over.

Another type of portable electric heater is the infrared spot heating lamp. They are used to focus warmth in a concentrated area. They have a variety of uses:

- heat therapy treatment of strained muscles

- providing heat for people working in a cold area

- keeping food hot on a serving table

- clustered in paint shops to quick-dry paint.

**FIGURE 2-5.** *Forced-air unit heater*

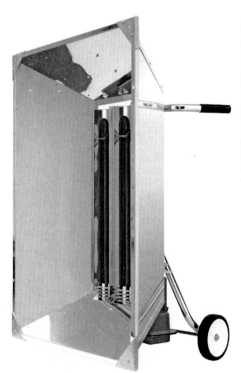

**FIGURE 2-6.** *Portable infrared heater*

Infrared lamps and heaters can heat a subject without heating much of the surrounding air. This makes them useful outdoors and in large, open, hard-to-heat indoor areas. They are used by garage mechanics, athletes on the bench, and people relaxing on the patio at home. To receive heat, the subject must be directly in front of the heater. These heaters may have a timer for automatic control. The timer cycles the heater on and off, or controls day and night schedules. Figure 2-6 shows a "rollaround" portable infrared heater.

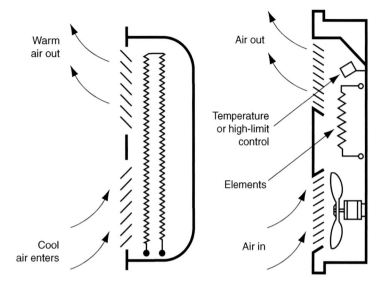

**FIGURE 2-7.** *Wall-mounted convectors*

### Wall-mounted heaters

*Wall-mounted* heaters, both radiant and convective, are similar to portable heaters. The major difference is that the wall-mounted units are permanently installed and supplied from an individual branch circuit of the electrical system.

*Radiant* wall heaters warm people and objects in their direct line of radiation. Some secondary heat is given off as warm air rising from the heater. Such heaters offer the advantage of instant concentrated heat. This makes them useful in bathrooms, entryways, and other areas where quick warmth is desired. They should be installed so that nothing will block the heat rays from the desired heating target or area. They must be able to "see" the heating target in order to heat it.

Wall-mounted warm air *convectors* offer the advantage of circulating the air throughout the room, thereby distributing warmth throughout the space. Fan or blower models give more positive circulation and more rapid heat distribution. Both types are shown in Figure 2-7. For best results, convectors should be installed where the circulation of air to the room will not be blocked. They should be placed so that fan motor and air movement noise, if any, do not affect the normal sound level.

Wall heaters are usually equipped with either wall-mounted or cabinet-mounted thermostats, whichever best fits the application. Approved heaters are equipped with a limit switch, which will shut down the heater and prevent overheating if air flow stops for any reason. Figure 2-8 shows a commercial-grade electric wall heater.

MARLEY ENGINEERED PRODUCTS

**FIGURE 2-8.** *Forced-air wall heater*

Hazardous location electric convection heaters are also available. They are used in areas with the potential for flammable gases or vapors, such as petroleum refineries, chemical manufacturers, dry cleaning plants, aircraft hangars, and fuel servicing areas. The utility pump house heater shown in Figure 2-9 is suitable for some hazardous locations.

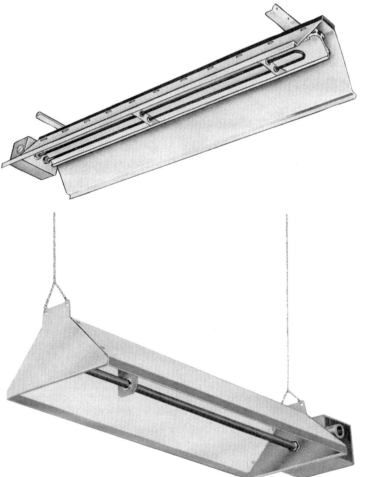

**FIGURE 2-9.** *Utility pump house heater*

MARLEY ENGINEERED PRODUCTS

### Ceiling heaters

*Ceiling* heaters appear in many different styles and types:

- embedded cable radiant heaters

- radiant panels

- combination heating and lighting units.

The embedded ceiling heating system is installed during building construction. Common ceiling heating cable is a continuous length of insulated resistance wire. It is pre-cut by the manufacturer to a specified heat output (wattage). As with other electric heating systems, ceiling cable system design starts with determining the amount of heat required in each room. This determines the amount of heating cable needed. From the length of cable, spacing for the grid pattern is computed. The pattern is marked off on the ceiling, and the cable stapled directly to the under-surface before the finished ceiling is applied. To avoid excessive heat loss, there should be extra insulation above the ceiling. There are also plasterboard sheets with heating elements already embedded. They are applied directly to the ceiling joists.

Ceiling cable installations offer some advantages. They are out of the usable room space, and therefore do not interfere with furniture or drapery location. Radiant heat

AITKEN PRODUCTS, INC.

**FIGURE 2-10.** *Infrared radiant overhead heaters*

is more efficient than convection heat, because there are no drafts and less infiltration. The warm mass of the total ceiling makes for uniform heat delivery. But, because of its large mass, the system cannot respond quickly to changes in demand. Ceiling cable gives room-wide distribution of heat. However, ceiling temperature limitations may prevent concentrating heat along windows and outer walls where most heat loss occurs. The radiant heat from the ceiling does not give full warmth under furniture or other obstructions. Ceiling cable installations are always controlled by wall-mounted thermostats.

Radiant glass or rubber panels are another ceiling-mounted radiant heat source. These panels come in a variety of physical sizes and heat output ratings. A common design is a heat-producing grid made of a stamped (or die-cut) sheet of resistance metal laminated between layers of glass. The panels are mounted at strategic locations in the ceiling to meet cold outer wall conditions and give the proper heat input and distribution.

Infrared heat-producing elements also may be mounted in ceiling fixtures. They may be suspended, surface-mounted, or recessed. Figure 2-10 shows two styles of electric infrared radiant overhead heaters that utilize metal sheath elements. They can be hung like fluorescents to spot heat, or grouped to heat an entire building. A common use is in commercial and industrial heating applications, where it is not practical to heat an entire working area. They are often used for auxiliary heat in a space that left unheated part of the time. Some other applications are machinists' work positions, doormen's stations, and loading docks. When used as auxiliary heat, the control may be a manual switch, a wall-mounted thermostat, or a percentage timer. Such a timer can be set to cycle the heater at any interval desired.

An infrared ceiling bulb is often used as a bathroom or dressing room heater. It is usually not the primary heat source. Instead, it is turned on when the occupant enters the room and turned off upon leaving.

The combination heating and lighting fixture is another popular ceiling unit. Some are recirculating heaters. They draw room air in through an intake grille, heat it, and expel it through discharge louvers. Other combination units provide infrared radiant heat and light. Still another type provides three functions—heating, ventilation, and lighting. Where extra lighting is not required, but fast, high-capacity heating is—in factories, stockrooms, and warehouses, for example—a vertical discharge unit heater like the one shown in Figure 2-11 may be used.

MARLEY ENGINEERED PRODUCTS

**FIGURE 2-11.** *Ceiling-mounted vertical discharge unit heater*

### Baseboard heaters

The *baseboard* heater, shown in Figure 2-12, is designed for general comfort heating. It is widely used in residences, commercial buildings such as motels, and similar applications. Baseboard sections are available in a wide range of heat output

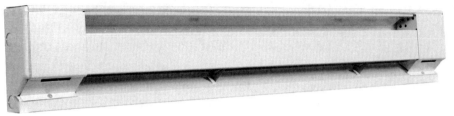

FIGURE 2-12. *Baseboard heater*

MARLEY ENGINEERED PRODUCTS

ratings. They can be radiant or convective. They may be used singly or joined to supply the heat needed for any space. This type of heater is installed at the floor line, usually on an outside wall under the windows.

Baseboard heaters have several advantages. They take up a minimum of space in the room. They deliver heat along a broad area at the outer perimeter of the room, where it is needed. They offer minimal interference with furniture placement. *Radiant* models heat directly. They must be located so that they "see" into the space they heat.

*Convectors* require free air movement throughout the room. In the convective model shown in Figure 2-13, room air flows in at or near the bottom. The air then flows around the heating elements, out through the top, and around the room. There is a similar unit of this type that has a blower. It forces air through the unit for better room air circulation and more rapid heat distribution.

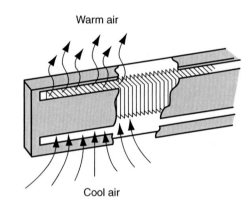

Warm air

Cool air

FIGURE 2-13. *Baseboard convector*

Electric *hydronic* baseboard heaters are filled with water and ethylene glycol. The fluid is heated by an immersion-type element built into the baseboard section. The heat storage capacity of the liquid tends to level the heat output. Heating can be both radiant and convective.

The baseboard heater in any of its forms is suited to control by a wall-mounted thermostat. However, some are manufactured with built-in thermostats. Many units now use a high-limit safety control along the full length of the heater. This protects against hot spots in case of blocked circulation.

### Floor heaters

*Floor* heaters, such as the drop-in model shown in Figure 2-14, are used for installations in which a floor location is preferred. One

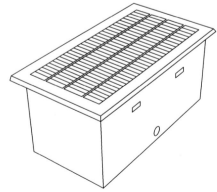

FIGURE 2-14. *Floor heater*

example is under ceiling-to-floor picture windows where there is no space for baseboard units. They are designed to heat by gravity convection of warm air from the heater into the room. They may have a built-in thermostat, but generally perform best if controlled by a wall-mounted room thermostat.

## CENTRAL HEATING SYSTEMS

*Central* electric heating systems use duct or piping systems to distribute heat. They include a central fan or water pump that forces the circulation. A typical electric hydronic system is shown in Figure 2-15. In a variation of this system, the circulator pump pumps water *away* from the boiler. This configuration eliminates many air problems, and allows the circulator to move the water better. Figure 2-16 on the next page shows a warm air counterpart.

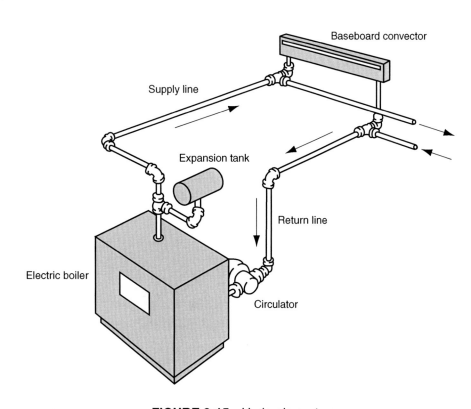

**FIGURE 2-15.** *Hydronic system*

Most central heating systems have a main or central heating plant as the source of heat. It can be an electric furnace, boiler, or heat pump. They operate much like any other warm air or hot water heating system. A special variation has a central fan and ductwork to provide circulation. But rather than a furnace providing heat, it is supplied by individual duct or register heaters for each room.

Thus, central electric heating can be divided into four basic categories:

- furnace

- boiler

- heat pump

- central fan with duct or register heaters.

The popularity of each varies with the section of the country and the type of home to be heated.

### Electric furnace

Electric furnaces are basically similar to fossil fuel furnaces. The difference is that electric resistance heating elements replace the burner. Generally, a number of elements are used. The furnace cabinet also encloses the air filter and a circulating fan. The fan forces the air through the heating section and ductwork to the various rooms. Temperature limit controls prevent the furnace from overheating. Comfort control of the system is provided by a low-voltage thermostat and a relay or sequencer and fan control.

The electric furnace, with a properly designed duct system, is easily combined with a central cooling system and an electronic air cleaner. Such a system provides complete year-round air conditioning.

### Electric boiler

The electric hot water boiler, as shown in Figure 2-17, is compact because the heating elements are immersed directly in the water being heated. All the heat from the elements goes directly to the boiler water. The water is then piped to the room radiators or convectors.

The control system for an electric boiler is similar to that of a furnace. It includes a room thermostat, relay, and circulator control. The boiler uses a fast-acting immersion-type high-limit control and a mechanical pressure-temperature relief valve. These eliminate overheating or building up a head of steam.

An adaptation of the electric boiler is a large storage vessel that permits off-peak water heating. Water is heated and stored when lower off-peak electrical rates apply. When the thermostat calls

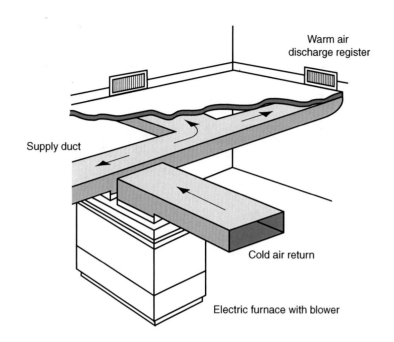

FIGURE 2-16. *Warm air system*

FIGURE 2-17. *Electric boiler*

for heat, heated water from this reservoir is circulated by a pump to the room units.

Electric hydronic boilers come in many sizes, including those for commercial applications. The hydronic installation is readily adaptable to zone control and to chilled water cooling systems for year-round air conditioning.

### Electric heat pump

The heat pump, shown in Figure 2-18, is a very special type of electric heating system. In winter, it "extracts" heat from outdoor air (or water) and transfers it indoors. Reversing the cycle in summer, it "absorbs" heat from indoors and disposes of it to outdoor air (or water). Heat pumps distribute heat or cooling to rooms through a central duct or piping system, as do other central systems.

It should be noted that the heat pump is usually sized for the *cooling* load. As a result, in some climates it is undersized for the heating load. In such cases, the system often is equipped with auxiliary resistance heating.

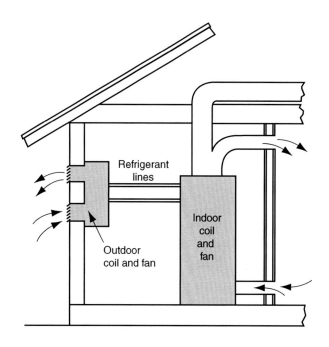

**FIGURE 2-18.** *Heat pump*

With the advent of two-speed compressors and variable-speed compressors, there are more options for sizing a heat pump. With a two-speed compressor, the heat pump can be sized for cooling on the low speed. For example, a 5-ton heat pump is rated for approximately three tons of cooling on the low speed. The heat pump can run on high speed in the winter and produce much more heat than a 3-ton heat pump. This is especially helpful in colder climates. With variable-speed compressors, there are even more options available. Heat pumps will be examined in more detail in the next Lesson.

### Central fan with duct or register heaters

Warm air duct or register heater systems do not have a central furnace as the major heat source. They do have a central circulating fan or blower and air-cleaning system. Such a system has a trunk and lateral ducts to each room. The heat supply for each room is from a heater in the duct or in the diffusing register in the room. In some systems there is a tempering heater at the fan, which prevents cold air from circulating to rooms with heaters off.

The central fan system offers advantages of individual room or zone control. Also, it is adaptable to central year-round air conditioning. A duct heater may supply one room or several rooms and be controlled by a zone thermostat. Register heaters in each room are controlled by individual room thermostats. Duct and register units can augment a heat pump system in extreme weather. They may be used similarly to supplement any ducted heating plant with hard-to-heat rooms or additions. Figure 2-19 shows a slip-in open-coil duct heater with its wiring exposed.

### SPACE HEATING

Most of the heating methods described in this Lesson are used primarily for residences, but they can apply to commercial and industrial heating as well. The following equipment, however, is intended chiefly for commercial and industrial buildings.

INDEECO

**FIGURE 2-19.** *Duct heater*

*Unit* heaters, of which Figure 2-20 is an example, are similar to some portable heaters described earlier. The main differences are in size and mounting methods. The unit heater always has a blower that moves a large volume of air. A unit heater is usually suspended from the ceiling or mounted high on a convenient post or pillar. It gives good heat distribution from this position, and the heat can not be readily blocked off.

Infrared heaters and lamps are growing in popularity in commercial, industrial, and farm applications. They are used on docks, in open work areas, at swimming pools, entryways, shop fronts, food counters, and in many other applications. In each case, it is the *subject* that is to be heated, not the air. These heaters and lamps come in a variety of types

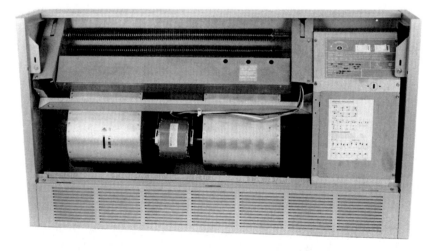

FOSTORIA INDUSTRIES, INC.

**FIGURE 2-20.** *Cabinet unit heater (with cover removed)*

and styles designed for specific heavy-duty applications. Their control is often on an automatically timed schedule. Figure 2-21 shows an infrared spot heater.

Some spaces require ventilation as well as heating. School classrooms are an example. For such use, various models of unit *ventilator* heaters are available. These heaters, pictured in Figure 2-22, provide for the proportional intake of outside air. It is mixed with room air, filtered, heated, and then discharged into the heated space.

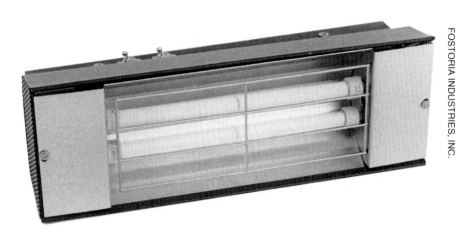

FOSTORIA INDUSTRIES, INC.

**FIGURE 2-21.** *Infrared spot heater*

Unit ventilators are available to satisfy just about every size and kind of installation. There are also models that include cooling. Automatic control is provided by a room thermostat, which is coordinated with controls in the unit. Heating, ventilating, and cooling is regulated in the desired sequence and within the recommended limits.

The so-called *blast coil* heater, or high-volume duct heater, provides a large amount of heated air for large air-handling systems. Its main application is in the higher-velocity ducts, where air temperatures must be raised rapidly as air passes through the ducts. Blast coil heaters are applied readily in zoned control

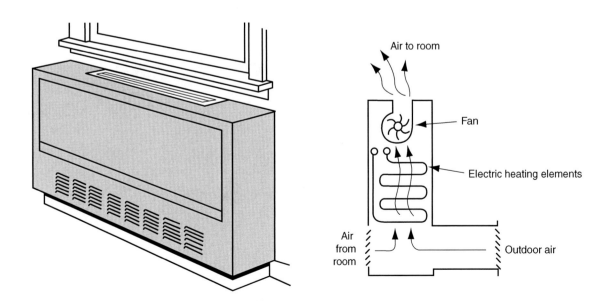

**FIGURE 2-22.** *Unit ventilator system*

commercial heating installations. They are turned on in stages, to satisfy the load for each zone. The zones are supplied with a constant volume of air, with only the temperature varied as necessary.

Electric *preheat* or *reheat* coils, diagrammed in Figure 2-23, are often an integral part of basic fan room equipment. They are used in air conditioning applications to reheat air that has been chilled to remove the moisture—or they may temper or preheat fresh, outdoor air before it is distributed through the system.

Another type of electric heater is the *makeup air* heater. This unit consists of a fan, which brings in outside air, and an electric heater similar to a duct heater. The purpose of the makeup air heater is to replace air that is exhausted by exhaust fans. Such fans may be over restaurant hoods, in bathrooms, or used for other process requirements.

The makeup air fan should be sized to "make up" for the air that the exhaust fans are removing from the space. First, the coldest design temperature must be determined. The next consideration is the desired discharge temperature. The temperature rise can then be calculated, and the electric heater should be sized based on the temperature rise desired.

For example, assume that the amount of air exhausted from the space is 5,000 cfm, the coldest outside design temperature is –10°F, and the desired discharge temperature is 70°F. The calculated temperature rise is therefore 80°F (–10 + 70 = 80).

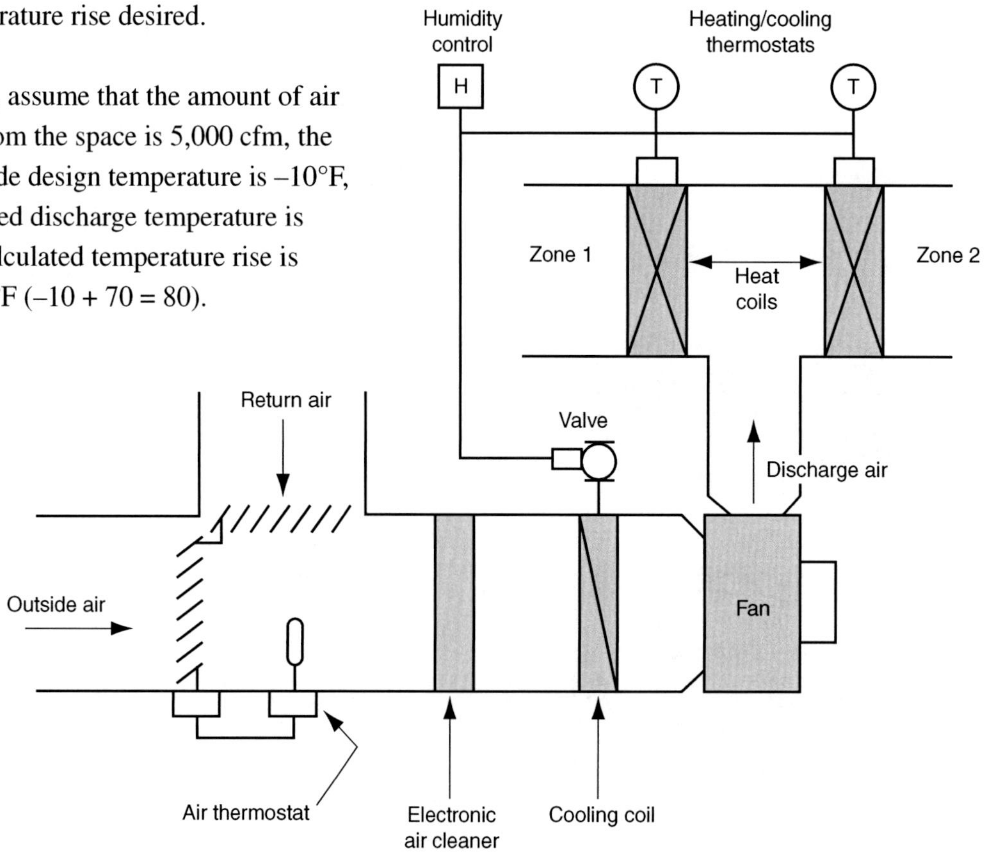

FIGURE 2-23. *Preheat or reheat coil*

The equation below can be used to calculate the Btuh output of the makeup air unit:

$$Btuh = 1.2 \times temperature\ rise \times cfm$$

$$= 1.2 \times 80 \times 5,000$$

$$= 480,000$$

The equation below can be used to calculate the required size of the electric heater (in kilowatts) when the Btuh output is known:

$$kW = \frac{Btuh}{3,412}$$

$$= \frac{480,000}{3,412}$$

$$= 140.7\ kW$$

## MELTING SNOW IN GUTTERS AND DOWNSPOUTS

Both insulated cable and insulated wire can be used to prevent heavy snow and ice accumulation on roof overhangs, and to prevent ice dams from forming in gutters and downspouts. Figure 2-24 on the next page shows a typical resistance wire or cable layout to protect a roof edge and downspout.

Resistance wire or insulated cable for this purpose is generally rated at approximately 3 to 16 watts per linear foot of roof edge. One foot of insulated wire per one foot of linear foot of gutter or downspout is usually adequate.

If the roof edge and/or gutters are heated, the downspouts also must be heated, in order to carry away water from the melted snow and ice. A heated length of wire should extend the full length of the downspout to a point below the frost line. Proper placement may require the use of weights, so extreme care should be taken that the wires do not cross. Some manufacturers make self-regulating heat cable, which lessens the risk of problems caused by crossed wires.

Lead wires should be spliced or plugged into the main power line in a waterproof junction box, and a ground wire installed from downspout or gutter to a good electrical ground. The National Electrical Code (NEC) also requires a 27-milliampere (mA) ground fault protector to protect the equipment. For personal shock protection, a 5-mA ground fault protector should be used.

Control is generally achieved by means of a manual switch with a pilot light. A thermostat that senses outdoor temperature is recommended to prevent system operation above 35°F.

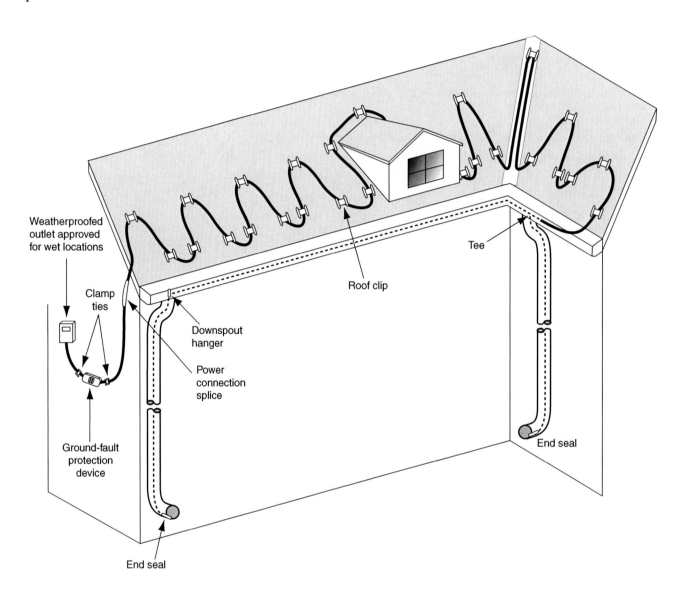

**FIGURE 2-24.**  *Heating cable for de-icing roofs, gutters, and downspouts*

1. What determines the amount of heat produced by an electric heater?

2. In what three ways may heat transfer be accomplished in an electric heater?

3. Are open wire elements replaceable in radiant heaters?

4. Where are rigid encapsulated heater elements generally used?

5. What characteristic of infrared rays makes them desirable for certain heating applications?

6. Name at least five different types of electric heaters.

7. Name one disadvantage of plug-in liquid-filled radiators.

8. Where are radiant wall heaters generally used?

9. What is the advantage of warm air convectors over radiant heaters?

10. Name three types of ceiling heaters.

11. When is embedded ceiling cable installed?

12. What are the advantages of ceiling cable heaters over other types?

13. Where are baseboard heaters generally used?

14. What are the advantages of baseboard heaters?

15. How do electric hydronic baseboard heaters work?

16. How is heat distributed in a central heating system?

17. Name the four basic categories into which central electric heating can be divided.

18. What is used to prevent overheating in an electric furnace?

19. Can an electric furnace be combined with a central cooling system?

20. Where are the heating elements located in an electric boiler?

21. A heat pump extracts heat from _____ during the winter.

22. Is a heat pump generally sized for the heating load or the cooling load?

23. Where is a duct heater located in a central system in which the heater supplies only one room?

24. What is used to augment a heat pump system in extreme weather?

25. Do unit heaters always contain a blower?

26. What is the conventional method of installing a unit heater?

27.     Where are blast coil heaters generally used?

28.     What is the purpose of a makeup air heater?

29.     What is the mathematical procedure for converting Btuh to kilowatts?

30.     The NEC requires a _____-mA ground fault protector to protect
        equipment used to melt snow in gutters and downspouts.

# Heat Pumps

## FUNCTION

The *heat pump* is a single unit that can both heat and cool a building, or one or more rooms in a building. A heat pump takes heat from an outside source (water, air, earth) and uses it to warm the conditioned space in the winter. In the summer, a heat pump removes heat from the conditioned space and discharges it to an outside *heat sink* (water, air, earth).

Units of the *air-to-air* type are commonly used for heating and cooling homes. The term "air-to-air" indicates that outside air is used as both the heat source and heat sink. Air is used as the heating medium and as the cooling medium.

Heat pumps have made a major impact in the heating and cooling of homes in recent years. They also have been used to supplement the heating of hot water in homes. They do so by using the wasted summer heat and using some of the converted heat in the winter.

The *ground source* heat pump is growing in popularity as an economical way of heating and cooling structures. One reason for its popularity is that people are willing to spend a little more money at first in order to reap the savings later. Another reason is that the installers and pipe manufacturers have worked together and reduced the ditching expense. This makes the outside loops for single homes reasonable in cost. In some cases, a ditching contractor will dig the ditch, install the liquid lines, and charge the lines with liquid. The contractor also may offer a leak-free warranty on the system to the heating and cooling dealer. Many systems have been installed in housing developments and office complexes that use a common ground source loop. This makes it economical to install and operate.

The U.S. government now requires an efficiency rating of 10 SEER (Seasonal Energy Efficiency Ratio) or higher on residential air conditioning or heat pumps sold after January 1, 1994. In the past, efficiencies were as low as 5 or 6 SEER. Most manufacturers now are building units that reach 13 or 14 SEER. A few are approaching 20 SEER with some special features. Efficiencies will be explained more later in this Lesson.

There is increasing use of heat pumps for year-round air conditioning in homes throughout the United States. There are many types of heat pump systems on the market today. Which one to choose is best decided by consulting with builders, engineers, electric power supply representatives, manufacturers' representatives, and heat pump equipment dealers.

### OPERATION

A heat pump works on the same principle as a household refrigerator or other refrigeration system. In effect, it transfers heat from one place or source at a relatively low temperature to another at a higher temperature.

Figure 3-1 shows how an air-to-air unit heats. Outside air passes over the cold evaporator coil. Heat is transferred from the air to the refrigerant in the coil. It is raised to a higher temperature by compression. It is discharged to the heating medium (air) at the condenser. A fan blows the warm air directly into the conditioned space or through ducts to the conditioned areas or rooms.

Figure 3-2 shows how an air-to-air unit cools. The heating and cooling cycles are identical except that the operation is reversed. Heat is taken from the warm air in the conditioned space or rooms. It is discharged to the outdoor air. Cool air is blown back into the space or rooms.

Heat pumps generally switch from heating to cooling, and vice versa, by *refrigerant reversal*. Valves (not shown in Figure 3-1) reverse the direction of refrigerant flow. The two heat exchange coils, in effect, trade jobs.

Heat pump operation is usually fully automatic. A thermostat is set for the desired temperature. Automatic controls then regulate operation. On a spring or

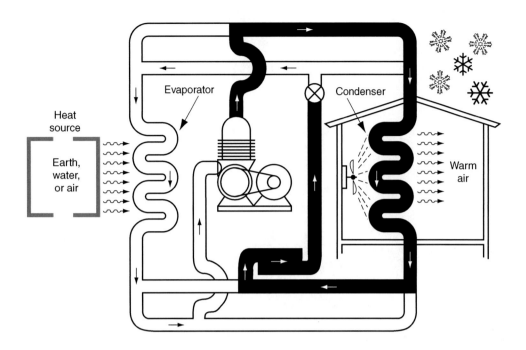

**FIGURE 3-1.** *Heating cycle of heat pump*

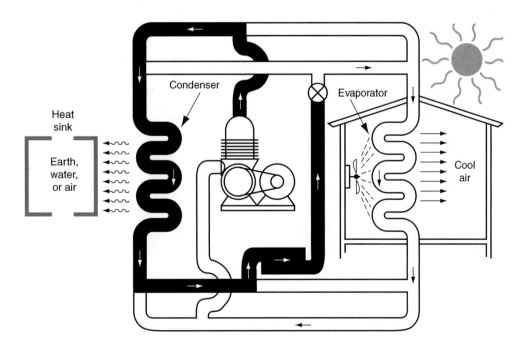

**FIGURE 3-2.** *Cooling cycle of heat pump*

fall day, the pump may heat during cool periods of the day and cool at other times. For fully automatic operation, the thermostat is set so that there will be a non-operative range of about 2 to 4°F between heating and cooling cycles. A closer setting might cause frequent cycling between the heating and cooling operations.

Heat pumps used in homes can be grouped into two types:

- room units

- central system units (split or packaged).

*Room units* heat and cool one or two rooms. They are designed for window, through-the-wall, and free-standing installation. They discharge the warm and cool air directly into the conditioned area.

*Central system units* heat and cool a number of rooms or the whole house. They are installed in some convenient place out of the main living area. They deliver the warm and cool air to the conditioned rooms through ducts.

Room units are of the self-contained, or *packaged*, type. These units contain all the components in one package, which includes the compressor, the two heat exchange coils (evaporator and condenser), the two fans or blowers for air handling, and the controls.

Central system units may be either self-contained or they may be split systems. As their name implies, *split-system* units consist of two separate sections. One section includes the indoor heat exchange coil, a blower, and electrical controls. It is installed inside the house. The other section includes the outdoor heat exchange coil, a fan, and controls. It is installed outside the house. The two sections are connected by refrigerant lines and electrical control wiring.

Heat pumps come in a variety of styles today. Some heat pumps use a single-speed compressor, a type of compressor which has undergone many changes in recent years to improve efficiency. Scroll compressors are used in other units. Two-speed and variable-speed compressors also are available now for heat pumps, a development that allows the compressor to match to load for both heating and cooling. The latest entry is a natural gas engine that drives the heat pump compressor.

Heat pumps are rated according to their heating capacity and their cooling, or heat removal, capacity. This rating usually is expressed in British thermal units of heat per hour (Btuh). Central system units may be rated in tons. A *ton* of cooling capacity equals 288,000 Btu per 24 hours, or 12,000 Btu per hour.

Room heat pump units are available in cooling capacities of up to about 20,000 Btuh. Larger self-contained, or packaged, units are available in capacities ranging from 1.5 to 30 tons. Split-system units are available in capacities ranging from 1.5 to 130 tons.

Most of the recent changes have been made to the central system units, including both split and packaged types. The newer units have many of the following features available:

- ability to match unit output with demand

- zone control for central units

- operation monitoring

- fault monitoring

- discharge air control of the air handler

- liquid-tolerant compressors

- scroll-type compressors

- dehumidification demand controlling ability

- multiple indoor sections for zoning with one outdoor unit

- higher efficiency

- greater dependability of equipment.

## OTHER TYPES OF HEAT PUMPS

*Water-to-air* and *water-to-water* are other types of heat pump systems that work very well. Their applications are not as common today as air-to-air or ground-source loop systems. Water is good heat source—possibly the best. But supply is a major problem. An inexpensive, adequate supply of good quality water may not be available in many areas.

## THE HEAT PUMP DEFINED

The heat pump can be defined as an air conditioning system arranged and controlled to move heat both *to* and *from* the conditioned area. Just as the more common air conditioning unit does, the heat pump moves heat from indoor areas where it is not wanted to outdoor areas where it bothers no one. Unlike the normal air conditioning unit, however, the heat pump can reverse itself. It can move heat from outside into the conditioned area when heat is required indoors.

It might seem that any air conditioner could do this if you simply take it out of the window and turn it around. However, air conditioners do not lend themselves to this type of reversing. The heat pump reverses the flow of heat by using a system of valves in the refrigerant system. They turn the refrigerant around and make it flow in the opposite direction.

As shown in Figure 3-3, heat pumps are classified by their source of heat and the medium to which they disperse heat during the heating season. The unit described earlier, which absorbs heat from the outside air during the heating cycle and rejects the heat into the air within the conditioned space, would be referred to as an *air-to-air* heat pump. Figure 3-4 shows a typical air-to-air heat pump.

Some heat pumps use water for their source of heat. The water could be a spring, lake, or swimming pool, for example. The outdoor coil may actually be immersed directly in the water. The indoor coil is in the conditioned air stream as before. This would be called a *water-to-air* heat pump—heat is absorbed into the system from water and rejected from the system into air.

Ground also may be used as a source of heat. And heat can be rejected to water rather than air. Many combinations are possible. For the sake of simplicity, this Lesson will confine itself to small air-to-air packages. They are by far the most common package in use today.

Let's look at the normal cooling operation of a small packaged air conditioner. In the top portion of

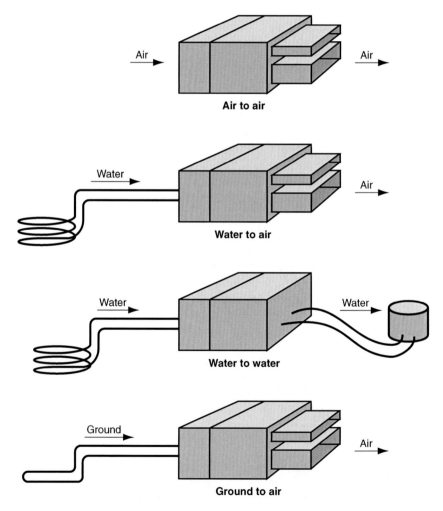

FIGURE 3-3. *Heat pump classifications*

Figure 3-5, the evaporator absorbs heat from the conditioned area. The condenser then rejects that heat to the outdoors.

Now consider what happens when we insert some valves in the refrigerant circuit and reverse the direction of flow of the refrigerant, as shown in the bottom portion of Figure 3-5. The refrigerant now absorbs heat from the outside air in what was the condenser. It rejects heat into the indoor conditioned area by using the original evaporator as a condenser.

In this arrangement, one coil is used for either condensing or evaporating the refrigerant. In a heat pump, therefore, you can't say that a coil is an *evaporator* coil or a *condenser* coil. It could be either, depending on whether the unit is on the heating or cooling cycle. In a heat pump, the coils are called *indoor* or *outdoor* coils. This term refers to the air source of the coil. The coil that has conditioned indoor air passing over it is the indoor coil. The coil using outside air as its air source is the outdoor coil. These terms always pinpoint the exact coil being referred to, regardless of whether the unit is heating or cooling.

YORK INTERNATIONAL CORPORATION

**FIGURE 3-4.** *Typical air-to-air heat pump*

## COEFFICIENT OF PERFORMANCE (COP)

Whenever heat pump economy is discussed, the abbreviation "COP" will be heard. The letters stand for *coefficient of performance*. Technically, the COP for a heat pump on the heating cycle may be defined as:

$$\text{COP} = \frac{\text{refrigeration effect} + \text{work input}}{\text{work input}}$$

Interpreted, that means:

$$\text{COP} = \frac{\text{the Btu you get out}}{\text{the Btu you pay for}}$$

The COP is nothing more than the heat available at the pump divided by the actual work required to produce or move this heat to the space where it will be used.

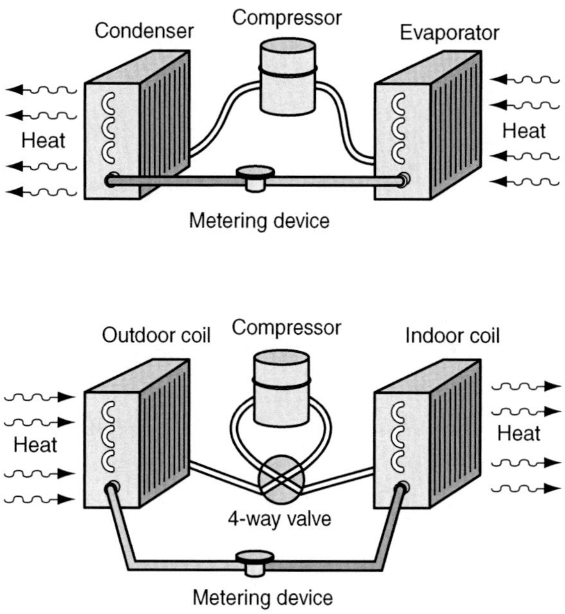


**FIGURE 3-5.** *Normal cooling operation*

The rating tables of a typical unit might indicate that it will supply 86,000 Btuh to the heat ducts. It may use 10 bhp (brake horsepower) in the compressor to do it. In this case, using 1hp as equal to 2,545 Btu, the equation for determining the COP would be:

$$COP = \frac{86,000 \text{ Btuh}}{10 \text{ bhp} \times 2,545 \text{ Btu}/\text{hp}}$$

$$= \frac{86,000}{25,450}$$

$$= 3.4$$

The 86,000 Btuh is the heating capability of the heat pump. It includes the heat being moved, and also the heat put into the refrigerant by the work of the compressor. This is the total heat available for heating purposes at the unit outlet. We divide this figure by the power input. Now we have a number that tells us just how well the unit is doing. A high number shows that the unit is moving a lot of heat, with little energy expended. A low number tells us that not too much heat is being moved. Auxiliary heat may be required to maintain the desired room conditions.

In direct resistance heat, for every Btu put into the heaters in electrical form, one Btu of heat is released. Obviously, in resistance heat, the COP is 1. It can never be higher. The COP of the heat pump, as long as even one Btu is being moved, can never be as *low* as 1. The COP can tell you quickly how good a job your heat pump is doing, in relationship to using the same work input as converting to heat with a direct resistance heater.

Let's examine the COP and find out what makes it vary. Remember a principle of basic refrigeration. With any given unit, as you lower the back pressure, less heat is absorbed into the system for each unit of energy used to drive the compressor.

The Department of Energy now requires heat pump manufacturers to rate their heat pumps at a high and low outside temperature, in order to evaluate heat pump performance better. The high-temperature COP is rated at 47°F outside temperature. The low-temperature COP is rated at 17°F outside temperature. The indoor temperature for both ratings is 70°F.

Let's look at the action of a heat pump for a moment. During the heating season, we get our heat from the outside air, using the outdoor coil as an evaporator. To get the heat to flow from the air into the evaporator, the evaporator temperature must be below that of the air. In other words, to extract heat from 15°F air, the evaporator temperature must be below 15°F. As you can see, with low outside air temperatures, evaporator temperatures can get quite low. Keep in mind that very low evaporator temperatures are likely during the heating season.

The problem with very low evaporator temperatures on the outside coil (evaporator coil) is that the compressor runs with higher compression ratios. This increases the discharge temperature. If the discharge temperature on the compressor is too high, it can damage the discharge valves. There are some checks that can be done to help prevent this problem. Make sure that there is approximately 450 cfm of air flow per ton, or 12,000 Btuh of cooling capacity, across the indoor coil. Check the superheat to see that it meets the manufacturer's parameters. Make sure that the defrost cycle for the outside coil works properly.

The lower the outdoor temperature, the less heat can be moved by the compressor. This means that the lower the outside temperature, the lower the COP. In addition, the lower the evaporator temperature, the greater the strain on the compressor. This has been overcome in newer heat pumps by using larger heat exchange coils on the evaporator and condenser. The suction pressures operate at a higher level than before. This also has raised the efficiency level of today's systems. It is important to note that in a heat pump on the heating cycle, the subject is no longer air conditioning duty, it is refrigeration duty. Installers and maintenance people must take care to provide proper operating conditions to ensure longer equipment life.

As far as the COP alone is concerned, most heat pumps operate within a range from about 1.5 to about 6. These should not be considered as limits, however, because some manufacturers will go beyond these "limits"—and others will not allow their pumps to reach them. The COP is a good performance indicator given any set of conditions, but what about the operation for a whole heating or cooling season?

If you were to take enough COP samples at different outdoor temperatures, you would have a good idea of how seasonal operation will vary. Such samples can be stated in "bins." You can take groups of temperatures in ranges of 5°F or less and call each a "bin." Take the past weather data and figure the number of operating hours for heating or cooling for each bin. Multiply the number of operating hours for each bin by the COP to calculate operational values. Add all the operational values together, divide by the number of bins, and you will have an average seasonal operational value. This is similar to how manufacturers determine their SCOP (Seasonal Coefficient of Performance) values. This can be applied to heating or cooling seasons.

## HSPF AND SEER

The industry today uses the terms HSPF (Heating Seasonal Performance Factor) and SEER (Seasonal Energy Efficiency Ratio) to replace the SCOP term. The "SEER" of a unit is the term that you will hear most often, because it is associated with the air conditioning unit. SEER is used more in warmer climates, and HSPF in colder climates. Usually, if you have a unit that has a higher SEER, the HSPF will also be higher.

The SEER of a system can be calculated with the following equation:

$$\text{SEER} = \frac{\text{(cooling) seasonal Btuh output}}{\text{(cooling) seasonal kWh input}}$$

The same applies for HSPF:

$$\text{HSPF} = \frac{\text{(heating) seasonal Btuh output}}{\text{(heating) seasonal kWh input}}$$

SEER and HSPF are determined by ARI and other testing groups that set guidelines. All equipment manufacturers must meet these guidelines in order to rate their equipment according to the same criteria.

## THE REFRIGERANT CIRCUIT AND DEVICES

Let's look at the refrigerant circuit itself. You'll find that it is not as different from a normal cooling unit as you might think. There are four requirements:

- First, we need valves to reverse the flow of refrigerant. In the case of small packages, this flow reversal is usually done with one valve, known as a *four-way* valve or *reversing* valve. Figure 3-6 shows a typical reversing valve.

- Second, another metering device is required for the outdoor coil, for use during the heating cycle. This may be a thermal expansion valve, a capillary tube, or an electronic expansion valve.

- Third, some method of routing the refrigerant is necessary if the metering device will not allow the refrigerant to flow both ways. There are many methods of doing this, but the device most commonly used is a check valve. (Many units that use capillary tubes or electronic expansion valves do not need check valves, because the refrigerant can flow either way through the metering device.)

- Fourth, a suction line surge accumulator is sometimes installed to protect the compressor against slop-over of liquid refrigerant during a change in cycle.

Let's examine a refrigerant circuit containing these four devices to find out where they fit and how they function. First, let's look at the heat pump refrigerant circuit with the refrigerant flow set for cooling, as shown in Figure 3-7. The heat is being moved from the conditioned interior space to the outside. The direction of flow is marked by the arrows.

Start at the indoor coil. During the cooling cycle, the indoor coil is the evaporator. Here, the low-pressure refrigerant picks up heat from the conditioned space and carries it to the four-way valve. The valve directs it into the compressor suction line, where it flows to and through the suction accumulator. It is compressed in the compressor. Then, the high-pressure gas is discharged to the four-way valve. From there it is directed to the outdoor coil, where it is condensed. The liquid refrigerant from the outdoor coil then flows through the check valve and bypasses the outdoor coil metering device. It continues through the liquid line to the metering device for the indoor coil or evaporator. Except for the additional mechanical devices inserted in the circuit, this is a standard cooling cycle.

In Figure 3-8, the flow of refrigerant is reversed. The heat pump is on the heating cycle. Heat is being extracted from the outside air and moved into the

**FIGURE 3-6.** *Reversing valve*

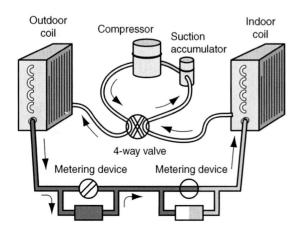

**FIGURE 3-7.** *Cooling*

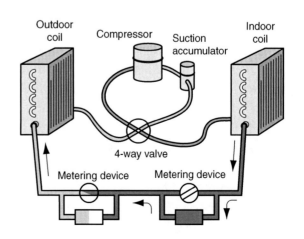

**FIGURE 3-8.** *Heating*

conditioned space for heating. The outdoor coil is now the evaporator. It absorbs heat into the system. The suction gas goes from the outdoor coil through the four-way valve to the suction accumulator. The gas goes from the accumulator to the compressor. There it is compressed, and the high-pressure gas is returned to the four-way valve. The valve directs this hot gas to the indoor coil, where it is condensed. Heat removed from the condensed refrigerant is transferred to the air for circulation throughout the conditioned area. The liquid refrigeration from the indoor coil uses a check valve to bypass the indoor coil metering device.

Note that the purpose of the two lines from the compressor to the four-way valve has not changed. The compressor discharge and suction lines always serve the same function. Because of this, the suction accumulator should always be used in the suction line to the compressor. On many of the newer models, the accumulator has been left out. This has been done in some cases because scroll compressors can pump some liquid, and in others because the compressor will flash the liquid into vapor as it enters the warmer motor winding section. However, it is still important to use good practices to prevent liquid or "wet" gas slopping into the compressor during cycle changeover. The compressor suction line is the best place to ensure this protection. Also, some units use capillary tubes or orifices for metering devices. Under certain loading conditions, they allow some liquid to leave the evaporator. This liquid will pass through the four-way valve and be collected in the accumulator.

Other than the fact that the refrigerant can flow in both directions, the heat pump refrigerant circuit is not the complex unit it may first seem to be. The basic knowledge required to service it is exactly the same as that required to service a normal cooling circuit.

The only really new device in the heat pump refrigerant circuit is the four-way valve. Figure 3-9 is a cutaway of a four-way valve, indicating how it functions. At the top of Figure 3-9, the valve piston is positioned for cooling. The discharge gas from the compressor is being directed through the valve to the outdoor coil. There it will be condensed and the heat removed. The compressor suction is drawing the low-pressure gas through the valve from the indoor coil. That is where the gas was evaporated and picked up heat from the area being conditioned.

At the bottom of Figure 3-9, the valve piston is positioned for heating. The discharge gas now leaves the valve through the line to the indoor coil. This coil becomes the

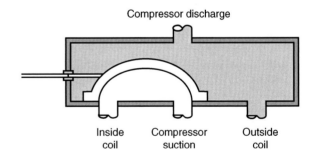

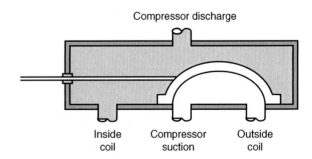

**FIGURE 3-9.** *Four-way valve*

condenser. The suction gas is now drawn from the outdoor coil. The refrigerant in this coil is evaporating and absorbing heat into the system. In theory, most four-way valves function in this manner. The major difference is in how the slide piston is moved.

Probably the most common method of redirecting gas flow in a four-way valve is the free-floating piston. It is moved back and forth by the refrigerant system pressures. The four-way valve shown in Figure 3-10 is an excellent illustration of this method. The compressor discharge is connected to the single-inlet side of the main valve cylinder. In this valve, therefore, there is always discharge pressure between the two end pistons.

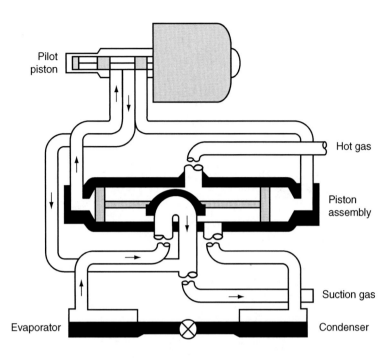

**FIGURE 3-10.** *Four-way valve (cooling)*

In each of the end pistons, there is a small orifice, or *bleed hole*. It allows the discharge gas to bleed slowly from between the pistons. In the drawing, as the gas passes through the right piston, it passes up the capillary until it is stopped by the small plunger in the pilot solenoid. This path is pointed out by the arrows. The gas passing through the right piston is trapped and cannot escape. Thus, the pressure behind the right piston will build up until it equals the discharge pressure, or the pressure between the pistons.

At the same time, gas is passing through the left piston orifice and into the left capillary tube. As the gas comes to the pilot solenoid valve, it is allowed to pass through the valve and into the suction line. The gas escaping through the left piston goes to the suction line. Thus, the pressure behind the left piston will remain lower than or equal to suction pressure.

With pressure behind the left piston low and pressure behind the right piston high, the piston assembly will be pushed to the left. Gas flow will be for the cooling cycle as shown.

When heating is required from the heat pump, the pilot valve solenoid is energized. The small solenoid valve piston is moved to the left, as indicated in Figure 3-11 on the next page. This closes off the flow of gas from the left capillary of the main valve. At the same time, it opens the right capillary to the suction line. The pressure that had been built up in the right capillary will be relieved.

With the left capillary closed, pressure behind the left piston builds up while pressure behind the right piston is being relieved. The pressure differentials are now reversed. The main valve piston is pushed to the right and the gas flow redirected for heating.

## AUXILIARY HEAT

Heat pumps are unable to move large amounts of heat at very low outdoor temperatures. Therefore, some form of supplementary or auxiliary heat is usually provided. In the past, this supplementary heat was normally in the form of electric resistance heaters. Now, it is becoming more common to use a gas or oil-fired furnace as a supplementary or auxiliary heat source. In a typical arrangement, a duct heater is installed in the air stream to provide the supplementary heat, if and when required. The size and number of supplementary electric resistance heaters is determined by the amount of heat required over and above that which the heat pump itself can supply.

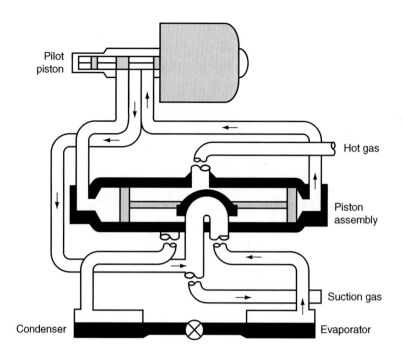

**FIGURE 3-11.** *Four-way valve (heating)*

The usual method of selecting a correctly sized heat pump is to select the unit on the basis of the cooling load. There are some areas where an unusual combination of climate and power rates make heat pumps practical for heating only. In this case, they are selected for their heating capacity—but such areas are greatly in the minority.

With the advent of two-speed compressors and variable-speed compressors, there are more options for sizing a heat pump. With a two-speed compressor, the heat pump can be sized for cooling on the low speed. For example, a 5-ton heat pump is rated for approximately 3 tons of cooling on the low speed. The heat pump can run on high speed in the winter and produce much more heat than a 3-ton heat pump. This is especially helpful in colder climates. With variable-speed compressors, there are even more options available.

After the pump has been selected on the basis of the cooling load, the amount of heat that it can deliver during conditions of maximum heating load is determined. The difference between what the heat pump can deliver and the maximum heating load is the *resistance* or *supplementary* heat load.

In colder climates, it is a good idea to figure the resistance heat for 100% of the heating load for emergency heat. One or more outside thermostats are used to stage resistance heat. If a gas or oil furnace is used as auxiliary heat, the furnace is sized to handle 100% of the heating load. This is done so that if there is a major problem with the heat pump, there is adequate heat until repairs can be made.

A simple example might be as follows. Say that the cooling load on a home is 36,000 Btuh, and the maximum heating load on the same home is 50,000 Btuh. But at the outdoor temperature at which the maximum heating load occurs, the heat pump can move only 20,000 Btuh. The difference is 30,000 Btuh (50,000 minus 20,000). This must be furnished by some form of supplementary heat. The maximum number or size of supplementary heaters that can be used is usually limited by electrical code approval or by the air resistance of the heaters.

When you use strip heaters for supplementary heating, their control presents an interesting problem. It costs more to get one Btu from direct resistance heat than to get one Btu from the heat pump cycle, so it is preferable to use the heat pump rather than resistance heat. The most common method of controlling strip heat is by using a two-step room thermostat, controlling as shown in Figure 3-12. Regardless of outside conditions, the strip heaters should not be turned on unless the compressor alone is not able to do the heating job. It is a simple matter to pass this information to the unit when a two-step room thermostat is used.

The first step of the thermostat will start the compressor. If the compressor cannot handle the load and the room temperature continues to drop, the second set of contacts in the thermostat will close. The second set of contacts will turn on the auxiliary heat, which may be furnished by electric strip heaters or by a gas or oil furnace. If electric strip heaters are used, in many cases one or more outside thermostats determine the number of heaters that come on. The outside thermostats are set so that the resistance heat matches the heat loss. This is particularly important if the electric utility has a demand rate.

The second step of the thermostat is usually set to close at about 1½ to 2°F below the first. If the compressor cannot move sufficient heat to maintain the temperature within the conditioned space, the temperature within the space will continue to drop. When it has dropped 1½ to 2°F below the room thermostat setting, the second step of the thermostat will close. This turns on the auxiliary heat.

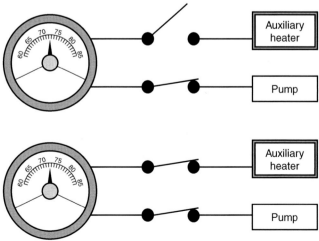

**FIGURE 3-12.** *Two-step room thermostat*

1.    In heat pumps, what does the term *air-to-air* indicate?

2.    How are low outside temperatures raised to higher temperatures for inside?

3.    When a heat pump is switched from heating to cooling, the operating cycle is _____.

4.    What different operations may a heat pump perform during the course of a spring or fall day?

5.    What are room units designed to do?

6.    What are central systems designed to do?

7.    Which heat pump components do *packaged* units contain?

8.    What does a *split* system consist of?

9.    Heat pumps are rated according to their _____ capacity and their _____ capacity.

10.   What is possibly the best heat source for a heat pump?

11.   What is a *water-to-air* heat pump?

12.   In a heat pump, why is it impractical to call a coil an *evaporator* or a *condenser*?

13.     In order for an evaporator to extract heat from the outside, what is the determining factor regarding temperature?

14.     As the outdoor temperature is lowered, is more or less heat moved by the compressor?

15.     Are heat pumps more efficient at higher or lower heat source temperatures?

16.     What is the typical COP range of heat pumps during heating?

17.     What type of valve reverses refrigerant flow in a heat pump?

18.     What is the function of an *accumulator* in a heat pump circuit?

19.     To what side of the reversing valve is the compressor discharge connected?

20.     How does the discharge gas bleed away in the reversing valve when it reverses?

21.     When is a pilot valve energized in a heat pump?

22.     How is the size and number of supplementary electric heaters determined for heat pumps?

23.     What is the most common method of controlling strip or resistance heat in a heat pump?

24. Regardless of outdoor conditions, when should supplementary resistance heat be used?

25. What does the first step of a room thermostat do?

26. How far is the second-stage thermostat usually set below the first?

# Radiant Heating Systems

Because some of the words and phrases associated with infrared heating may be new to you, this section will define those terms with which you should be familiar. The following paragraphs will discuss three in particular—*black body*, *wavelength*, and *emissivity*.

### Black body

A *black body* is any material which, theoretically, can absorb all the thermal radiation impinging upon it, while reflecting none of these energies. A black body is not necessarily black. If you could make a list of black bodies, a whitewashed wall would be near the top of the list as something that comes close to meeting the required characteristics. The color is far from black, yet this material absorbs infrared energies at near the black body rate. There are other materials with similar characteristics, but they fall short of the black body rating of 1.

Do not confuse *radiation* with *reflection*. A black body has an *emissivity* of 1. This means that it absorbs all the thermal radiation directed at it (none bounces off, or reflects). Conversely, a black body can send or radiate all those energies away. On the other hand, a sheet of polished aluminum is highly reflective. It rejects much of the infrared energies directed at it, because the infrared rays bounce off. But it does absorb a small quantity of these energies. If the polished aluminum reflects 95% of the infrared impinged upon it, then it absorbs 5% of those energies. This would account for 100% of the energy that contacts it. Because of its reflectivity, polished aluminum is used extensively in both high- and low-intensity infrared units. Aluminum panels are used to deflect the infrared rays for a more compact or concentrated pattern. This gives more definition to the area that these units are able to cover.

Black bodies are only theoretical. However, many surfaces can absorb a large percentage of the infrared energies directed at them. Others, like the polished aluminum, will reflect a high percentage of this energy. You should keep this in mind when working in the infrared heating field.

### Wavelength

Heat may be lost from a body, even though no substance is in contact with it. Such energy is sent from the surface in every direction. Take the sun, for example. It is theoretically in contact with no matter. It throws off heat, which is intercepted by the earth. The heat cannot be seen. Nevertheless, it is transmitted millions of miles by electromagnetic waves. Much of this passage is through a vacuum (outer space).

Infrared, ultraviolet rays, gamma rays, x-rays, radio, and visible light are transported the same way. However, these energies all travel in different wavelengths, or impulses. A *wavelength* is the distance measured in the progression of a wave from one point to the next point. It is much the same as the waves in the ocean as they travel across the surface of the water. Infrared wavelengths are measured in microns. A *micron* is one one-millionth of a meter.

For comparison, visible light travels in wavelengths of 0.4 to 0.8 microns. Infrared travels within a range of 0.8 to 400 microns. From a practical standpoint, infrared heating wave lengths are found in the 2 to 20-micron range. However, infrared heating devices operate most efficiently within the 2 to 7-micron range.

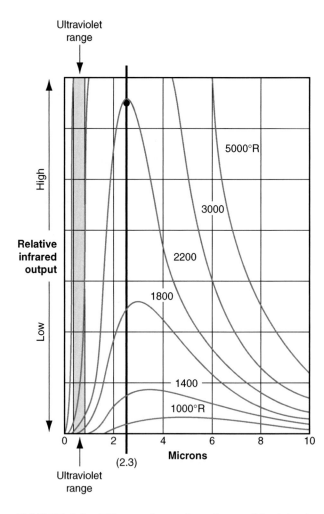

**FIGURE 4-1.** *Effects of wavelength on a black body*

Infrared rays to not lose their energy until they are intercepted by liquids or solids. Air does not absorb the rays. Therefore, none of the energy is lost to air.

This explains why, with infrared heating, the air in the space is slow to heat upon start-up. The air finally warms as the objects heated by the infrared source give off some of their heat through convection.

Figure 4-1 shows the effects of wavelength on the emitting power of a black body. Note that a black body at 2,200°R (1,740°F) has peak radiation (Btuh output) at a wavelength of about 2.3 microns. Also note that the peak output of a given temperature is at a lower micron level. The shaded portion of the graph is the ultraviolet range. As you can see, the output level descends sharply as it approaches the ultra-violet range. This means that wavelengths in the ultraviolet range are not effective for providing heat.

### Emissivity

*Emissivity* is the relative power of a surface to emit heat by radiation. A surface is rated based on its ability to radiate compared to a black body. By comparison, a black body has an emissivity value of 1. This value of 1 is the basis for all studies relating to the emitting power of a given surface. It is used in formulating not only the emission rates, but also the ability of a surface to absorb radiated heat. As the emissivity of a material decreases from 1, its reflecting quality increases. For instance, a material with an emissivity of 0.9 reflects 10% of the infrared energies impinging upon it. No material has an emissivity greater than 1.

Assume that a material with an emissivity of 0.8 radiates 25,000 Btuh. That same material contains heat in the amount of 31,250 Btuh. Conversely, the same material impinged upon by 31,250 Btuh will absorb 80% of this quantity, or 25,000 Btuh. About 20% (6,250 Btuh) will reflect, or bounce away, from the material. Table 4-1 shows a list of various materials and their approximate emissivity values. In general, a rough surface with no sheen whatsoever will have a comparably high emissivity rate, while a smooth surface that is highly polished will have a relatively low emissivity rate. Both emissivity and reflectivity values are shown for each material.

| Material | Emissivity | Reflectivity |
|---|---|---|
| Aluminum (polished) | 0.07 | 0.93 |
| Aluminum alloy | 0.33 | 0.67 |
| Asbestos board | 0.96 | 0.04 |
| Brick (rough red) | 0.93 | 0.07 |
| Glass | 0.90 | 0.10 |
| Gravel | 0.28 | 0.72 |
| Iron (cast) | 0.44 | 0.56 |
| Iron (rusted) | 0.61 | 0.39 |
| Lacquer (flat black) | 0.96 | 0.04 |
| Lacquer (flat white) | 0.80 | 0.20 |
| Marble | 0.56 | 0.44 |
| Plaster | 0.91 | 0.09 |
| Sand | 0.76 | 0.24 |
| Sandstone | 0.83 | 0.17 |
| Sawdust | 0.75 | 0.25 |
| Slate | 0.67 | 0.33 |
| Steel (galvanized) | 0.45 | 0.55 |
| Steel (sheet) | 0.66 | 0.34 |
| Steel (18-8 stainless) | 0.45 | 0.55 |
| Stonework | 0.93 | 0.07 |
| Varnish (glossy) | 0.89 | 0.11 |
| Water | 0.68 | 0.32 |
| Wood (planed oak) | 0.91 | 0.09 |

**TABLE 4-1.** *Emissivity and reflectivity values of various materials*

Stefan Boltzman suggested that the total radiation from a heated body is proportional to the fourth power of its absolute temperature. Ludwig Boltzman furthered this theory through thermodynamic reasoning. The following equation may be reliably adapted:

$$e(bb) = KT^4$$

where:

> e(bb) = emissive power of a black body
> > K = Stefan Boltzman constant
> > > $= 0.172 \times (10)^{-8}$
> > > $= 0.00000000172$
> > T = absolute temperature in degrees Rankine
> > > = degrees Fahrenheit − 460.

**Example:** Determine the emission rate (Btu/ft²/hr) of a black body that has an area of 1 ft² and a temperature of 1,600°F.

> $e(bb) = KT^4$
> $e(bb) = 0.00000000172 \times (1,600 - 460)^4$
> $e(bb) = 30,974$ Btuh/ft²

Using the Stefan Boltzman constant and adding the emissivity value of a material, the following equation can be used:

$$e = KT^4 \times E$$

where:

> e = emissive power
> E = emissivity value (%) of the material.

If the material in the example above had an emissivity of 0.8, then *e* would be 30,974 × 0.8, or 24,779 Btu/ft²/hr.

## TYPES OF ELECTRICAL RADIANT HEAT

### Metal sheath heater

The *metal sheath* heater is composed of a resistor embedded in an electrical insulating refractory contained within a metal tube. It is the most rugged of the three sources discussed here. It stands up well against impact, vibration, and splashing. Metal sheath heaters can be mounted horizontally, vertically, or at any angle between.

The response time of the metal sheath heater is about 2 to 5 minutes. This permits the use of a simple percentage input timer control to maintain any temperature from full ON to full OFF fairly consistently because of the thermal mass storage of the element during the OFF period. At full operation, the heaters emit a dull red glow. There is no glare even at maximum wattage.

Reduced-voltage operation is not normally recommended because of the drastic reduction of radiating efficiency. Metal sheath radiant heaters are normally designed for about 50 W per inch of $\frac{3}{8}$-in. diameter tube. Lower intensities are readily attained at the sacrifice of radiant efficiency. Higher intensities are readily attained at the sacrifice of life expectancy. A more frequent means of attaining higher intensity is by doubling up length with a hairpin element. This also affects space requirements and fixture design.

### Quartz tube filled with air

The *quartz tube* consists of a coiled element within a fused quartz tube. The space inside the tube is air-filled. The element is supported by the tube itself. The tube is capped (not sealed) by porcelain or metal terminal blocks. It stands up well against splashing. It has medium resistance to vibration, and low resistance to impact.

The tube's primary advantage is flexibility. It is easy to match exactly to heat, voltage, and length requirements. It has a quicker response time than the metal sheath heater, but with similar low luminosity. It can be controlled by a simple percentage input timer. The pulses will be particularly noticeable visually only on low-percentage settings.

Quartz tubes are normally designed for about 35 W per inch of $\frac{3}{8}$-in. diameter tube. Lower intensities are readily attained at the sacrifice of radiant efficiency, higher intensities at the sacrifice of life expectancy. A more frequent means of attaining higher intensity is to increase the diameter of the tube. For example, the $1\frac{1}{2}$-in. tube can provide up to 125 W per inch. However, the greater space requirements affect the design of the fixture.

### Quartz lamp filled with inert gas

The *quartz lamp* is a coiled resistor positioned in a straight line and away from the quartz tube by round tantalum spacers. The filament is sealed into the ends of the $\frac{3}{8}$-in. diameter quartz tube. The tube is exhausted and filled with inert gas.

Quartz lamps are normally designed for 100 W per inch of ⅜-in. diameter lamp. Special high-temperature testing lamps (unsuited for continuous duty) are made at 200 W per inch. Special construction is available at extra cost for the popular 100 W per inch lamps. They can operate in horizontal or vertical positions, or at any angle in between when used in suitably ventilated fixtures.

Except for this special construction, with lamps over 500 W installed vertically, the filament will collapse to one end, causing the lamp to fail. The upper seal will also overheat, although proper ventilation (required on all ratings) may be able to overcome this.

## APPLICATION OF INFRARED HEATERS

Application instructions presently refer to watts per square foot density of installation as the criterion for use. Without a more definitive measure of the heat available, this is perhaps the best that can be used. However, consider the following facts regarding the application of infrared comfort heaters:

- Radiant energy is converted to heat upon absorption by the receiving surface. The radiant efficiency of an element is the ratio of the energy radiated to the energy input. The radiant efficiency of a system (or fixture) is the ratio of the radiant energy, directed where desired, to the input. The radiant efficiency of an installation is the ratio of the energy absorbed by receiving surfaces to the input.

- The radiant efficiency of each source may be different. Generally, the higher the element temperature, the higher the radiating efficiency and the shorter the wave length. The wavelength distribution of two energy sources is shown in Figure 4-2.

- The reflectance of reflectors varies with the type of material, and with the design and maintenance of the reflecting surface.

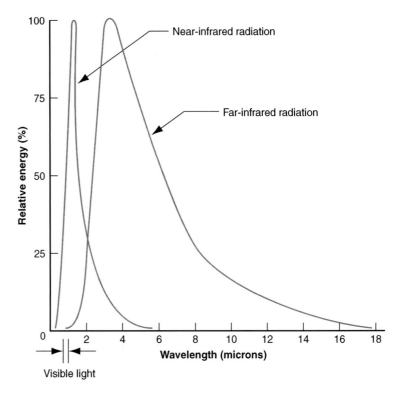

**FIGURE 4-2.** *Radiating efficiencies of two energy sources relative to wavelength*

- The shape of the reflector and the relative position of the element and reflector greatly affect the efficiency of the fixture. A broad distribution curve and *spill radiation* may lose much of the potential value of infrared heating when heat sources are more than a few feet away from personnel being heated.

- Low-temperature sources emit less radiant heat and more convection heat proportionately than high-temperature sources. Convection heat is used only in increasing the ambient temperature. This occurs usually above the *living level*.

- Color sensitivity varies. You probably have noticed that black or dark colored surfaces absorb more of the available radiant heat from any source, regardless of the wavelength. Lighter colored objects generally absorb less radiant heat. This *color sensitivity* effect is reduced in the far-infrared portion of the spectrum. The importance of color sensitivity and the relative value of near-infrared and far-infrared are points of discussion among experts.

- Watt density input is merely an indication of heat available from the infrared source. It is not an accurate measure of the ability to radiate heat to personnel or surroundings. The efficiency of the fixture, the radiating efficiency of the element, the receiving efficiency of personnel (light or dark colored clothing) all affect effectiveness of the installation. The best way to find the actual requirement is by testing on a sample installation—or observe several installations with similar weather exposures. Do so in the company of an experienced observer and system designer.

## INFRARED SNOW-MELTING SYSTEMS

### Infrared fixture layout

The same infrared fixtures used for human comfort heating installations are used for snow-melting systems. The are major differences in target area design procedure and infrared fixture selection. This is because of the emphasis on the horizontal surfaces involved with snow melting. In personal comfort applications, the human body's vertical surfaces are most important. When snow melting is the prime design concern, fixtures with narrow beam patterns confine the radiation energy within the target area to a greater extent. This permits more efficient operation. Often, asymmetric reflector fixtures are used near the sidelines of the target area. They aim the radiation primarily to one side of the fixture centerline.

Infrared fixtures usually have a longer energy pattern parallel to the long dimension of the fixture rather than at right angles to it. Therefore, fixtures are generally mounted in a row, parallel to the longest dimension of the area. Where the target area is 8 ft or more in width, fixtures should be located in two or more parallel rows. This arrangement also gives a better personal comfort heating effect. Radiation is directed from both sides across the target area. This provides a more favorable incident angle.

### Radiation spill

Watt density and distribution in the snow-melting area depend on the number, wattage, beam pattern, and mounting height of the heating fixtures, and on their relative positions to the pavement. In theory, the best energy distribution would be uniform throughout the snow-melting target area at a density equal to the design requirement. The heating fixture reflector design determines the percentage of the total fixture radiant output scattered outside of its target area.

Even the best designed controlled beam fixture will not have a completely sharp cutoff at the beam edges. If uniform distribution were maintained for the full width of the area, much radiant energy would fall outside the target area. Therefore, infrared snow-melting systems are designed so that intensity on the pavement decreases before reaching the edge of the area. This design procedure keeps stray radiant energy losses to a minimum.

Table 4-2 shows the values obtained in a sample snow-melting problem. The target area is 8 ft by 15 ft, with each square foot shown on the table. The area is irradiated by four single-element fixtures using quartz infrared lamps. Mounting height is about 10 ft. The units are located as shown in Table 4-2. The sample design average is 45 W per square foot. You can see that the central part of the target area has an incident watt density above the design average value. The peripheral area has radiation densities below the average.

For distribution similar to Table 4-2, snow will collect at the edges of the area as the energy requirements approach or exceed the capacity of the system. As snowfall lessens, the snow will again be melted to the edges of the area—and possibly beyond if system operation continues.

### Target area watt density

Theoretical target area wattage densities for snow melting with infrared systems are the same as commercial applications of embedded element systems. However, theoretical density values are for radiation incident to the pavement surface. You cannot simply multiply the recommended wattage density by the

**Infrared intensity on the pavement from four fixtures, in watts per square foot**

| | | | | | | | | | | | | | | |
|---|---|---|---|---|---|---|---|---|---|---|---|---|---|---|
| 14.7 | 16.0 | 19.75 | 23.7 | 25.5 | 27.5 | 28.2 | 28.0 | 28.2 | 27.5 | 25.5 | 23.7 | 19.75 | 16.0 | 14.7 |
| | | | | Fixture | | | | | Fixture | | | | | |
| 23.7 | 24.8 | 28.7 | 31.7 | 35.7 | 38.2 | 38.5 | 39.4 | 38.5 | 38.2 | 35.7 | 31.7 | 28.7 | 24.8 | 23.7 |
| 25.7 | 31.7 | 37.5 | 42.7 | 46.4 | 49.4 | 52.2 | 53.0 | 52.2 | 49.4 | 46.4 | 42.7 | 37.5 | 31.7 | 25.7 |
| 28.2 | 34.3 | 42.8 | 46.7 | 51.2 | 55.7 | 58.5 | 63.0 | 58.5 | 55.7 | 51.2 | 46.7 | 42.8 | 34.3 | 28.2 |
| 28.2 | 34.3 | 42.8 | 46.7 | 51.2 | 55.7 | 58.5 | 63.0 | 58.5 | 55.7 | 51.2 | 46.7 | 42.8 | 34.3 | 28.2 |
| 25.7 | 31.7 | 37.5 | 42.7 | 46.4 | 49.4 | 52.2 | 53.0 | 52.2 | 49.4 | 46.4 | 42.7 | 37.5 | 31.7 | 25.7 |
| 23.7 | 24.8 | 28.7 | 31.7 | 35.7 | 38.2 | 38.5 | 39.4 | 38.5 | 38.2 | 35.7 | 31.7 | 28.7 | 24.8 | 23.7 |
| | | | | Fixture | | | | | Fixture | | | | | |
| 14.7 | 16.0 | 19.75 | 23.7 | 25.5 | 27.5 | 28.2 | 28.0 | 28.2 | 27.5 | 25.5 | 23.7 | 19.75 | 16.0 | 14.7 |

**TABLE 4-2.** *Watt per square foot densities throughout an 8-ft by 15-ft target area*

square feet of pavement area to find the total power input for the system. There is a rule of thumb based on actual practice for estimating the total input wattage needed in the infrared fixtures above the target area. Multiply the commonly used snow-melting watt densities shown in Table 4-2 by the target area in square feet. Then multiply the result by a correction factor of 1.6. The additional wattage compensates for the radiant efficiency involved, and for radiation falling outside the snow melting area. For small areas, or when the fixture mounting height exceeds 16 ft, the multiplying factor can be as large as 2.0. Large areas with sides of about equal lengths can have a factor of about 1.4.

The point-by-point method is the best way to calculate the heating fixture requirements. For this method, divide the target area into a grid pattern of 1-ft squares. Then cumulatively add the watt per square foot radiant energy from each infrared fixture on each square foot of grid, as shown in Table 4-2. Find the radiant energy distribution of a given infrared fixture from the equipment manufacturer. Follow all recommendations for fixture size and placement.

### System operation

With infrared energy, the target area can be preheated to snow-melting temperatures in 20 to 30 minutes unless the air temperature is well below 20°F or there is high wind velocity. With this fast warm-up time, the system does not need to be turned on until snow begins to fall. It can be turned on manually, or automatically with a snow detector. A timer is sometimes used to turn a system off four to six hours after the snow stops. This allows time to dry the pavement completely.

If snow accumulates before the system is turned on, there will be a delay in clearing the pavement. This is also the case with embedded systems. Note that the infrared energy is absorbed in the top layer of snow, not by the pavement surface. The time needed to clear the snow depends on the depth of the snow and the atmospheric conditions. Generally, a system will clear accumulated snow in about the same time that it melts falling snow. For example, assume that a system keeps pavement clear by melting one inch of snow an hour as it falls. Under the same conditions, this system will take one hour to clear one inch of accumulated snow.

Infrared snow-melting systems need little maintenance, primarily cleaning. For maximum efficiency, clean the reflectors at least once a year. The best time is the beginning of winter.

### Controls

A simple ON/OFF switch with a pilot light is normally used to activate electric snow-melting equipment. For heavy current loads, the ON/OFF switch controls a magnetic contactor. It, in turn, makes or breaks the snow-melting circuit. The operator turns the system on in anticipation of snow, and off when it is cleared. An outdoor thermostat in the control system can prevent accidental operation in summer. It will turn the system off when outdoor ambient temperature exceeds 35°F.

For critical applications, the high watt density capacity is needed only for extreme snow conditions. There is a way to limit the energy waste from this excess capacity during normal and light snow conditions. Add a low-temperature range thermostat, with remote slab temperature sensing bulb, to the control circuit. Install the remote bulb midway between cable or wire runs or between mats in the slab. Set the thermostat at 40°F. During mild weather snow conditions, the system will cycle on and off at slab temperature as the sensing bulb reaches 40°F.

### Automatic sensing

There are several fully automatic control devices. In general, these devices detect precipitation and sense air temperature at the same time. One method is to set a thermostat for a 35°F air temperature. Arrange for the signal from this thermostat to activate a heating element on a receptacle. This warm receptacle collects the precipitation, and melts it if it is frozen. The water then runs into a sensor collecting cup and activates a pilot circuit. This, in turn, can energize the snow-melting system power contactors. Another thermostat can be used to control the surface temperature of the snow-melting slab.

## HEATING WITH HIGH-INTENSITY ELECTRIC INFRARED HEATERS

An intervening heat transfer medium is not required to transfer energy by radiation. This fact allows high-intensity radiant heaters to be used in space heating very effectively. Heat is transferred by three methods—conduction, convection, and radiation. In conventional methods of space heating, air is the intervening medium for transferring energy from its source to the people or objects to be heated. Such a system uses conduction, convection, and, to a lesser degree, radiation. Energy is transmitted from the flame by conduction, radiation, and convection through a heat exchanger, generally to air or water. The energy is then distributed by convection to the area to be heated.

Air currents at less than body temperature passing over an individual cause a cooling sensation. Therefore, when convection is used to heat a space, air from the heat exchanger must be much higher than body temperature. This is essential for preventing a chilling effect on the occupants. The temperature required makes the air *buoyant*, or lighter than the surrounding air. This causes it to rise toward the ceiling. In most convection applications, because of the buoyant effect of the warm air, temperatures at the top of the building are higher than those at floor level.

Electric infrared heaters actually use two heat exchangers to distribute energy. The emitting surface of the infrared element is a radiant heat exchanger. It transmits energy to the various absorbing media around it. Energy absorbed by those media is immediately converted to heat. The heated materials that have absorbed the infrared energy then heat the air close to them. In effect, the floor and other equipment and structures in the building absorb the infrared energy. They all form a large heat exchanger, reflector, and re-radiator for the infrared energy.

There is one important difference in an infrared system. The floor and other objects that become the heat exchanger are at a much lower temperature than the heat exchanger in a convection heater. The air circulating around them cannot be heated higher than the temperature of the objects themselves. Therefore, air heated in an infrared system does not have the same buoyant effect as air in a convection system.

Since energy has been distributed by a radiant method of heat transfer, no high-velocity air circulation is required. Such circulation would create uncomfortable conditions because of the relatively low air temperature. Because of the low energy level of the air, it is not so buoyant. And remember that it cannot be heated any warmer than the heat exchanger from which it received its heat. Thus, the heat must be concentrated in the working area of the building, instead of rising to the roof. Since the air is warmest closest to the floor and other absorbing media, it must decrease in temperature as it attempts to rise. Heat loss through walls and ceilings of the building is decreased because of lower ambient temperatures on the upper portion of the walls and the ceiling.

One of the most significant factors in the application of infrared high bay heaters is that infrared energy from the heaters is not transferred to the air to an extent that allows it to cause high ceiling temperatures. Air is heated by the emitted energy because it circulates over the objects and materials that have absorbed the energy. The air cannot reach a higher temperature than these objects or materials. As the air moves away from these solid absorbing materials, it must become cooler. Therefore, it does not contribute to a higher energy level in the regions of the building above the occupied zone. Heat loss is decreased due to the lower ambient temperatures in the upper part of the building. To a lesser degree, additional heat is conserved since the internal surface coefficients are decreased. This occurs because of the lack of air movement resulting from the use of infrared heaters.

When the occupants of an area are exposed to direct radiation, lower ambient temperatures can be maintained to accomplish the same degree of comfort. The effect of radiation on the sensation of warmth is of most interest in space heating applications. The human skin absorbs infrared radiation almost like a black body. The absorption for wavelengths greater than 2 microns is between 0.97 and 0.98. Visible rays and the shorter infrared waves are reflected to a greater extent.

Radiation at wavelengths greater than 2 microns penetrates the skin, but is absorbed in less than 0.0008 in. Visible rays and the shorter infrared waves travel deeper before being absorbed. Studies show that a change in radiation of about 2 Btuh per square foot gives a sense of warmth.

In an IR (infrared) heating system, as heat loss per square foot of floor area increases, heater input can usually be reduced. This is because of the increase in flux density of the infrared energy over the area. With more direct radiation available, the air temperature can be lowered, thus decreasing heat loss.

As an example, consider building X with an area of 10,000 ft$^2$. It has a heat loss of 30 Btuh/ft$^2$. Under such conditions, a typical radiant intensity on the floor is about 15 Btuh/ft². The ambient temperature needed for comfort might be 70°F. Then consider building Y of 10,000 ft². It has a heat loss per square foot of 80 Btuh. Under these conditions, a typical radiant intensity may be 40 Btuh/ft².

With the increase in radiant intensity, a lower ambient temperature will maintain comfort. In this case, a temperature as low as 60°F could probably maintain comfortable working conditions. The ability of an infrared system to create comfortable conditions at lower ambient temperatures is an important factor in determining the total heat input requirement. This fact accounts for some of the economy of operation expected in a properly applied infrared heating system.

## SPACE HEATING WITH ELECTRIC RADIANT HEATERS

When an entire space is heated with radiant heaters, comfort is governed by two factors:

- the direct radiation on the subject from every heater that the body "sees"

- the warming of the air in the space, which takes place by convection heat transfer from the floor and other surfaces that are heated.

AITKEN PRODUCTS, INC.

There is a balance between the two heating effects within which the body can adjust for comfort. Where infiltration rates are high, comfort should depend on direct radiation. This will minimize the cost of heating the infiltrating air. At very high air change rates produced by industrial ventilation, a makeup air system may be used to temper the incoming air required to maintain a suitable pressure balance.

**FIGURE 4-3.** *Typical ceiling-mounted electric radiant heater used in a space heating application*

Where infiltration is minimal, and the building is well-insulated and has relatively low ceilings, the air temperature will closely approximate normal room temperatures. Direct radiation is of minor consequence. However, the more you depart from such ideal conditions, the more direct radiation becomes a factor in total comfort conditions. Figure 4-3 shows one type of electric radiant heater that can be used for space heating.

## FULL BUILDING HEATING WITH INFRARED HEAT

Infrared units can heat all types of commercial and industrial buildings successfully. The placement, number, and size of the units are extremely important for a good application. The following paragraphs discuss these factors in greater detail.

When heating with infrared, keep in mind that floors (slabs) and stationary objects will be heated. They will then radiate, conduct, and convect their heat to the space. Therefore, it is important that the infrared rays are wisely directed. They should not be wasted on walls—particularly outside walls or windows. The placement, angle of installation, and intensity patterns are important to be sure that the heat is put to its best use.

Another noteworthy facet of infrared full building heating is start-up. When you heat the floor (slab) and other stationary objects, it takes time to generate a build-up, particularly from a cold start. At start-up during the winter, it may take one or two full days of heating with infrared before such a build-up (heat sink) is obtained. Once the heat sink area is established, comfortable conditions should prevail for the entire heating season with normal cycling of the heating equipment.

In many facilities, doors must be opened frequently. Others may have the kind of construction that permits high levels of infiltration (leaks of outside air into the space). It is in these types of buildings that the heat sink infrared method is best appreciated. Others that come to mind are those that have walls with high rates of heat loss, such as uninsulated steel buildings. In all cases, when the heat from the infrared units is directed into the floor (slab), the heated floor, in turn, provides heat to the space. For this reason, the slab should have ample edge insulation. This limits the conduction of heat from the slab into the surrounding grade.

## FULL BUILDING HEAT LOSS

As with other types of heating applications, you first must determine the Btuh needs when planning to use infrared heating. For buildings, such information is often available from the architect or engineer involved in the building design. If not, you will have to develop it on your own, or with the aid of someone knowledgeable in heat loss studies. The following paragraphs will help you generate much of your own heat loss information for commercial and industrial buildings.

### Building heat losses

Buildings lose their internal heat by radiation, convection, conduction, and by infiltration (outside air leaking into the building). These losses occur when the outdoor temperature is lower than the indoor temperature.

### Design temperature

To determine heat loss through a wall, roof, or other parts of a building enclosure, the design temperature difference ($\Delta T$) is used in the final calculation. The outdoor temperature at winter design conditions is needed.

Winter outdoor design temperatures are available from ACCA's Manual N or from ASHRAE heat loss calculation books. There are also computer programs that contain ACCA's Manual N heat load calculations. With electric infrared heaters, the heat load calculation is adjusted by multiplying by 0.85. Heat output of electric infrared heaters is calculated by multiplying the input (in kilowatts) by 3,413. The result is the Btu output of the heaters. The Btu output figure is divided into the adjusted heat load to find the number of heaters needed to heat the space.

The indoor temperature is often a matter of choice. Sometimes, it may depend on the use of the building. For example, some warehouses are unheated—or the temperature may be kept just above freezing for the protection of the materials or equipment stored within. However, for comfort conditions, most building owners or users currently observe an indoor design temperature of 68°F. This offers adequate heating, yet provides the most economical fuel costs. By subtracting outdoor temperature from indoor temperature, you can find the $\Delta T$ (temperature difference) to be used in heat loss calculations.

### Surface losses by convection and radiation

The outside surface of all buildings loses the heat stored inside. Building construction dictates at what rate this occurs. All building materials have a certain resistance to the flow of heat. To compute heat losses, you must know the heat flow rate through the outer shell.

Heat flow rates are expressed in several ways. A "K" factor is the flow of heat, expressed in Btuh through one square foot of a specific material that is 12 in. thick. It is based on a temperature difference of 1°F. However, most buildings have partitions much thinner than 12 in. They very often are made of various layers of differing materials. Thus, the "K" factor is not a very practical or efficient tool for determining heat loss.

Another measure of the resistance of heat flow is known as the "R" factor. This is a rating assigned to insulation. It identifies, by number, the ability of the insulation to resist the flow of heat. The higher the "R" number, the greater the resistance. However, the "R" factor alone is not sufficient for computing heat loss.

The "U" factor is a value expressed in Btuh/ft$^2$/°F. It represents the amount of heat that will flow through one square foot of a material of a specific thickness in one hour. Further, it is based on a 15-mph wind effect on the cold side. The values are scientific expressions that advise anticipated loss when there is a temperature difference ($\Delta$T) of 1°F between the two sides. "U" factors are given for individual materials and for specific wall and roof constructions which may or may not include insulation. Therefore, the "U" factor provides the best heat flow information for computing heat loss. Table 4-3 on page 82 lists some types of construction with "U" factors. For materials not listed, refer to the ASHRAE guide or other sources.

The "R" factor can be converted to a "U" value by dividing the R number into 1. (Example: R19 = $\frac{1}{19}$ = 0.05 Btuh/ft$^2$/°F.) However, insulation is never singularly used in construction. You should use this information only to make comparisons between insulations when studying fuel consumption. For instance, let's assume that a ceiling with a surface area of 10,000 ft$^2$ is under study. The objective is to choose the most cost-effective insulation. If R10 and R19 are being considered, you first must convert the R factors to Btuh/ft$^2$:

$$R10 = \tfrac{1}{10} = 0.1 \text{ Btuh/ft}^2$$
$$R19 = \tfrac{1}{19} = 0.0526 \text{ Btuh/ft}^2$$

With a $\Delta$T of 70°F (indoor = 70°F, outdoor = 0°F), calculate the Btuh loss for each as follows:

$$R10 = 70 \times 10,000 \times 0.1 = 70,000 \text{ Btuh loss}$$
$$R19 = 70 \times 10,000 \times 0.0526 = 36,820 \text{ Btuh loss}$$

Use the following equation to compute the annual fuel consumption for each insulation:

$$\frac{\text{HL} \times 24 \times \text{DD}}{\text{Eff} \times \Delta\text{T}} = \text{annual fuel consumption in Btu}$$

where:

HL = hourly heat loss for area studied
DD = annual degree days
Eff = efficiency of heating equipment
$\Delta$T = temperature difference at design.

For this example, we will use 90% heater efficiency, and 6,000 annual degree days (approximate for 0° design). Therefore, for R10:

$$\frac{70,000 \times 24 \times 6,000}{0.90 \times 70}$$

$$=\frac{10,080,000,000}{63}$$

$$= 160,000,000 \text{ annual Btu consumption}$$

And for R19:

$$\frac{36,820 \times 24 \times 6,000}{0.90 \times 70}$$

$$=\frac{5,302,080,000}{63}$$

$$= 84,160,000 \text{ annual Btu consumption}$$

To determine fuel costs, first convert the Btu to kilowatt-hours (kWh). Then determine the maximum amount of electricity used for the demand rate period. It varies from utility to utility. The calculations must be made on a month-by-month basis, since most electric utilities bill demand rate on a monthly schedule.

For example, let's use a demand rate of $5.00 per kilowatt and a rate per kilowatt-hour of 5 cents. The assumption is that with R10 insulation, the heat loss is 70,000 Btu per hour. With R19 insulation, it is assumed to be 36,820 Btu per hour.

If the heat loss is 70,000 Btu per hour, let's assume that the month is a cold month and the average Btu loss per hour is one-third of 70,000 Btuh, or 23,333 Btuh. One kilowatt is 3,413 Btu, so:

$$\frac{70,000}{3,413} = 20.5 \text{ kW for the demand rate}$$

$$20.5 \times \$5.00 = \$102.50$$

$$\frac{23,333}{3,413} = 6.8 \text{ kW per hour for the month}$$

$$6.8 \times 30 \times 24 = 4,896 \text{ kWh per month}$$

$$4,896 \times \$0.05 = \$244.80$$

R10 costs are $244.80 per month, plus $102.50 for the demand rate, or a total of $347.30 for that month

If the heat loss is 38,820 Btu per hour, let's assume that the month is a cold month and the average Btu loss per hour is one-third of 38,820 Btuh, or 12,940 Btuh. Again, since one kilowatt is 3,413 Btu:

$$\frac{38,820}{3,413} = 11.4 \text{ kW for the demand rate}$$

$$11.4 \times \$5.00 = \$57.00$$

$$\frac{12,940}{3,413} = 3.8 \text{ kW per hour for the month}$$

$$3.8 \times 30 \times 24 = 2,736 \text{ kWh per month}$$

$$2,736 \times \$0.05 = \$136.80$$

R19 costs are $136.80 per month, plus $57.00 for the demand rate, or a total of $193.80 for that month. Therefore, the savings for that month would be $347.30 minus $193.80, or $153.50 for the additional insulation.

To do accurate calculations, you would need daily temperature readings for every winter month over a ten-year period. This is called *bin data*. It is available from the U.S. Weather Bureau. A decision on which insulation to use must be made based on insulation cost difference versus fuel cost during years of amortization.

### Surface area

To develop surface area for an entire building, first list the various construction types found in the shell of the building. This includes the following.

- wall construction (there may be several different types of construction employed, so be sure to list them all)

- type of glass (list each type separately)

- ceiling or roof construction

- doors (list each size or type separately)

- basement or slab.

For each of the various surfaces or edges, measure carefully so that accurate areas or lineal dimensions can be developed. Be sure to deduct windows and door areas from the wall surface. Next, review Table 4-3 on page 82 and find the proper "U" factor for each different construction type listed. When the ΔT, "U" factor, and surface area are known, surface losses can be calculated as follows:

area (in square feet) $\times$ ΔT $\times$ U = Btuh loss for area studied

The sum of all surface area losses is the total radiational and convectional losses for the building under study.

### Infiltration

In all buildings, there is some infiltration of outside air. This unheated air enters through cracks, usually around windows and doors. It can seep through loosely constructed walls and joints. Such leakage adds considerably to the total heat loss. It is difficult and time-consuming to determine the amount of infiltration. There are devices that measure such leakage, but at great cost. An accurate assessment of infiltration is best compiled by the architect or engineer. If this information is unavailable, most estimators will arbitrarily use an infiltration rate based on the volume of the building. For small buildings (less than 100,000 cubic feet) an infiltration rate of one air change per hour is generally used. For larger buildings, the air change rate is lower—but never less than one-third the volume of the building.

A more exacting method of determining infiltration rates is available from the ASHRAE guides and other sources. In these studies, lineal feet measurements of all window and door edges are needed. Also considered are the types of joints used in the construction of the building, potential wind velocities, and prevailing wind directions.

If you use the air change method, simply multiply the building volume in cubic feet times 0.018 times ΔT. This gives the Btuh loss for one air change of infiltration. If you use other than one air change, or if you use the ASHRAE method, you must make this adjustment before completing the above calculation. The infiltration loss will be added to the total radiational losses determined earlier. If you use ACCA's Manual N heat load calculation, or a computerized version of it, the infiltration will be calculated as part of the heat loss.

### Exhausts and ventilation

Many industrial and commercial buildings are equipped with exhausters to get rid of unwanted contaminants. Also, many of these buildings require ventilation.

| Surface | Area, square feet | | "U" | Btuh loss |
|---------|------------------|---|-----|-----------|
| Brick wall | 3,320 | (partial doors deducted) | 0.41 | 78,949 |
| Steel wall | 97,320 | (doors, windows deducted) | 0.21 | 118,535 |
| Roof | 30,000 | | 0.05 | 87,000 |
| Windows | 480 | | 0.70 | 19,488 |
| Doors (service) | 60 | (deduct from brick wall) | 0.20 | 696 |
| Doors (service) | 24 | (deduct from steel wall) | 0.20 | 278 |
| Doors (rollaway) | 120 | (deduct from brick wall) | 0.59 | 4,106 |
| Doors (rollaway) | 264 | (deduct from steel wall) | 0.59 | 9,034 |

Total radiational losses = . . . . . . . . . . . . . . . . . . . . . . . . . . . . . . . . . . . . . . . . . . . . . 318,086

Infiltration = volume × ½ air change = 600,000

600,000 × 0.5 = 300,000

300,000 × 0.018 × 58 = . . . . . . . . . . . . . . . . . . . . . . . . . . . . . . . . . . . . . 313,200

Slab edge loss = 700 lineal feet × 58 × 0.3 = . . . . . . . . . . . . . . . . . . . . . . . . . . . . . 12,180

Hourly heat loss in Btu = . . . . . . . . . . . . . . . . . . . . . . . . . . . . . . . . . . . . . . . . . . . 643,466

**TABLE 4-3.** *Sample heat loss calculations*

Both exhaust and ventilation are supplied under power to ensure that the volume is as prescribed. Flow rates are expressed in cfm (cubic feet per minute). If the building you are evaluating for heat loss includes either or both of these functions, observe the following rules.

If the infiltration rate (cfm) is greater than the exhaust cfm and/or ventilation cfm, then calculate only the infiltration losses. Calculate infiltration cfm by dividing the volume of infiltration (cubit feet) by 60 (minutes).

If the infiltration rate (cfm) is less than the exhaust and/or ventilation cfm, then calculate the losses associated with these functions. Add this to the radiational losses determined earlier. Be sure to omit the infiltration losses.

Calculate exhaust and ventilation Btuh losses with the following equation:

$$\text{cfm} \times 1.085 \times \Delta T = \text{Btuh loss}$$

### Loss by conduction

Conductive losses occur at grade. They are greatest in buildings that have a slab rather than a basement. It is important that the slab edges are insulated to guard against excessive losses at this point. This is particularly important when using infrared as a heat source, since a basic objective with infrared is to heat the slab.

To calculate Btuh loss for the edges of the slab, use the following:

- slab with uninsulated edge: 0.91 Btuh × lineal feet × ΔT

- slab with insulated edge: 0.30 Btuh × lineal feet × ΔT

This quantity is added to the radiation, infiltration, or exhaust and ventilation losses determined earlier. The total represents the hourly building Btu loss at design conditions.

### Heat loss study

To help you understand heat loss calculation more fully, the following sample heat loss study is offered in Table 4-3:

| | |
|---|---|
| **Building:** | Commercial, measuring 200 ft × 150 ft × 20 ft high |
| **Walls:** | Split construction, 5 ft of 8-in. common brick (two rows of 4 in.), 15 ft of sheet metal with 1 in. expanded polystyrene |
| **Roof:** | Flat, built up with 6-in. R19 insulation |
| **Windows:** | 30, measuring 48 in. × 48 in. each, double-insulated with steel sash |
| **Doors:** | Three service doors, 7 ft × 4 ft insulated steel, and two rollaway doors, 12 ft × 16 ft steel (1.75 in.) |
| **Floor:** | Slab on grade with edge insulation |
| **Infiltration rate:** | ½ air change |
| **Outdoor design:** | +10°F |
| **Indoor design:** | 68°F |
| **ΔT:** | 58°F |

Total heat loss for the example is 643,466 Btuh.

For convection-type heating, this is the amount of heat that must be supplied to the building under design conditions of +10°F outdoors and 68°F indoors.

The convection-type heaters would have to be sized based on their Btuh output rating. These ratings are listed in the manufacturer's specifications.

However, when heating with infrared, you can reduce the calculated heat loss by 15%. Also, you size the units based on their input rating. Therefore, $643,466 \times 0.85 = 546,946$ Btuh. The 15% reduction is permissible because with infrared you avoid direct radiation against the ceiling and outside walls. This, in effect, keeps the $\Delta T$ at a minimum. That is why it is important not to direct the infrared rays against outside walls, windows, and doors. Of course, with the reflectors, no infrared energies should contact the ceiling or roof.

## INFRARED APPLICATION FOR TOTAL BUILDING HEATING

The first consideration in selecting infrared heaters is the available mounting height. Low mounting heights dictate that larger numbers of small, high-intensity units may be required (or low-intensity units). High mounting heights may require fewer large, high-intensity units, and may rule out low-intensity units altogether. Remember that the most effective application will allow the intensity patterns of adjacent units to overlap. Voids between unit patterns give less than ideal results.

Let's continue with the sample heat loss example, and make our unit selections. The ceiling height is 20 ft. However, this does not mean that you will install the units at or near this height. First, you must check clearances from combustibles. You may find that there are combustible materials in the built-up roof. Then you must observe the manufacturer's recommended clearances. This is the closest you dare install the selected units. (Fire hazard clearances are clearly stated. They will vary for each manufacturer and each individual unit. You must know these dimensions before planning any unit selections or installations.)

Let's assume that high-intensity units require a top clearance of 24 in., and low-intensity units 12 in. Thus, the maximum mounting height for high-intensity units is 18 ft, and for low-intensity units 19 ft. This distance is from the floor to the top of the unit. Remember, the building in our example has 700 lineal feet of wall. With this data, you can analyze your equipment selections.

High-intensity infrared units come in sizes ranging from 30,000 to 160,000 Btuh input, with three or four sizes in between. Low-intensity units generally come in sizes ranging from 75,000 up to 150,000 Btuh input, with two or three sizes in between. Determine exactly what sizes are available from the manufacturer.

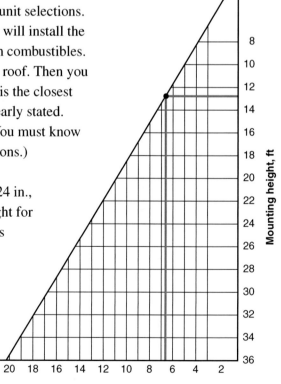

**FIGURE 4-4.** *Minimum unit centerline-to-wall distance (in feet) for a high-intensity infrared heater installed at a 30° angle*

For our example, let's see how many of the largest and smallest units might be needed. You can also find the initial centerline distance (CLD) required between units. For a high-intensity application:

546,946 ÷ 30,000 = 22 units          700 ÷ 18 = 38.9 ft CLD

546,946 ÷ 100,000 = 6 units          700 ÷ 6 = 116.6 ft CLD

### High-intensity application

The 30,000-Btuh high-intensity infrared unit has the shortest CLD. Also, remember the mounting height limit in our example building (18 ft). Let's proceed with this unit. It is best to plan on the greater number of units, and hope to get total coverage of the perimeter. Now you must find the mounting height and the centerline distance from the wall. For a 15-ft mounting height, Figure 4-4 shows that the units should be 7 ft 9 in. from the wall.

Figure 4-5 shows a proposed layout for the 30,000-Btuh high-intensity units. This size was selected for optimum perimeter coverage. With larger units, there would be many pattern voids because of the limited mounting height and greater CLD.

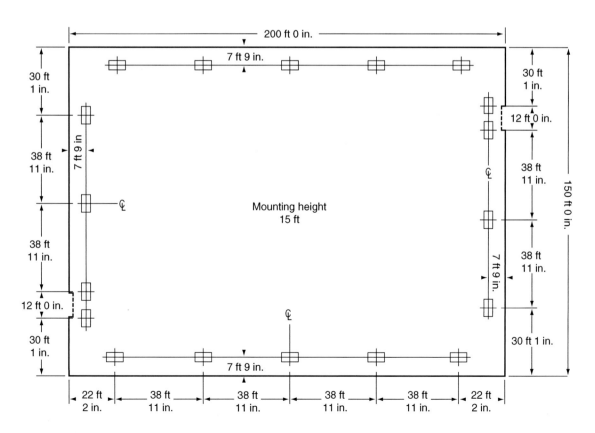

**FIGURE 4-5.** *Sample layout of 18 high-intensity units of 30,000 Btuh at a 30° angle*

As mentioned earlier, this would give less than ideal heating characteristics. Note that liberties were taken with unit placement so that there is a concentration of heat at the rollaway doors. Otherwise, the CLD of 38.9 ft was observed and the units are at a 30° angle, facing the center of the building.

Two adjacent heaters at 38.9 ft CLD give intense floor coverage over about 30 ft of the CLD. This leaves 8.9 ft of diminished intensity (void). But line-of-sight intensities will give a small amount of heat to this area. As an alternate, you may choose to use more heaters for a shorter CLD.

There is a better solution. We can close the CLD by changing units to a horizontal position. This requires moving farther from the wall. Look at Table 4-4. The recommended distance between heater and wall is 18 ft with the unit at a 14-ft height.

Figure 4-6 shows how the layout would appear. Note that on the 200-ft walls there are no intensity voids. The 150-ft walls, however, will have voids of 6 in. You could plan on the line-of-sight intensities to cover these.

Therefore, there are three choices of installation:

| Horizontal mounting height (ft) | Suggested long-axis distance from wall (ft) |
| --- | --- |
| 8 | 8 |
| 10 | 10 |
| 12 | 14 |
| 14 | 18 |
| 16 | 21 |
| 18 | 25 |
| 20 | 28 |
| 22 | 32 |
| 24 | 35 |
| 26 | 38 |
| 28 | 42 |
| 30 | 46 |
| 32 | 49 |
| 34 | 53 |
| 36 | 56 |

**TABLE 4-4.** *Recommended distance from wall at different mounting heights*

- 18 units, 30° tilt, with 8.9 ft of void between units. Since the number of units matches the heat load, you may choose to rely on line-of-sight intensities to fill the voids. Mounting height is 15 ft.

- 24 units, 30° tilt, with no voids. This requires six additional units. They give a 33% increase in input beyond the calculated heat loss. Mounting height is 15 ft.

- 20 units, horizontal installation. This is a 11% increase in capacity over the calculated heat loss (two additional units). Mounting height is 14 ft.

Let's assume that the locations of all three systems are acceptable. If so, then the third strategy should be selected to guarantee solid perimeter coverage.

### Location of infrared heating units

- Position one row of the heaters along each exposed wall. The minimum total input of the heaters should be no less than the transmission loss of

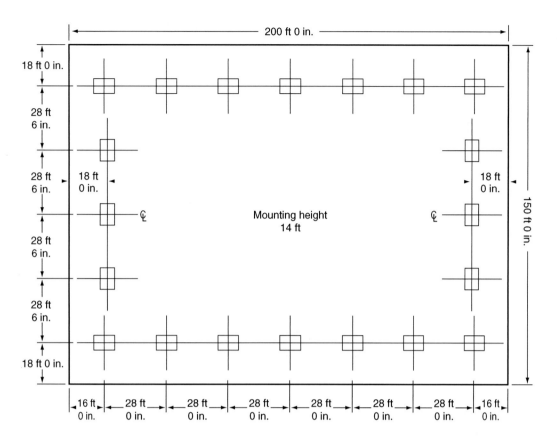

**FIGURE 4-6.** *Sample layout of 20 high-intensity units of 30,000 Btuh installed horizontally*

the wall combined with the infiltration loss of the building. Mount the heaters according to the placement chart in the manufacturer's application or installation manual.

- Doors that open periodically permit large amounts of infiltration. Treat such door areas as a spot heating problem. The direct radiation gains to the workers should offset the reduced air temperatures.

- Locate the remaining units in a pattern that gives uniform distribution of radiation in spaces normally occupied.

- Avoid locations where structural members and machinery will cast cold shadows on the subject. They will absorb or reflect the infrared energy, which will not reach the subject.

- Place units so that combustible materials and sensitive equipment are not overheated. Too much heat can be from direct radiant heat transfer or by contact with the heater. Shielding with aluminum sheets protects from radiation.

## CONTROLLING INFRARED UNITS USED FOR TOTAL SPACE HEATING

Direct radiant heating systems are controlled with ordinary room thermostats with suitable radiation shielding. You can set the thermostat to maintain a predetermined air temperature in the occupied space, or set it to the temperature found by experience to provide the most comfortable conditions. With this type of control, air temperature can be changed to adjust for the direct radiation actually received by the subjects.

Avoid the undesirable effect of all radiant heat being turned off at once. Couple alternate heaters to separate thermostats. Then, on an initial rise of inside air temperature, only part of the radiant heat is turned off. The remaining coverage of radiation should provide comfort conditions at the higher air temperature. Should the temperature continue to rise, the remaining heaters would be extinguished. Eventually, with a continued rise in temperature, all the heaters would be off. If the temperature settles at some intermediate point, a given number of heaters would continue to operate to add direct radiation to the area.

This type of control is accomplished by wiring alternate heaters into different thermostats set at slightly different temperatures. It is desirable to break the control system down into small units. It allows the system to maintain better comfort conditions—if one area has reached comfortable conditions, it would not have to be overheated because an adjoining area requires more heat. Avoiding overheated areas creates economies in operation. The additional cost of the controls is more than offset by the fuel savings.

### Placement of thermostats

Mount internal air thermostats on walls or building columns about 5 ft from the floor. Shield them from direct radiation. Some thermostats may control a large group of heaters around a doorway. Mount them internally so that they operate the heaters automatically when cold air enters the doorway. A manual override can also be used for this function.

## SPOT HEATING WITH ELECTRIC INFRARED HEATERS

When occupant density is low and work stations relatively static, spot heating is an economical solution. It offers both low initial cost and operational savings. Spot heating generally assumes that heat is not required for other purposes. A high infiltration rate combined with limited work stations also suggests spot heating. In spot heating applications, there should be radiation from two sides of the worker, if practical. Direct the major amount of the radiation below the subject's head.

### Spot heating with high-intensity infrared

When a high-intensity infrared has reached peak temperature, the surface glows brightly. The material has reached a temperature of about 1,650 to 1,850°F. The intensity is great near the surface. It is impractical or even dangerous to expose objects or materials at close distance. When you draw away from this surface, you find more acceptable levels of radiation. The intensity diminishes as the inverse square of the distance. It can calculated using the following equation:

$$\frac{T1}{T2} = \frac{(D2)^2}{(D1)^2}$$

where:

T1 = known Btuh/ft² intensity
D1 = distance at which T1 was measured
T2 = new Btuh/ft² intensity
D2 = new distance.

The intensity recedes as you move away from the source. However, this does not mean a reduction of total output. It does show that the focus widens as the distance increases. Therefore, the Btu are spread over a larger area. This reduces the temperature at the greatest distances from the source, while the original output is constant.

When you recognize the distance/intensity relationship of infrared heat, it is easier to understand the importance of the correct mounting height. Btu intensities vary with the size, surface temperatures, and infrared patterns of the heater. Thus, specific mounting height versus Btu intensity is found only through testing of a particular model and size of heater. For this reason, mounting height information varies with manufacturers. They often provide a recommended minimum mounting height chart. An example is shown in Table 4-5.

Some high-intensity infrared heater manufacturers publish flux density graphs. You can interpret these to find the desired mounting height. Even better, the manufacturer may interpret the flux density graph for you and publish a Btuh per square foot table, as shown in Figure 4-7 on the next two pages. These tables give specific mounting heights based on the Btu required at

| Recommended minimum mounting height | | |
|---|---|---|
| | Heater position | |
| Size, Btuh | Horizontal | 30° angle |
| 30,000 | 11 ft 0 in. | 10 ft 0 in. |
| 50,000 | 13 ft 6 in. | 12 ft 6 in. |
| 60,000 | 14 ft 6 in. | 13 ft 0 in. |
| 90,000 | 16 ft 0 in. | 14 ft 6 in. |
| 100,000 | 17 ft 0 in. | 15 ft 0 in. |
| 120,000 | 17 ft 6 in. | 15 ft 6 in. |
| 150,000 | 18 ft 6 in. | 15 ft 7 in. |
| 160,000 | 19 ft 0 in. | 17 ft 0 in. |

**TABLE 4-5.** *A common recommendation for minimum mounting heights*

the floor or at a specified height. They also provide horizontal distance in an easy-to-interpret format. Generating such graphs and tables requires testing on each specific model, size, and potential variation of the heater. As a result, this type of specific information is often not available. When flux density graphs or Btuh per square foot tables are available, use them to find the mounting height for the heat required. If they are not, find the best height from the recommended minimum mounting height chart and the floor coverage required.

There is a simple rule to follow in floor coverage. The coverage of a horizontal unit is two times the mounting height. At a 30° angle, the length of dispersion is four times the mounting height. While this distance/intensity relationship applies to mounting height, it also affects the intensity pattern of the infrared dispersion or floor coverage.

The first step in spot heating with high-intensity infrared is to find the Btu level needed. Most spot heating is used to provide comfort for people. With this in mind, let's look at how Btu requirements vary under different ambient conditions, and as the people change activities.

Figure 4-8 on page 92 is a *surface heat loss nomograph*. It shows Btu levels needed to provide comfort conditions for people working in a given area. Note that the activity level, ambient temperature, air movement, and clothing all affect the Btu lost from the body. The greatest influence is activity level. As the activity level rises, fewer comfort Btu are required. The body

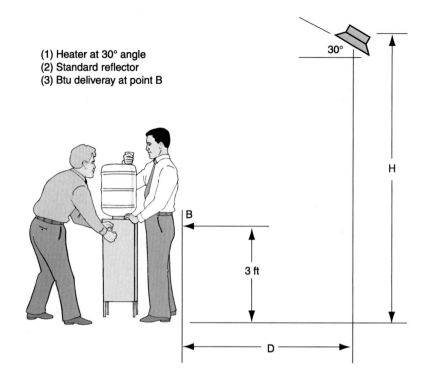

(1) Heater at 30° angle
(2) Standard reflector
(3) Btu deliveray at point B

| H | D (ft) | | | | | | | | | | | |
|---|---|---|---|---|---|---|---|---|---|---|---|---|
| (ft) | 2 | 4 | 6 | 8 | 10 | 12 | 14 | 16 | 18 | 20 | 22 | 24 |
| 7 | 212 | 174 | 105 | 66 | 43 | 29 | 20 | 15 | 11 | 9 | 7 | 6 |
| 9 | 70 | 99 | 77 | 55 | 39 | 29 | 22 | 17 | 13 | 10 | 8 | 7 |
| 11 | 29 | 53 | 54 | 44 | 33 | 26 | 20 | 16 | 13 | 11 | 9 | 7 |
| 13 | 15 | 30 | 36 | 34 | 28 | 23 | 18 | 15 | 12 | 10 | 9 | 7 |
| 15 | 9 | 17 | 24 | 25 | 23 | 19 | 16 | 14 | 12 | 10 | 8 | 7 |
| 17 | 5 | 11 | 16 | 18 | 18 | 16 | 14 | 12 | 10 | 9 | 8 | 7 |
| 19 | 4 | 7 | 11 | 13 | 14 | 14 | 12 | 11 | 10 | 8 | 7 | 6 |
| 21 | 2 | 5 | 8 | 10 | 11 | 11 | 10 | 10 | 9 | 8 | 7 | 6 |
| 23 | 2 | 4 | 6 | 7 | 8 | 9 | 9 | 8 | 8 | 7 | 6 | 6 |
| 25 | 1.4 | 3 | 4 | 6 | 7 | 7 | 7 | 7 | 7 | 6 | 6 | 5 |
| 27 | 1.0 | 2 | 3 | 4 | 5 | 6 | 6 | 6 | 6 | 6 | 5 | 5 |
| 29 | 0.8 | 1.7 | 3 | 3 | 4 | 5 | 5 | 5 | 5 | 5 | 5 | 4 |
| 31 | 0.7 | 1.4 | 2 | 3 | 3 | 4 | 4 | 5 | 5 | 4 | 4 | 4 |
| 33 | 0.5 | 1.1 | 1.7 | 2 | 3 | 3 | 4 | 4 | 4 | 4 | 4 | 4 |

Model RIH 60

**FIGURE 4-7.** *Btuh heat delivery (check the accompanying tables for the value of H and D for three specific Reznor models)*

REZNOR

generates much of its own heat requirements. As the activity level decreases, more comfort Btu must be added. These changes are shown in the small inset at the upper right on the chart. They must be added or deducted from the surface heat loss shown in the left column. A sample application later will put this chart to use.

Figure 4-7 illustrates examples of Btuh/ft² tables. Such tables give radiating capability and mounting heights based on testing of specific heaters. These tables are for specific Reznor models of high-intensity infrared heaters. Each table is based on testing of the heater installed in the most common spot heating application—a 30° angle measuring the Btu intensity 3 ft above the floor.

Most infrared units have standard reflector systems. They define the radiation pattern. In effect, they provide a better concentration of Btu intensities. Figures 4-9 and 4-10 on page 93 show the long axis pattern and the short axis pattern, respectively. The maximum spread of 12 ft is typical, but will vary with unit size. Also, the manufacturer has selected these dimensions based on acceptable intensity levels for the average installation. Intensities beyond these dimensions exist, but in many cases they are considered fringe Btu that do not figure into considerations for spot heating.

**Line of sight**

**Model RIHV 100**

| H (ft) | D (ft) | | | | | | | | | | | |
|---|---|---|---|---|---|---|---|---|---|---|---|---|
| | 2 | 4 | 6 | 8 | 10 | 12 | 14 | 16 | 18 | 20 | 22 | 24 |
| 7 | 354 | 290 | 174 | 110 | 72 | 49 | 34 | 25 | 18 | 14 | 12 | 9 |
| 9 | 116 | 165 | 129 | 91 | 66 | 49 | 36 | 28 | 22 | 17 | 13 | 11 |
| 11 | 49 | 88 | 90 | 72 | 56 | 44 | 34 | 27 | 22 | 18 | 15 | 12 |
| 13 | 25 | 49 | 59 | 56 | 46 | 38 | 31 | 25 | 21 | 18 | 15 | 12 |
| 15 | 14 | 29 | 39 | 41 | 38 | 32 | 27 | 23 | 19 | 16 | 14 | 12 |
| 17 | 9 | 18 | 26 | 30 | 30 | 27 | 24 | 20 | 17 | 15 | 13 | 12 |
| 19 | 6 | 12 | 18 | 22 | 23 | 22 | 20 | 18 | 16 | 14 | 12 | 11 |
| 21 | 4 | 9 | 13 | 16 | 18 | 18 | 18 | 16 | 14 | 13 | 11 | 10 |
| 23 | 3 | 6 | 9 | 12 | 14 | 15 | 15 | 14 | 13 | 12 | 10 | 9 |
| 25 | 3 | 6 | 9 | 12 | 14 | 15 | 15 | 14 | 13 | 12 | 10 | 9 |
| 27 | 2 | 4 | 5 | 7 | 9 | 10 | 10 | 10 | 10 | 9 | 9 | 8 |
| 29 | 1.4 | 3 | 4 | 6 | 7 | 8 | 9 | 9 | 9 | 8 | 8 | 7 |
| 31 | 1.1 | 2 | 3 | 5 | 6 | 7 | 7 | 8 | 8 | 7 | 7 | 7 |
| 33 | 0.9 | 1.8 | 3 | 4 | 5 | 5 | 6 | 6 | 7 | 7 | 6 | 6 |

**Model RIHV 150**

| H (ft) | D (ft) | | | | | | | | | | | |
|---|---|---|---|---|---|---|---|---|---|---|---|---|
| | 2 | 4 | 6 | 8 | 10 | 12 | 14 | 16 | 18 | 20 | 22 | 24 |
| 7 | 531 | 435 | 262 | 164 | 108 | 73 | 51 | 37 | 28 | 22 | 17 | 14 |
| 9 | 174 | 248 | 193 | 137 | 98 | 73 | 54 | 42 | 32 | 25 | 20 | 16 |
| 11 | 74 | 133 | 135 | 109 | 84 | 66 | 51 | 41 | 33 | 27 | 22 | 18 |
| 13 | 38 | 74 | 89 | 84 | 70 | 56 | 46 | 38 | 31 | 26 | 22 | 18 |
| 15 | 22 | 44 | 59 | 62 | 58 | 48 | 40 | 34 | 29 | 24 | 21 | 18 |
| 17 | 14 | 28 | 40 | 45 | 45 | 41 | 36 | 30 | 26 | 23 | 20 | 17 |
| 19 | 9 | 18 | 27 | 33 | 34 | 34 | 31 | 27 | 24 | 21 | 18 | 16 |
| 21 | 6 | 13 | 19 | 24 | 27 | 28 | 26 | 24 | 22 | 19 | 17 | 15 |
| 23 | 4 | 10 | 14 | 18 | 21 | 22 | 22 | 21 | 19 | 18 | 16 | 14 |
| 25 | 3 | 7 | 11 | 14 | 17 | 18 | 18 | 18 | 17 | 16 | 14 | 13 |
| 27 | 3 | 5 | 8 | 11 | 13 | 15 | 15 | 15 | 15 | 14 | 13 | 12 |
| 29 | 2 | 4 | 6 | 9 | 11 | 12 | 13 | 13 | 13 | 13 | 12 | 11 |
| 31 | 2 | 3 | 5 | 7 | 8 | 10 | 11 | 11 | 11 | 11 | 11 | 10 |
| 33 | 1.3 | 3 | 4 | 6 | 7 | 8 | 9 | 10 | 10 | 10 | 10 | 9 |

**FIGURE 4-7.** *Btuh heat delivery (continued)*

Btuh/ft² intensity tables are based on extensive testing. The values and boundaries are considered by the manufacturer as the most useful. However, the infrared pattern extends beyond these boundaries by simple "line-of-sight" considerations. If you can see the glowing surface, there will be energies, however small, radiated to the point of sighting. Figure 4-11 shows the typical line-of-sight pattern for both long axis patterns and short axis patterns. Intensities are small but do exist. Keep this in mind when selecting a room thermostat location.

### Spot heat sample

Remember, spot heating is most often used for personal comfort in buildings with partial or no heating. Many warehouses fall into this category. Warehouses are often unheated, or only partially heated to guard against freezing of product or sprinkler systems. We will use such a building for our example. There is a spot heating requirement because one person works in the building. The worker, who packages product for shipment, is in a small section of the warehouse. Here are the pertinent design criteria.

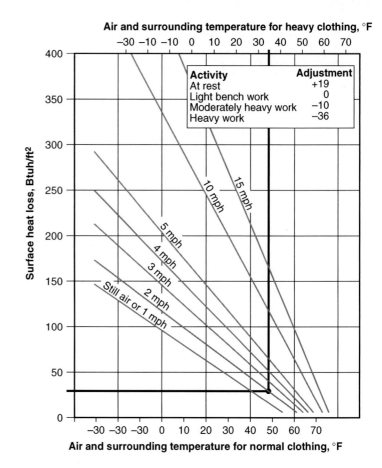

**FIGURE 4-8.** *Surface heat loss nomograph*

| | |
|---|---|
| **Building:** | Medium-sized warehouse |
| **Surrounding temperature:** | 35°F |
| **Work area:** | 8 ft × 8 ft |
| **People:** | One (standing) |
| **Clothing:** | Heavy* |
| **Activity:** | Light bench work |
| **Available mounting height:** | 20 ft maximum, no minimum |
| **Available mounting space:** | 20 ft × 40 ft |
| **Air velocity in building:** | 2 mph |

*Light clothing consists of undershirt, cotton shirt, shorts, and cotton trousers. Heavy clothing would be double this amount.

Every person loses body heat, even when asleep. As activities increase, the body generates additional heat. This heat warms the individual, even under extremely cold conditions. Most of this body heat is lost through convection, radiation, and perspiration. When activity is reduced and the surrounding temperature is below

70°F, some type of heat must be added, or the individual must be protected against the cold in some way. It is the purpose of spot heating to provide the heat that the body is not generating so that comfortable conditions exist.

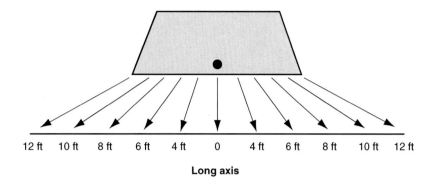

**FIGURE 4-9.** *Long axis radiation pattern*

Refer to the surface nomograph in Figure 4-8. From it, find the surface (clothing) loss for our example. Follow the 35°F temperature line down from the "Heavy clothing" line at the top. When this line intersects the 2-mph line, move directly horizontal to the Btu/ft² line. The value at that location is 25 Btuh. Now refer to the "Activity adjustment" table. For light bench work there is no Btu adjustment. Assume that the subject had been engaged in heavy work. If so, there would be no need for heat

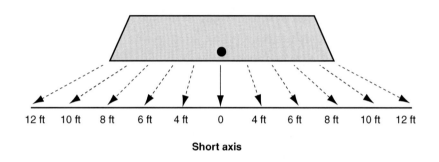

**FIGURE 4-10.** *Short axis radiation pattern*

whatsoever, since you must deduct 36 Btuh from the 25 Btuh value just found. Conversely, if the subject were at rest, you would add 19 Btu to the 25 Btu value.

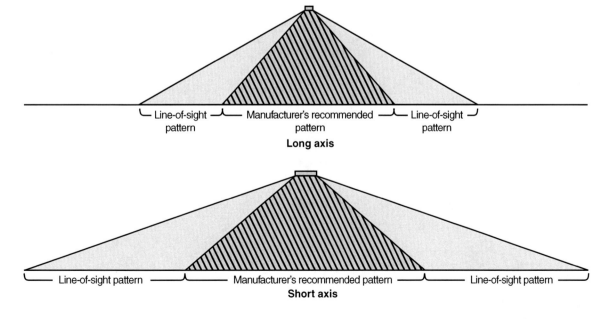

**FIGURE 4-11.** *Typical line-of-sight patterns*

For safety of design, multiply the 25 Btuh by 120%. This gives a Btu/ft$^2$ value of 30 as our target intensity requirement. Therefore, you must direct 30 Btuh/ft$^2$ at the subject at a point 3 ft above the floor. This is about belt height for a standing person. If the person were seated, the distance above the floor would be 2 ft. Ideally, the subject should be covered from all four sides. However, spot heating may be adequate from only two infrared units, installed as shown in Figure 4-12.

High-intensity infrared for spot heating is most often installed at an angle. Most units are certified for both angular or horizontal installation. According to the recommended minimum mounting height chart, a 30,000 Btuh heater at a 30° angle should be at a height of 10 ft. With spot heating used to heat a person, consider activity and clothing and also the normal position of the person. If the subject is standing, direct the infrared heat at a point 3 ft above the floor, as shown in Figure 4-13. If the subject is seated, use a point 2 ft above the floor. For our example, a mounting height of 13 ft 3 in. is used, with the heater at a 30° angle.

**FIGURE 4-12.** *Two units used for spot heating*

Thus, the mounting height has been determined. Now refer to the graph shown in Figure 4-14 for the horizontal distance of the unit from the subject. From the 10¼-ft height line (on the vertical axis) move right until you intersect the sloped "0" line. You should have a reading of approximately 6 ft. This dimension, when doubled, gives you the center-to-center distance (12 ft) between the two infrared units. They will be located as shown in Figure 4-13.

If you wish to cover all four sides of the subject, you will use four units rather than two. Figure 4-15 shows a plan view of the four-unit layout. Remember, the same height of 13¼ feet is used with either two or four units.

**Larger work area**

Now let's expand our example. Assume that the work area is larger and that there

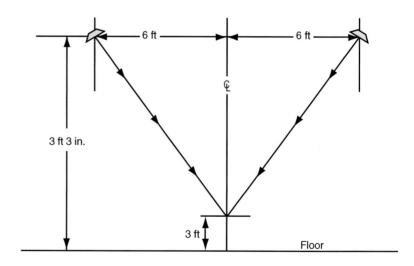

**FIGURE 4-13.** *End view of location of two units*

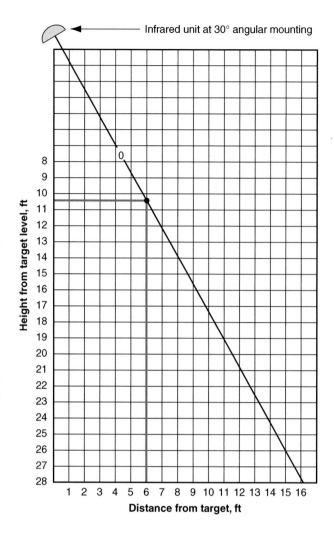

**FIGURE 4-14.** *Finding the horizontal distance from the target subject*

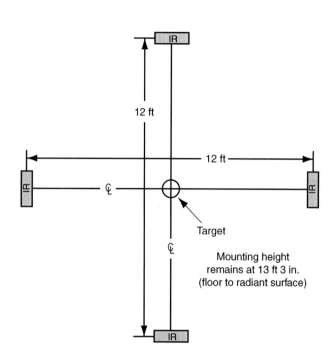

**FIGURE 4-15.** *A four-unit layout*

are more workers. You must first find the coverage area. Let's assume that there are three workers doing the same work. The area is expanded from 8 ft × 8 ft to 8 ft × 30 ft.

You must plan on at least two units on each side of the workers. Also, you must not create too much intensity by overlapping the focus of the units. Remember, your original findings required a 30-Btu/ft² intensity at a recommended minimum of 10 ft. (This example uses 10 ft 3 in., plus 3 ft for standing workers, or a mounting height of 13 ft 3 in.)

The coverage (measured at 3 ft above the floor) is about twice the mounting height. Figure 4-16 on the next page shows two heaters with a centerline distance of 20 ft. Since the coverage overlaps, the average of the total Btu radiated will increase. This allows for a slightly higher mounting height to reach the same

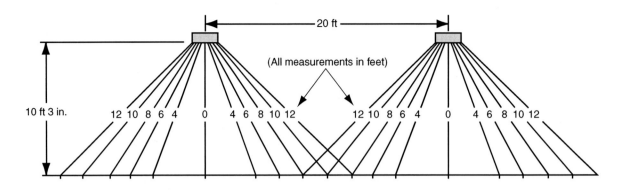

**FIGURE 4-16.** *Two-unit installation with overlap*

comfort level. Refer back to Figure 4-14. Note that if mounting height changes, the distance from the target also changes. Figure 4-17 shows an example of a plan view using four units.

Other manufacturers make asymmetrical units as well as symmetrical units. Metal sheath elements do not radiate as much infrared energy as quartz infrared heaters. Refer to Tables 4-6 and 4-7 at the end of this Lesson.

Consider economy when heating open areas, such as areas near doors or an open loading dock. Locate the heaters so that they direct a minimum amount of radiation toward the open air, while still providing the required intensity on a subject working in the area. In this way, the surrounding surface is warmed and contributes to the overall comfort level. Direct heat loss to the surroundings is minimized.

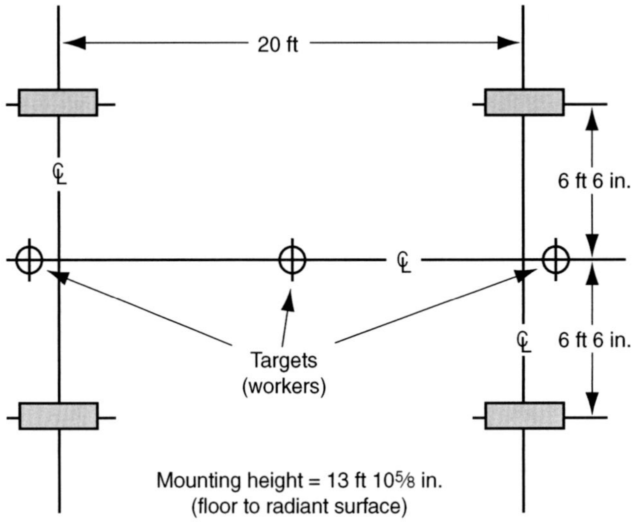

### Control for spot heating

Controls are used to reduce the radiation rate as the ambient temperature increases. The increase may be due to a build-up from the heaters, or it may be caused by milder weather. The control should be local for each work station when there are more work stations than workers, or if workers move from one station to another. A preferred method in spot heating is to control each heater with a manually operated switch. When several units spot heat an area, one or more can be turned off as temperature increases. With portable heaters, you can vary radiant energy density by repositioning the heater.

**FIGURE 4-17.** *A four-unit, two-bank application*

## ADDITIONAL RADIANT AND INFRARED USES

This discussion has concerned infrared heating in industrial plants. This is one of the most common applications for infrared systems. However, infrared heating units can be applied to various process applications, thawing operations, paint drying, etc.

Infrared heating systems have many features that commend their use for total comfort heating and spot heating. However, as in all systems, they require intelligent design and application. When properly applied, infrared heating systems can solve heating problems considered impossible or impractical with conventional heating means.

Another form of radiant heat is in-floor electric radiant heat. In such a system, electric cable is laid out in a grid on a subfloor. It is covered with a pourable floor underlayment. The cable heats the underlayment and the floor above it. Heat radiates from the floor into the entire room.

As noted earlier, this type of low-temperature heat does not create buoyant air that rises rapidly. It operates without air currents throughout the room. The effect is the same as using infrared radiant heaters mounted above the floor. The floor is heated and it, in turn, heats the air just above it. The heated air slowly rises, and cools as it does so. Temperatures from floor to ceiling remain fairly even.

Much of the material contained in this Lesson was provided courtesy of Reznor. Used with permission.

**Heat distribution of quartz infrared heaters, delivered in watts per square foot**

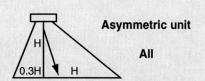

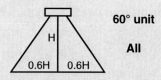

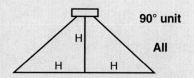

| Height (ft) | Area | ft² | W/ft² From 3.2 kW | W/ft² From 5 kW | Area | ft² | W/ft² From 3.2 kW | W/ft² From 5 kW | Area | ft² | W/ft² From 3.2 kW | W/ft² From 5 kW |
|---|---|---|---|---|---|---|---|---|---|---|---|---|
| 1 | 1.3 × 2 | 2.6 | 1,020 | 1,540 | 1.2 × 2 | 2.4 | 1,104 | 1,667 | 2 × 2 | 4 | 663 | 1,000 |
| 2 | 2.6 × 4 | 10.4 | 255 | 385 | 2.4 × 4 | 9.6 | 276 | 417 | 4 × 4 | 16 | 166 | 250 |
| 3 | 3.9 × 6 | 23.4 | 113 | 171 | 3.6 × 6 | 21.6 | 123 | 185 | 6 × 6 | 36 | 74 | 111 |
| 4 | 5.2 × 8 | 41.6 | 64 | 96 | 4.8 × 8 | 38.4 | 69 | 104 | 8 × 8 | 64 | 41.4 | 62.5 |
| 5 | 6.5 × 10 | 65.0 | 41 | 62 | 6.0 × 10 | 60.0 | 44 | 67 | 10 × 10 | 100 | 26.5 | 40.0 |
| 6 | 7.8 × 12 | 93.6 | 28 | 43 | 7.2 × 12 | 86.4 | 31 | 46 | 12 × 12 | 144 | 18.4 | 27.8 |
| 7 | 9.1 × 14 | 127 | 21 | 32 | 8.4 × 14 | 117 | 23 | 34 | 14 × 14 | 196 | 13.5 | 20.4 |
| 8 | 10.4 × 16 | 166 | 16 | 24 | 9.6 × 16 | 153 | 17 | 26 | 16 × 16 | 256 | 10.4 | 15.6 |
| 9 | 11.7 × 18 | 210 | 13 | 19 | 10.8 × 18 | 194 | 13.7 | 20.6 | 18 × 18 | 324 | 8.1 | 12.4 |
| 10 | 13.0 × 20 | 260 | 10 | 15 | 12.0 × 20 | 240 | 11.0 | 16.7 | 20 × 20 | 400 | 6.6 | 10.0 |
| 11 | 14.3 × 22 | 314 | 8.4 | 12.7 | 13.2 × 22 | 290 | 9.1 | 13.8 | 22 × 22 | 484 | 5.5 | 8.3 |
| 12 | 15.6 × 24 | 374 | 7.1 | 10.7 | 14.4 × 24 | 345 | 7.7 | 11.6 | 24 × 24 | 576 | 4.6 | 7.0 |
| 13 | 16.9 × 26 | 440 | 6.0 | 9.1 | 15.6 × 26 | 402 | 6.6 | 10.0 | 26 × 26 | 675 | 3.9 | 5.9 |
| 14 | 18.2 × 28 | 510 | 5.2 | 7.8 | 16.8 × 28 | 470 | 5.6 | 8.5 | 28 × 28 | 780 | 3.4 | 5.1 |
| 15 | 19.5 × 30 | 585 | 4.5 | 6.8 | 18.0 × 30 | 540 | 4.9 | 7.4 | 30 × 30 | 900 | 3.0 | 4.4 |

NOTE: These figures are based on the most reliable engineering data available. However, the manufacturer is not to be held responsible for the performance of any special installation. Refer to your consulting engineer for all recommended layouts.

**TABLE 4-6.** *Radiant efficiency of quartz lamps at 80%*

AITKEN PRODUCTS, INC.

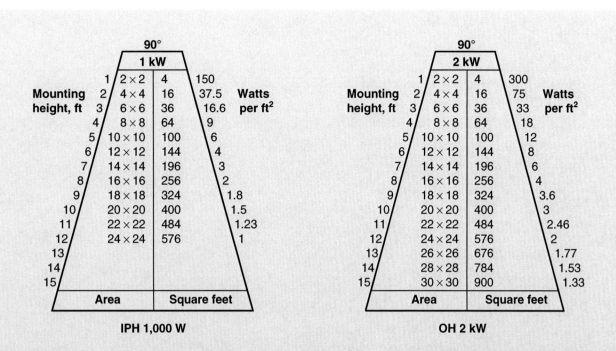

Watts per square foot is computed at 60% of input watts, which is the accepted efficiency of metal sheath elements. This means that for each 100 W of input, 60 W is delivered by the element as radiant energy and directed at the target. The balance (40%, or 40 W) is given off as convected or conducted heat, which is built up in the fixture itself and is of some benefit, although not readily measurable.

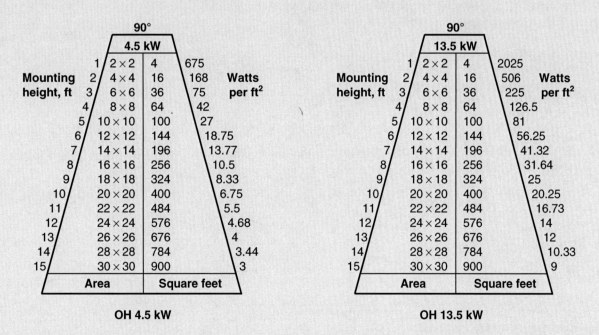

**Example:** 60% of 1,000 W = 600 W ÷ 4 ft² = 150 W/ft² @ 1-ft mounting height, and so on. (For quartz lamps, use 80% efficiency, and for quartz tubes, use 60%.)

**TABLE 4-7.** *Pattern distribution and watt density for various 90° metal sheath heaters*

99

1.     How is a metal sheath heater constructed?

2.     What are the advantages of using metal sheath heaters for radiant heating systems?

3.     What are the primary advantages of quartz tube heaters?

4.     The radiant efficiency of an element is the ratio of _____ to _____ .

5.     What effect does the element temperature have on radiant efficiency?

6.     What is the effect of radiant heat on light colored objects?

7.     What type of fixtures should be selected when snow melting is the primary design concern?

8.     How are infrared fixtures generally mounted?

9.     What rule of thumb based on actual practice is used to estimate the total wattage of infrared fixtures used for melting snow?

10.    What is the best method of calculating the fixture requirements for an infrared heating installation?

11.    How much time is required to heat a surface to snow-melting temperatures with infrared energy?

12.    What is the advantage of a fast warm-up?

13.    How is the equipment turned on?

14.    What should be done to the reflectors to ensure maximum efficiency of operation?

15.    What should be done to prevent accidental operation of the system in summer?

16.    How does room air circulation differ when radiant heat is used in place of conventional heat?

17.    How does human skin react to infrared radiation?

18.    What important characteristics account for the economy of operation with a properly applied infrared heating system?

19.    How are electric infrared units sized to heat a building?

20.    Why should infrared heaters *not* be located where structural members and machinery cast shadows on the subject?

21.    Combustible materials and sensitive equipment may be protected from radiation and the effects of overheating by shielding with _____.

22.    How can the undesirable effect of shutting down all radiant heat at one time be avoided?

23.    How are internal thermostats usually mounted?

24.     Where is spot heating generally required?

25.     What is the preferred method of control in spot heating applications?

# Duct Heaters and Furnaces

## DUCT HEATER APPLICATIONS

D uct heaters, such as the one shown in Figure 5-1, are used in several ways in forced air systems. They can be primary heat sources or supplemental heaters. They can be used for preheating and/or reheating in central trunk ducts or branch ducts. Most duct heaters are pre-engineered, factory-assembled units. Such units consist of a standard frame section, metal sheathed heating elements, and a pre-wired terminal box. They are available in a wide range of frame sizes to fit standard duct dimensions, with various heating capacities and staging increments for operation on ac voltage ratings of 120 to 550 volts.

### Location recommendations

The standard duct heater is inserted in a rectangular opening in the side of a horizontal or vertical duct. The heater itself can form a part of the duct. To do so, a special frame is added to the heater. Upstream and downstream duct sections are then attached to the frame.

BTU ELECTRIC HEATERS

**FIGURE 5-1.** *Typical duct heater*

103

### Pre-wired heating units

Duct heaters are available with built-in automatic reset or manual reset thermal cut-outs, and with pre-wired contactors, line fuses, and transformers. The only field connections for such heaters are power wiring to the heater terminal box and control wiring from a thermostat. They are available without these components when the installation specifies a remotely mounted power and control panel.

### Installation requirements

The application and installation of duct heaters must conform to all local codes, laws, and regulations in effect at the job site. The Canadian or U.S. National Electrical Code (NEC) also governs installations. Many construction and installation aspects are prescribed by Underwriters' Laboratories (UL) requirements.

## KEY TECHNICAL TERMS

All technologies use descriptive terms. It is important for you to be familiar with these terms and know how to use them. They will help you understand specifications and installation details. The following list contains some common terms that describe components and functions of electric heating:

**Air flow.** The volume of air passing a given point (in an air duct), usually expressed in cubic feet per minute (cfm).

**Air velocity.** The speed of air passing a given point (in an air duct), usually expressed in feet per minute (ft/min).

**Aluminized steel.** Steel coated with aluminum for corrosion resistance.

**Ambient.** Surrounding or encompassing, as in *ambient temperature*.

**Automatic.** Self-acting, operating by its own mechanism, having been actuated by some influence, such as a change in current flow, pressure, temperature, or mechanical configuration.

**Auto reset (thermal cut-out).** The primary thermally operated safety switch. It opens a circuit when a predetermined air temperature is reached. It automatically closes the circuit when the temperature drops below this point.

**Branch circuit.** That portion of a wiring system between the final over-current device protecting the branch circuit and the duct heater.

**Btu.**   British thermal unit (3,413 Btu = 1 kW). Nominally, the quantity of heat required to raise one pound of water one degree Fahrenheit.

**Contactor.**   A device used for repeatedly establishing and interrupting the electric power circuit to the duct heater. Usually electromagnetically operated.

**Control circuit.**   An electric circuit that controls a power circuit through a relay or equivalent device. In other words, the circuit that includes the thermostats, holding coils of the contactors, and the auto or manual reset thermal cut-out.

**Face area.**   The area of a duct heater inside the duct.

**Fan interlock.**   A means for preventing duct heater operation unless the fan motor supplying air through the duct is also operating.

**High-limit switch (thermal cut-out).**   A thermally operated safety device. It automatically opens the circuit when the air temperature within the duct reaches a pre-set high limit.

**Holding coil.**   The wire coil of an electromagnet. When energized, it causes the electrical contacts to relays or contactors to change position.

**Internal (safety) circuit.**   The portion of the wiring system within the duct heater between the staging contactors and the line-voltage terminal blocks. These circuits are limited to 48 amperes (A) maximum by the National Electrical Code. Internal circuits consist of staging circuits that are combined up to the 48-A limit.

**Kilowatt (kW).**   1,000 watts (1 kW = 3,413 Btu).

**Manual reset (thermal cut-out).**   The back-up or secondary thermally operated safety switch. It opens a circuit when a pre-set air temperature is reached. The circuit remains open until a reset button or plunger is manually pushed back into the closed position.

**Open coil element.**   Heating elements with the electrically live coiled resistance wire exposed directly to the flow of air through the heater. Figure 5-2 on the next page shows exposed heating elements.

**Pressure drop.**   The drop in air pressure in a duct. Usually caused by resistance to air flow from elbows, filters, or duct heater heating elements.

**Relay.**   A thermal or electromagnetically operated device with electrical contacts for controlling various operating functions of a system. Normally, the term *relay* refers to devices rated at 15 A or less. A relay can control a contactor, but not vice versa.

**Safety contactor.** A contactor whose holding coil is operated by the manual reset thermal cut-out. The contactor must disconnect a sufficient number of conductors to interrupt current flow to the heater.

**Sequencer.** A time delay contactor that controls a fan or blower, plus one or more electric heating elements. The time delay between energizing electric heating elements is generally 10 or more seconds. One reason for using a sequencer is to prevent light dimming. Dimming may occur if all heating elements come on at once.

**FIGURE 5-2.** *Heating elements in a duct heater*

**Staging.** Providing power circuitry and controls that divide the full output of a heater into segments. Each segment is energized separately, according to the demand for heat.

**Staging circuit.** The portion of the wiring system located within the duct heater and controlled by the staging contactor.

**Staging contactor.** A contactor that controls only one segment (stage) of the total heating capacity. Its holding coil is controlled by a thermostat or switch and the automatic reset thermal cut-out.

**Static pressure.** The outward push or pressure of air against the walls of a duct.

**Temperature gradients.** Temperature variations, generally a rise in temperature from floor to ceiling.

**Transition.** Increasing or decreasing the cross-sectional size of the ductwork to accommodate the dimensions of a duct heater.

**Ventilated.** Provided with a means to circulate enough air to remove excess heat.

**Watt density.** The watts of electric heat produced within a given area. For duct heaters, generally expressed in kilowatts per square foot of face area.

**Zero clearance.** When used with duct heaters, this term means that air space or thermal insulation is not required around the ductwork at the point where the heater is inserted. Combustible materials may butt right up to the duct. Duct heater control or terminal panels must be accessible.

## MECHANICAL CHARACTERISTICS

### Installation of ductwork

Installation of ductwork that will accommodate a duct heater must adhere to one of the following:

- Standards of the National Fire Protection Association (NFPA) for the Installation of Air Conditioning and Ventilating Systems of Other than Resident Type (Pamphlet 90A)

- Residential-Type Warm Air Heating and Air Conditioning Systems (Pamphlet 90B).

Duct dimensions may exceed the insert heater dimensions. If so, the area beyond the insert-type heater dimensions must be filled with wire mesh, or expanded or perforated sheet metal of 50% open area. This maintains a uniform air velocity across the face of the duct. For electric duct heaters, air stream static pressure drops are small compared to steam and water coil pressure drops. Figure 5-3 shows the static pressure drop as a function of velocity.

When installing a duct heater where the insert dimensions exceed the insert-type heater dimensions, you must meet certain objectives.

First, *discharge air temperature* from the duct heater must be less than the maximum discharge air temperature allowed by the manufacturer. If a heat pump is involved, you must know the *maximum inlet air temperature* to the duct heater. If you know the inlet temperature and the cfm, you can calculate the outlet temperature for

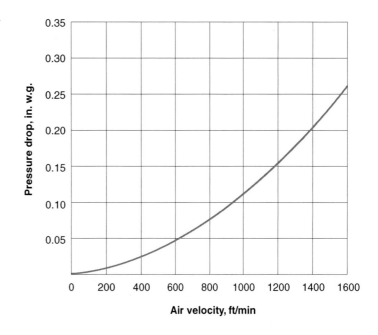

**FIGURE 5-3.** *Static pressure drop for electric duct heaters*

107

the duct heater (assuming you know the duct heater kW). In some cases, you may have to install an outside thermostat to keep the duct heater from coming on until the outside temperature is cold enough. This prevents the temperature rise of the heat pump and the duct heater from causing a discharge temperature higher than the maximum allowed by the manufacturer.

The material that blocks the area between the duct and the insert dimensions of the heater must not restrict the air flow through the duct excessively. If the duct rating is 1,200 cfm, it must deliver 1,200 cfm when the installation is complete. If the space is filled with expanded metal, perforated metal, or wire mesh, install an access door upstream of the heater. This allows you to check the filler material for restriction by dirt and lint, and clean it if needed.

### Zero clearance

Zero clearance between the flange-type heater frame or between the duct and surrounding combustible building material is allowed. However, there must be adequate clearance around the terminal or control box for service and inspection. If the ductwork is insulated, the insulation must not cover any part of the terminal box.

### Provision for service

Equipment service may be required at some future time. Space should be provided for such service. Enough clearance is recommended so that you can remove or replace equipment as a complete assembly without dismantling.

### Other equipment

A duct system may require accessories such as insulation, sound absorbers, filters, and fire dampers. They do not normally affect the operation of the duct heater itself. However, be sure that they do not add resistance to air flow that is not compensated for by the fan system.

### DUCT HEATER INSTALLATION

The following guidelines apply to most duct heater installations:

- Never install duct heaters from the bottom or top of the duct. Install them only from the sides of the duct, as shown in Figures 5-4 and 5-5.

- Always install heaters on the discharge side of any air handler equipment. Heaters are suitable for both horizontal and vertical duct systems.

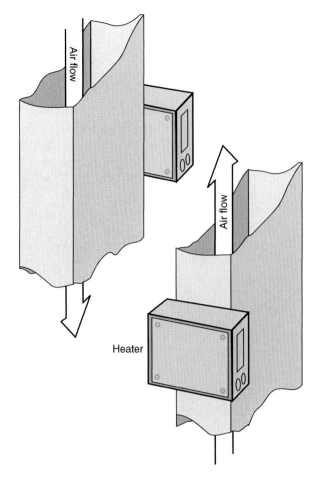

**FIGURE 5-4.** *Vertical duct*

**FIGURE 5-5.** *Horizontal duct*

- Install only one duct heater in any one duct. The capacity required may exceed the output of one heater. If so, select the total number of heaters and proportion them in separate run-outs or separate ducts from the plenum.

- Locate a duct heater at least 4 ft from the nearest surfaces of a heat pump or a central cooling air conditioner that may be used in conjunction with a duct heater.

- Keep the heater at least 18 in. away from any canvas duct connector. If located closer, replace the canvas with a high-temperature connector.

- Control enclosures of the duct heaters must be completely accessible. They should be located to provide ventilation at all times.

- Install the air duct according to applicable directives. These are the Standards of the National Fire Protection Association for the Installation of Air Conditioning and Ventilating Systems of Other than Residence-Type (Pamphlet No. 90A), and Residence-Type Warm Air Heating and Air Conditioning Systems (Pamphlet No. 90B).

- Provide each duct heater with a fan relay. Wire the heater and fan motor so that the duct heater cannot operate unless the fan is on.

- Wire the coil of the secondary contactor (general-purpose, continuous duty-rated 6,000 cycles) in series with manual reset limit control.

To install the heater, cut an opening 6½ in. × 7⅛ in. on 8 in. × 16 in. ducts. Cut an opening 6½ in. × 11⅛ in. on 12 in. × 18 in. ducts. Remove the terminal box cover and slide the heater into the duct. Use the control box as a template to drill the mounting screw holes. Mount the heater to the duct with screws (supplied by the installer).

### Mounting limitations

UL does not permit the mounting of multiple duct heaters in series or tandem in a single duct. However, for larger horizontal or vertical ducts, from two to six flanged heaters may be combined into *heating banks*. Figures 5-6 and 5-7 show typical examples. The maximum duct size is 120 in. × 240 in. The maximum capacity for each individual heater is 150 kW, or a maximum total capacity of 900 kW. When specified, splice brackets are furnished to join the heaters together.

You may locate duct heaters at any point in the duct system except for those limitations shown in Figure 5-8. Do not put duct heaters closer than 4 ft from the downstream side of a turn (see Figure 5-9) unless turning vanes are installed in the turn. The turning vanes will straighten out the air flow so that it will be uniform over the face of the heater. Duct heaters closer than 2 ft from the upstream side of the turn also may require turning vanes.

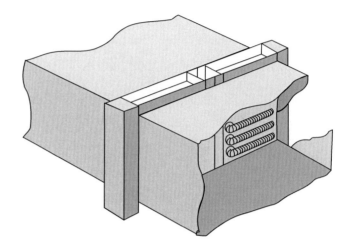

**FIGURE 5-6.** *Heating bank example*

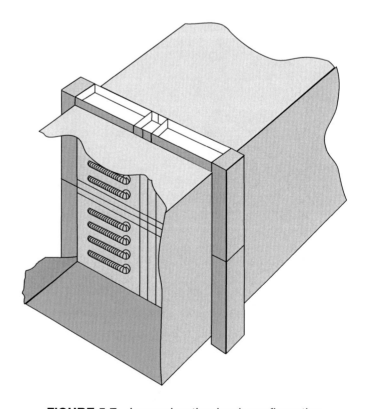

**FIGURE 5-7.** *Larger heating bank configuration*

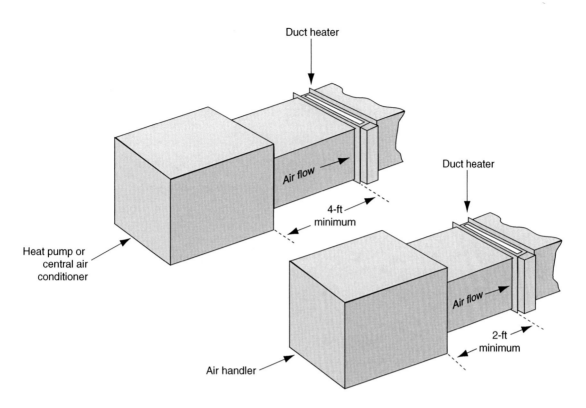

**FIGURE 5-8.** *Mounting guidelines in straight runs*

A duct heater may have to be installed near a flexible duct connection, as shown in Figure 5-10 on the next page. If so, be sure that there is a 4-in. minimum distance between the duct heater and the flexible connector. The connector must be suitable for 190°F temperatures.

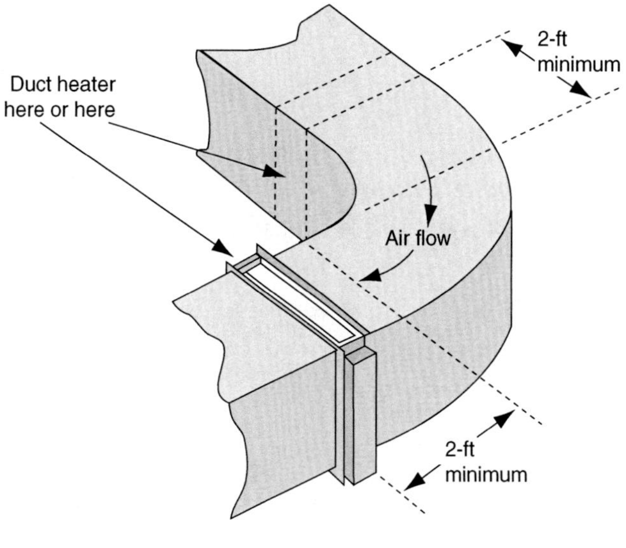

In some air distribution systems, the duct heater may be larger than the ductwork. If so, the duct area must be increased by a sheet metal *transition*. The slope of the transformation piece on the upstream side of the equipment is limited to 30°, as shown in Figure 5-11 on the next page. On the leaving side, the slope should not be more than 45°.

**FIGURE 5-9.** *Mounting guidelines in turns*

### Air velocity—an important factor

The minimum air flow through a duct heater directly relates to the inlet air temperature. Consider both the air flow across the heater and the inlet temperature. The amount of supplementary heat required is expressed in terms of kW, as follows:

$$kW\ required\ =\ \frac{Btu\ heat\ loss}{3{,}413}$$

Each kW produces 3,413 Btuh. Divide the Btuh of heat needed by 3,413 to find the kW needed. Use the chart in Figure 5-12 to find the minimum air flow needed. You will need to know the maximum inlet air temperature of the heater. The outlet air from a heat pump (sometimes 110°F) would be the inlet air to an auxiliary heater. You also must know the kW per square foot of the minimum duct area (kW/ft$^2$ MDA) for the heater. An example is worked out below:

**Example.** A 12-kW heater designed for a minimum duct size of 8 in. × 16 in. is the only heat in a residence. You expect inlet air to the heater will be 77°F maximum. Divide the 8 in. × 16 in. area (128 in$^2$) by 144, and you find that you have 0.888 ft$^2$ of heater minimum duct area design.

Next, divide the 12 kW by the 0.888. Your answer equals 13.5. This is the kW/ft$^2$ MDA. Locate 13.5 along the bottom side of the chart in Figure 5-12. From there, draw a vertical line upward to intersect with the 77°F inlet air line. From the point of intersection, draw a horizontal line to the left side of the chart . The answer is 800 ft/min (velocity) of air minimum required over the heater.

To convert to cfm, multiply the answer by the square feet of the heater minimum duct area design. In this example, 800 multiplied by 0.888 would be 710 cfm.

These minimum air flow requirements should be met at any point over the face of the heater. Heaters may be used in ducts larger than the heater minimum duct design. If so, reliable means should be used to ensure proper air flow through the heater.

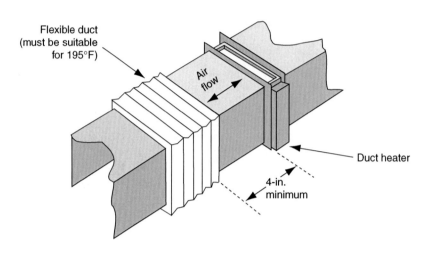

**FIGURE 5-10.** *Mounting guidelines near flexible duct connections*

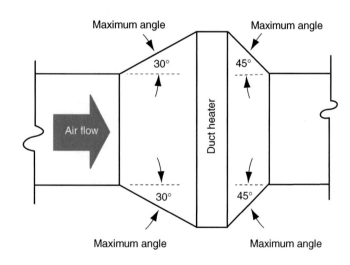

**FIGURE 5-11.** *Increasing duct area with a transition*

## ELECTRICAL CHARACTERISTICS

### Kilowatt-hour ratings

Electric duct heater capacities are rated in kilowatts (kW). This rating is then translated into Btu output. The following steps are used for this translation:

1 kilowatt = 1,000 watts

1 kilowatt = 3,413 Btu

Btu × 0.293 = watts

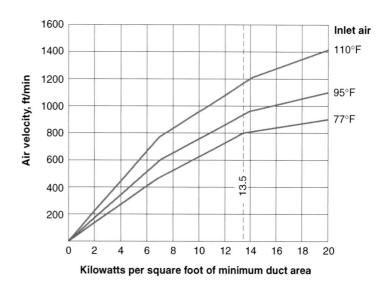

**FIGURE 5-12.** *Performance data*

With an ohmmeter and the following equation, taken from the Ohm's Law wheel in Figure 5-13, you can find the kilowatt output of a duct heater:

$$P = \frac{E^2}{R}$$

Here are some examples.

**Example A**. A duct heater of unknown kW output is rated for 240 V single-phase. Resistance is measured with an ohmmeter at 12.02 Ω on each of two coils. Since the resistance changes as the coil heats up, a correction factor of 1.065 is used:

12.02 × 1.065 = 12.8 hot

Using the equation for power:

$$P = \frac{240^2}{12.8}$$

$$= \frac{57,600}{12.8}$$

$$= 4,500 \text{ W, or } 4.5 \text{ kW}$$

Two coils at 4.5 kW each = a 9-kW heater.

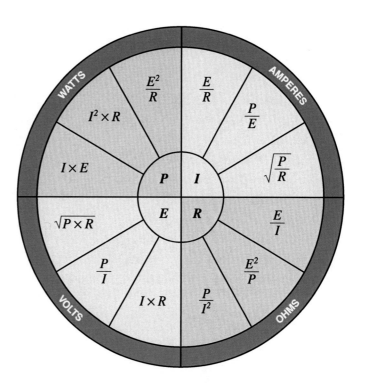

**FIGURE 5-13.** *Ohm's Law wheel*

**Example B**. A duct heater marked 240 V three-phase has three coils, wired in a delta configuration, that measure 20.29 Ω cold.

$$20.29 \times 1.065 = 21.61 \text{ hot}$$

Plugging the new figures into the equation for power:

$$P = \frac{240^2}{21.61}$$

$$= \frac{57,600}{21.61}$$

$$= 2,665 \text{ W, or } 2.67 \text{ kW}$$

Three coils at 2.67 kW each = a 7.99-kW heater.

Efforts are always being made to simplify calculations. The field of electric heat is no exception. Using Table 5-1 is a time-saving way to determine watt/kilowatt output. You can use it to skip the mathematical calculations shown in the preceding examples.

### Watt density

The maximum *watt density* (see the definitions earlier in this Lesson) allowed in a duct heater is 22.5 kilowatts per square foot of duct area. This equals 0.156 kW per square inch of duct area. Normal duct heater design has about 60 watts per square inch of wire surface for most applications. Multi-zone applications require de-rating to 25 watts per square inch of wire surface. Single-zone applications require de-rating to 35 watts per square inch of wire surface.

### Wiring data

All wiring for electric duct heaters must comply with local and U.S. National or Canadian codes. Use Type RH wire, or its equivalent, suitable for 75°C, for connections to heater terminals or control boxes.

|      | 120 V | 138 V | 208 V | 240 V | 277 V | 480 V |
|------|-------|-------|-------|-------|-------|-------|
| kW   | Cold resistance in ohms | | | | | |
| 0.5  | 27.04 | 35.76 | 81.25 | 108.17 | 144.09 | 432.68 |
| 1.0  | 13.52 | 17.88 | 40.62 | 54.08 | 72.05 | 216.35 |
| 1.5  | 9.66  | 11.92 | 27.08 | 36.06 | 48.03 | 144.22 |
| 2.0  | 6.76  | 8.94  | 20.31 | 27.04 | 36.02 | 108.17 |
| 2.5  | 5.41  | 7.15  | 16.25 | 21.63 | 28.82 | 86.54 |
| 3.0  | 4.51  | 5.96  | 13.54 | 18.03 | 24.02 | 72.11 |
| 3.5  | 3.86  | 5.11  | 11.61 | 15.45 | 20.58 | 61.81 |
| 4.0  |       | 4.47  | 10.16 | 13.52 | 18.01 | 54.08 |
| 4.5  |       |       | 9.03  | 12.02 | 16.01 | 48.08 |
| 4.8  |       |       | 8.46  | 11.27 | 15.00 | 45.07 |
| 5.0  |       |       | 8.12  | 10.82 | 14.41 | 43.27 |
| 6.0  |       |       | 6.77  | 9.01  | 12.01 | 36.06 |

**TABLE 5-1.** *Use ohms to find unknown kilowatt output*

[]

The current (amperage ) load of electric duct heaters in a single circuit should not exceed 48 A. Existing electrical codes state that duct heaters drawing more than 48 A total load must be subdivided into internal circuits. Each circuit may not exceed 48 A load. Also, each internal circuit must be protected by an overcurrent device or fusing at not more than 60 A. This is in addition to the branch circuit fusing required.

To meet this provision, each subdivided heater circuit must have fuses or circuit breakers, as shown in Figure 5-14. If the heater's total load is 48 A or less, branch circuit protection alone is adequate, as shown in Figure 5-15.

U.S. and Canadian electrical codes have a further requirement. They state that: "Duct heater controller equipment shall be accessible, with the disconnecting means installed at, or within sight of, the controller." This means that a circuit breaker or fused disconnect switch must be installed so that anyone servicing the heater can easily disconnect it.

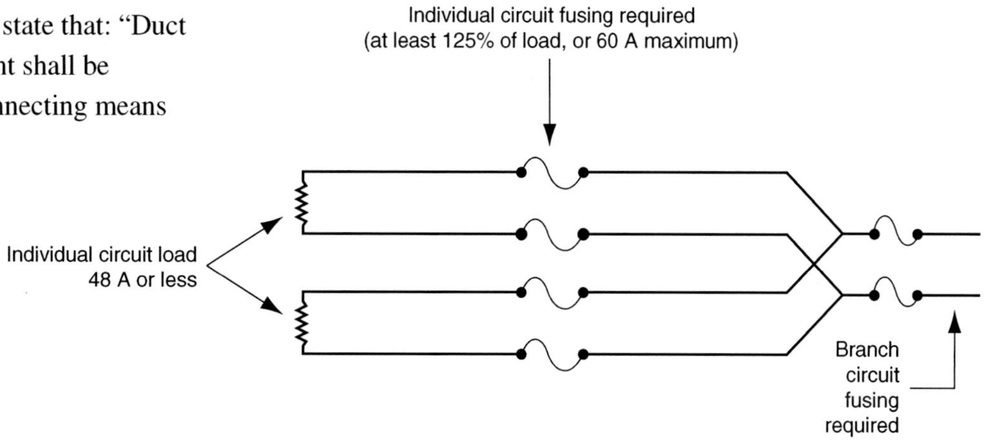

Individual circuit fusing required
(at least 125% of load, or 60 A maximum)

Individual circuit load 48 A or less

Branch circuit fusing required

**FIGURE 5-14.** *Total load of more than 48 A*

Figures 5-16, 5-17, 5-18, and 5-19 on the next several pages show typical wiring diagrams for various applications of electric duct heaters. Each has a single-phase 240-V ac source. Each example shows branch circuit protection as being adequate. Therefore, you can assume that the total heater load in each case does not exceed 48 A.

Figure 5-16 is a wiring diagram for a single-stage, one-element heater. Figure 5-17 shows a two-stage, two-element heater. Figures 5-18 and 5-19 depict two-stage, three-element and three-stage, three-element heaters, respectively.

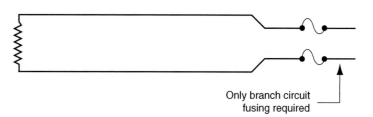

Only branch circuit fusing required

**FIGURE 5-15.** *Total load of 48 A or less*

You can assume that the total amperage load of the heaters in the wiring diagrams is 48 A. This is a good chance to explore their kilowatt output and its translation into Btu of sensible heat.

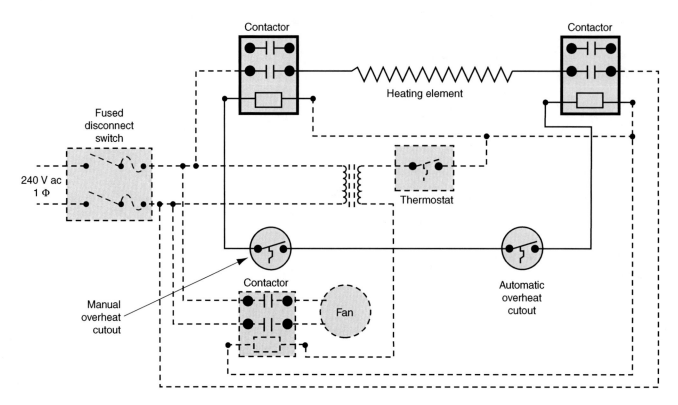

**FIGURE 5-16.** *Single-stage, one-element heater*

The graph in Figure 5-20 below is used for this calculation:

■ Select the line in Figure 5-20 drawn from 0 to 240 V. Find the point where this line crosses the vertical dotted line, which is the 48-A maximum load point. From there, draw a horizontal line back to the left side of the graph showing kilowatts.

■ From the position of the horizontal line, you see that the output is about 12 kW.

■ Now refer to the previous formula, 1 kW = 3,413 Btu. The Btu output of the heaters can be established as 40,956 Btuh.

For single-phase circuits, you can find the watts by measuring the voltage and the amperes for the circuit. Multiply the

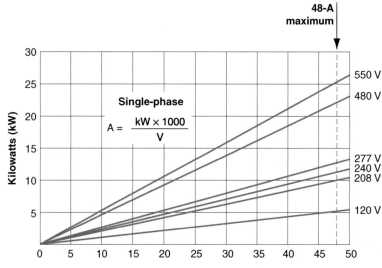

**FIGURE 5-20.** *Calculating kW output in a single-phase circuit*

volts times the amperes to obtain the watts. Divide the watts by 1,000 to obtain kilowatts.

### Three-phase wiring

There are duct heaters with internal three-phase circuits for use with three-phase (3 Φ) service. They consist of three (or some multiple of three) fin tubes, wired in "wye" or "delta" configurations. Other wiring configurations (series-parallel, three-phase unbalanced or open delta, and single-phase staging for three-phase supply) are also available. A neutral terminal is generally not furnished unless requested. Multiple-stage heaters are wired to distribute heat output evenly over the face of the heater when only partially energized.

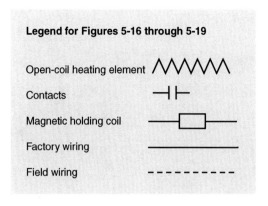

**Legend for Figures 5-16 through 5-19**

Open-coil heating element

Contacts

Magnetic holding coil

Factory wiring

Field wiring

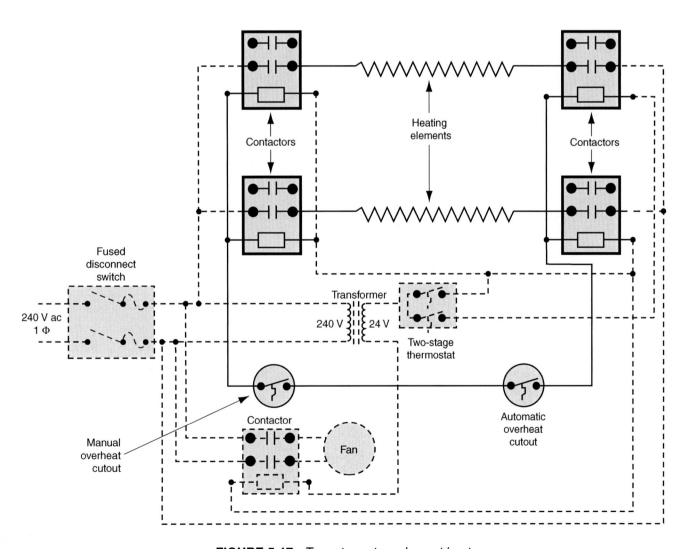

**FIGURE 5-17.** *Two-stage, two-element heater*

117

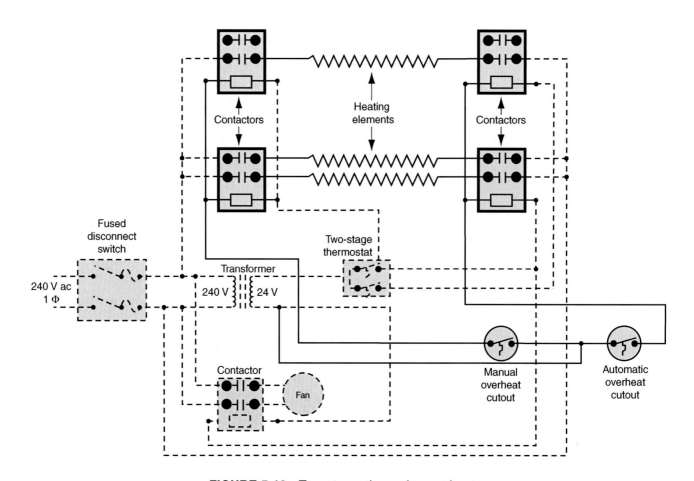

**FIGURE 5-18.** *Two-stage, three-element heater*

In three-phase wiring, 240 V and below is normally delta. Wiring above 240 V is normally wye. Figure 5-21 on page 120 shows typical basic three-phase heating coil wiring. Completed wiring would, of course, include required contactors, overload protection, and controls.

In a delta configuration, as shown in Figure 5-21A, both line and coil voltage will be the same, as indicated in Table 5-2. In a wye configuration, as shown in Figure 5-21B, coil voltage is lower than line voltage as a result of the wiring method. Table 5-2 also shows this differential. It allows the use of a wye connection to use heavier-gauge heater wire to get the desired output per coil. Heavier wire produces a lower surface temperature and longer service life. A wye connection is often used to get more kW output in a smaller area. Figure 5-21C shows wiring in a four-wire, three-phase configuration. Figure 5-21D shows connections for single-phase staging of a three-phase heater.

| Delta voltages | | Wye voltages | |
|---|---|---|---|
| Line | Coil | Line | Coil |
| 208 V 3 Φ | 208 V | 298 V 3 Φ | 129 V |
| 240 V 3 Φ | 240 V | 240 V 3 Φ | 138 V |
| 480 V 3 Φ | 480 V | 480 V 3 Φ | 277 V |

**TABLE 5-2.** *Voltage comparison of delta and wye wiring configurations*

The graph in Figure 5-22 on the next page shows how to find kilowatt output for a 48-A maximum at various three-phase voltages. The procedure is the same as for determining kW values in a single-phase circuit.

For three-phase circuits, you can determine watts by measuring voltage and amperes for the circuit. Multiply volts times amperes. Then multiply that answer by 1.73. This gives the watts for a three-phase circuit. Divide the watts by 1,000 to get kilowatts. This works well if the ampere reading on all three phases reads the same. If there is a difference in the ampere readings, you will get better accuracy by averaging the voltage and ampere readings. To average the three voltage or amperage readings, simply add the three readings together and divide by 3.

### Connecting to lower voltages

When a heater with fixed resistance in ohms is connected to a lower-than-rated voltage, the wattage and Btuh output, as well as amps, will be reduced. This is shown in Table 5-3 on page 121.

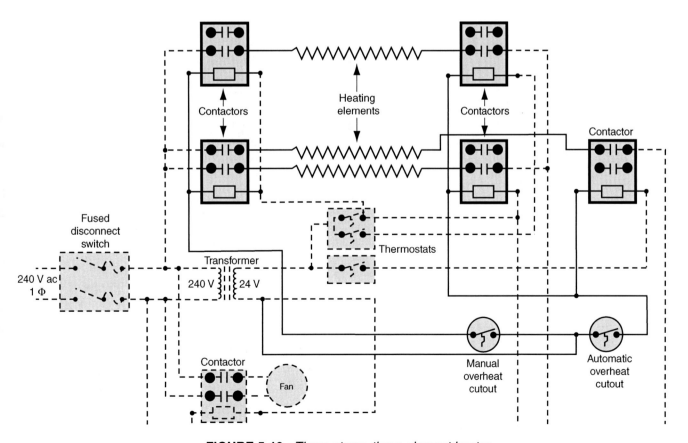

**FIGURE 5-19.** *Three-stage, three-element heater*

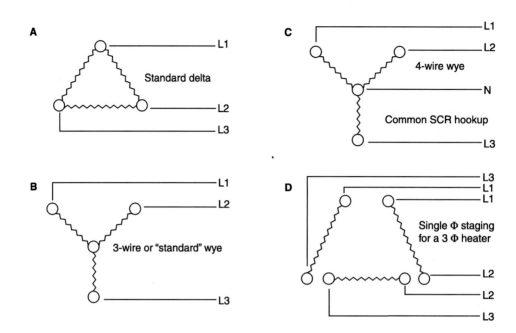

**FIGURE 5-21.** *Typical coil connections*

## Over-voltage factors

Increasing voltage, without changing resistance, increases wattage. For example, a 208-V, 3.75-kW heater will produce about 5 kW at 240 V. This almost 25% increase could lead to burned out coils and other problems:

- The ampere draw may be over the 48 A per circuit allowed by UL and the NEC.

- The element output is now ⅓ more than the factory design limit.

- The contactor and other component capacities may be exceeded.

- Safe wattage density may be exceeded. This could cause the heater to short cycle.

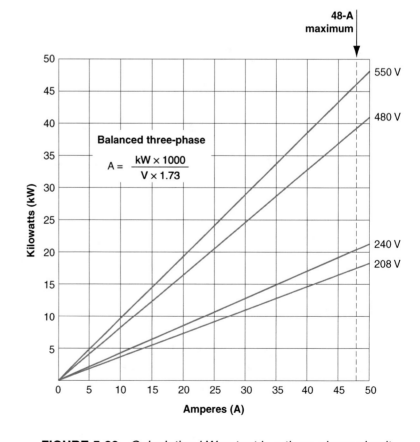

**FIGURE 5-22.** *Calculating kW output in a three-phase circuit*

- UL label and manufacturer's warranty become void.

- Product liability passes from the manufacturer to you.

### Temperature controls

A single-phase, single- or multiple-stage heater may be controlled directly by a remote line-voltage thermostat. This is true if the ampere rating of the heater is below the ratings of the thermostat and the 15-A rating of the automatic reset thermal cut-out in the heater circuit. The 15 A will give the following maximum kW at standard voltages:

| Volts, single-phase: | | | | |
|---|---|---|---|---|
| 120 | 208 | 240 | 277 | 480 |
| **Maximum kW at 15 A:** | | | | |
| 1.8 | 3.1 | 3.6 | 4.1 | 7.2 |

| Heater rated voltage | Lower applied voltage | % of heater wattage and Btuh | % of heater data plate amps |
|---|---|---|---|
| 600 | 575 | 92% | 96% |
|  | 550 | 84% | 92% |
| 480 | 460 | 92% | 96% |
|  | 440 | 84% | 92% |
| 277 | 265 | 92% | 96% |
|  | 254 | 84% | 92% |
| 240 | 230 | 92% | 96% |
|  | 220 | 84% | 92% |
|  | 208 | 75% | 87% |
|  | 201 | 70% | 84% |
| 208 | 200 | 92% | 96% |
|  | 190 | 84% | 92% |
| 120 | 115 | 92% | 96% |
|  | 110 | 84% | 92% |

**TABLE 5-3.** *Lower applied voltages produce lower wattage and Btuh outputs*

Single-phase heaters that exceed these ratings, and all three-phase heaters, require a contactor. A separate contactor is required for each internal circuit and heating stage. The contactor holding coils are generally 24 V. They can be controlled by low-voltage thermostats.

As pointed out earlier, 48 A is the maximum current draw permitted in an internal circuit. Therefore, it is the number of internal circuits that determines the number of branch circuits required to meet the total amperage draw of the combined heater circuits.

When related to kW ratings, the 48-A limit results in the following:

| Volts | Single-phase | Three-phase |
|---|---|---|
| 120 | 5.8 kW | |
| 208 | 10.0 kW | 17.3 kW |
| 240 | 11.5 kW | 19.9 kW |
| 277 | 13.3 kW | |
| 480 | 23.0 kW | 39.8 kW |
| 550 | 26.4 kW | 45.6 kW |

## SAFETY PROTECTION

Duct heater installations must have sufficient protection to meet all safety requirements. The 1996 U.S. Electrical Code and the Canadian electrical code give guidelines for the installation of duct heaters. Also, you must check with local governing bodies to know what codes have been adopted and are required. Underwriters' Laboratories and the Canadian Standards Association also have standards for installing duct heaters.

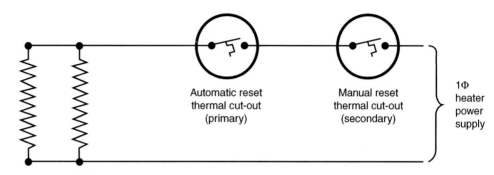

Total 1Φ load 15 A or less

**FIGURE 5-23.** *Over-temperature protection for single-phase heaters*

### Over-temperature limit controls

Acceptable *over-temperature protection* is an automatic reset thermal cut-out, which limits delivered temperature to 170°F. For single-phase heaters, the cut-out may be wired in series with the heater. However, as shown in Figure 5-23, the load may not exceed the 15-A electrical rating of the cut-out.

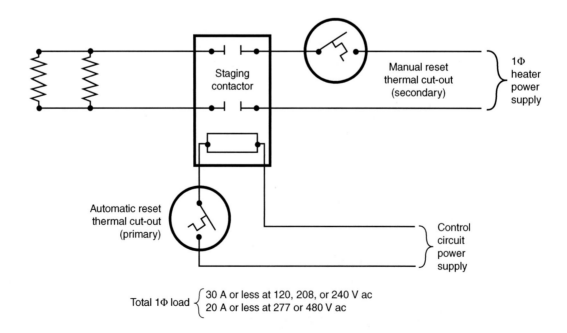

Total 1Φ load { 30 A or less at 120, 208, or 240 V ac
20 A or less at 277 or 480 V ac

**FIGURE 5-24.** *Over-temperature protection for larger single-phase heaters*

122

For larger single-phase heaters and all three-phase heaters, the cut-out must be wired in series with the staging contactor holding coil. This is shown in Figures 5-24 and 5-25. Secondary over-temperature protection is also required. It may be satisfied by installing a manual reset thermal cut-out. This is a single-pole, pilot duty cut-out. It is normally used with built-in or remotely mounted safety contactors.

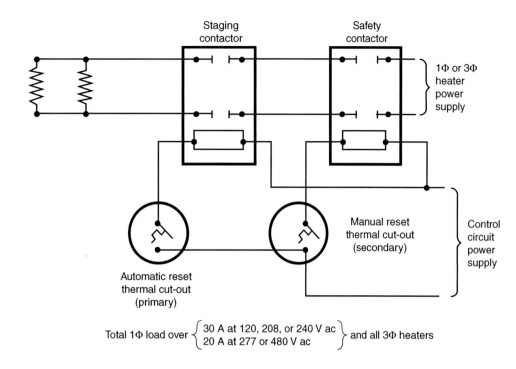

Total 1Φ load over $\left\{\begin{array}{l}\text{30 A at 120, 208, or 240 V ac}\\ \text{20 A at 277 or 480 V ac}\end{array}\right\}$ and all 3Φ heaters

**FIGURE 5-25.** *Over-temperature protection for three-phase heaters*

When a single-phase heater load does not exceed the 30 A (at 120, 208, or 240 V ac) or 20 A (at 277 or 480 V ac) electrical rating of the manual cut-out, it may be wired directly in series with the heater. This is shown in Figures 5-23 and 5-24. For larger loads, one or more safety contactors controlled by only the manual cut-out are required. This is shown in Figure 5-25. Safety contactors controlled by the manual cut-out must be UL-listed for at least 6,000 cycles of operation.

National codes generally permit de-energizing rather than disconnecting line power, but some local codes require that all ungrounded conductors be disconnected. To comply with all requirements, install contactors disconnecting all ungrounded conductors.

### Air failure protection

In addition to over-temperature protection, U.L. requires *air failure protection*. This is accomplished in one of two ways:

■    Electrically interlock the blower circuit with the control circuit of the
     heaters. This can be handled in several ways. The most positive method
     is to take the power for the heater control circuit directly from the blower
     circuit power supply through auxiliary contacts in the blower magnetic

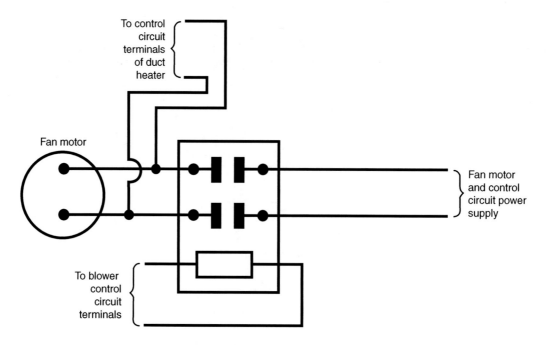

**FIGURE 5-26.** *Air failure protection*

starter or the load side of blower contactor, if used. This arrangement is shown in Figure 5-26.

- Interlocking heater controls and blower controls may involve extensive wiring. If so, it may be more practical to use a single-pole air flow or pressure differential switch wired in series with the automatic reset thermal cut-out. In this way, the heater control circuit cannot be energized unless both the cut-out and the air failure switch are closed. This arrangement is shown in Figure 5-27.

### Checking coil wire temperature

Acceptable wire temperature can be determined by visual inspection. With the duct heater installed, remove a limit control from the proximity of the heater (with the power supply off), but leave it in the circuit. When looking at the coils with the blower running and the heater energized, a maroon color between the insulators is acceptable (approximately 800 to 1,000°F). A bright red or orange color indicates overheating. It should be corrected by increasing air flow.

### Time delay

Time delay between stages is sometimes used to meet local code requirements. These codes are usually written to limit the number of kW switched on at one time. This eliminates light bulb dimming, etc.

EAA and NEMA have a joint committee to establish a uniform national standard. They propose a per stage maximum of 24 A, with not less than 10 seconds delay between the operation of each load-switching device.

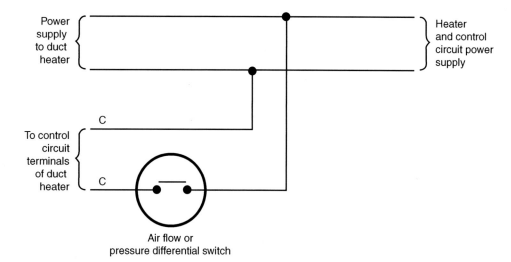

**FIGURE 5-27.** *Air failure protection using an air flow or pressure differential switch*

**Transformer selection**

Choose a low-voltage transformer with a VA (volt-ampere) rating that exceeds the combined total (VA) of all loads connected to the transformer. In order to compensate for the in-rush current required to close a contactor, add 50% to the total.

For example, assume that you are using two Honeywell R850B contactors at 16.7 VA each:

$$2 \times 16.7 = 33.4$$

Adding another 50%:

$$33.4 + 16.7 = 50.1$$

Thus, a 50-VA transformer could safely be selected.

**Temperature rise calculation**

Use the following equation to calculate *temperature rise* across a duct heater:

$$\text{temperature rise} = \frac{\text{kW} \times 3,081}{\text{cfm}}$$

For example, assume that you are using a 10-kW duct heater with an air velocity through the duct of 650 cfm:

$$\text{temperature rise} = \frac{10 \times 3,081}{650} = \frac{30,810}{650} = 47.4^\circ \text{F}$$

However, the cfm figure alone does not tell the whole story. The 650 cfm in the preceding example would produce 650 ft/min in a 1 ft × 1 ft duct. The same 650 cfm in a 2 ft × 2 ft duct would be only 162.5 ft/min. See the heater manufacturer's performance data chart for air velocity requirements for satisfactory performance.

## ELECTRIC FURNACES

Anyone considering central electric heating installation work should understand the *electric furnace* and how it is controlled. Capacity and control considerations are critical to economical, comfortable operation.

Basically, an electric furnace is made up of an enclosure that contains heating elements, an electric blower, and an air filter. Operation is controlled by a thermostat placed at a central location in the structure. Heat is distributed through a duct system. The system provides for both supply and return air. So far, it is much the same as any other type of furnace.

But here the similarity stops. The electric furnace has many other component parts. These include relays, transformers, step or proportional controllers, and limit controls. These are added for safety purposes and to ensure adequate heat distribution.

The electric furnace is still common in some areas, especially in manufactured homes, but the electric utilities are not promoting it. They are encouraging the use of the more efficient heat pump.

The energy crisis of the 1970s brought action by the federal government, which passed laws that made the power companies promote the wise use of energy. Although the electric furnace was a good source for home heating, it is being used less as a single heat source. Some utility suppliers have special rates where an electric furnace works well. It requires that energy management controls be installed to shift the use to keep on-peak demands to a minimum.

### Sizing

Regardless of the type, brand, and location of the furnace, the size of the heating elements is of prime importance. It is incorrect to think that if a given amount of heat is sufficient, then a larger amount is better. A grossly oversized furnace will:

- cost more to purchase

- cause higher fluctuation in room temperature

■ cost more to operate

■ require a larger electric service and branch circuit wiring materials.

Relating the Btu size of a fossil fuel furnace with an electric furnace will lead to oversizing of electric units. Other types of furnaces have combustion and flue losses. The electric furnace is a compact, self-sufficient unit. It needs nothing more than an electric cable to energize it.

To determine the proper size furnace, the heat loss of the building must be calculated by qualified personnel. As is true for all electric heat, the home must be insulated to specifications written for electrically heated dwellings. Your local utility will usually have a department to help in these areas. It can provide:

■ insulation recommendations

■ heat loss calculations for the building

■ other information related to the heating system.

Select the size of the furnace on the basis of the heat loss indicated. The Nebraska Iowa Electrical Council (NIEC) recommends that the total capacity of an electric furnace should not exceed the heat loss for the dwelling by more than 20%. The installed capacity may have to exceed this limitation for some reason, such as the unavailability of the proper size. If so, NIEC recommends that capacity in excess of 10% over the heat loss should be treated as emergency replacement equipment and left unconnected unless needed. This will save on oversizing of wiring and service entrance.

NIEC also recommends that the heater stages should not exceed 10 kW (34,000 Btuh) per stage. It suggests that the best rating is somewhere between 4.5 to 6 kW per stage. Multi-level homes may benefit from the installation of one furnace for each level. This permits the home to be zoned, and the temperature on various levels can be reduced as changes occur in the living habits of the occupants.

### Selection

The choice of electric furnace type depends on:

■ the type of building involved

■ the location of the furnace in the building.

Most furnaces are designed to deliver air through a duct system with a low-velocity cfm air distribution system. In the past, furnaces with high-velocity distribution systems were used, but they are rarely found today. High-velocity distribution usually consists of small outlets in the ceiling and a central air return.

NIEC recommends that the thermostat base and the control wiring provide for continuous fan operation. Higher cfm is usually required during cooling than during heating. Because of this, NIEC also recommends a provision for changing fan speed. This can be done by using a multi-speed motor or a variable-speed pulley.

Most manufacturers of electric furnaces offer models for the four basic installation possibilities:

- upright

- counterflow

- attic

- crawlspace.

### Power and control circuits

In an electric furnace, power and control circuits are identical in assembly and function to their counterparts in a duct heater installation. All electric furnaces are controlled in steps. An electric furnace has banks of elements. They may vary from three to six kW (3,000 to 6,000 W) each. The elements are arranged in *banks* or *stages*. For example, a 22,000-W furnace could have four 5,500-W elements.

When the thermostat calls for heat, the furnace is energized in four steps through a system of relays. The steps of 5,500 W each are a few seconds apart. This eliminates a large in-rush or load on the electric system within the building. Don't confuse this common procedure with staging of the electric furnace banks or elements.

There are line-voltage controls for low-wattage furnaces, but for practical purposes most controls are low-voltage. A small transformer is used to reduce line voltage to 24 V to operate the furnace controls. When the thermostat calls for heat, it energizes a relay that brings on the first element. After 30 to 45 seconds, the second element is turned on by the time delay relay of the first step.

In this manner, all banks or elements of the furnace are turned on. With the first step of heat, the fan is also started. High-limit controls provide protection against excessive temperature or voltage drop.

With two-stage control, the capacity of the furnace is divided into two stages. Using the previous example, two banks of 5.5 kW each would be on one stage, and the other two elements on the second. On the first signal for heat, the thermostat turns on half of the total steps of the unit.

The second half will not be energized until the thermostat gives a second signal. It has two bulbs that must tip to bring on the total heating system. The two bulbs are usually positioned 2 or 4° apart. Don't confuse this method with modulating control, which will be described later.

Another form of two-stage control is the outdoor bulb controller. Here the single-stage indoor thermostat energizes the first two 5.5-kW elements. The second bank is energized by an outdoor thermostat. It is set to prevent total heating until the outdoor temperature has dropped below a given setting. The setting is usually between 0 and 30°F. All of this can be done on large-capacity furnaces simply by dividing the furnace into more banks.

Thus far, examples have used the simple two-position thermostat. Another type of step control is a *modulating thermostat* piloting a multi-stage device that switches power to the furnace. This method is more accurate than simple two-position control. The simpler method puts two or more two-position thermostats under one cover. This results in a thermostat with excessive *droop* and a total differential of up to 8° in three to four-stage models.

The modulating step controller, depending on the number of steps and stages, can be set to be more accurate than a two-position controller. It applies continuous heat based on the load requirement and does not have the droop of a two-position control. In this system, the thermostat drives a small motor and makes and breaks a series of switches. As this is done, the switches turn the various steps or banks of heating elements on or off. This gives full step control in relationship to the demand of the occupied space.

Multi-step control often is used in commercial or larger residential installations. In the past, *modulating* control was used, but now has given way to *electronic* control In function, such controls act like modulating control. Electronic control can control up to ten stages of heat, and possibly more. The way the electric utility charges for electricity also may have an impact on the type of controls that are used. Some electric companies have a demand rate for residential customers as well as commercial customers.

Several manufacturers have developed a solid-state control system that responds quickly to changing climatic conditions. In this system, a sensing device constantly emits a signal. The signal is proportionate to the difference between room air temperature and pre-set instrument temperature. A circuit board inside the furnace interprets this signal. It activates one or more elements to provide the right amount of heat. Figure 5-28 shows such an electric heat sequencer.

## THE DUCT SYSTEM

The sheet metal work involved in the design and manufacture of air duct systems is complex. It requires a great deal of skill and training. But anyone involved in central warm air heating should be familiar with some basic principles.

There are several factors to consider in the design and installation of a good duct system—the space required, the location, heat loss, noise, and, of course, cost. Once supply outlets and return grilles are located, follow these rules for duct installation:

HONEYWELL INC.

**FIGURE 5-28.** *Electric heat sequencer*

- Avoid connections with high equivalent lengths—they are poor performers. *Equivalent lengths* of fittings are expressed in feet of straight duct that would have the same resistance to air flow. Figure 5-29 shows a typical main duct configuration. For each fitting, a letter identifies the type and numerals show the equivalent length in feet of straight pipe. For example, "A-40" refers to a type-A fitting with an equivalent straight length of 40 ft.

- Run main ducts as directly and as straight as possible.

- Transitions should be streamlined.

- Elbows should have an inside radius equal to at least one-third of the duct width.

- Use turning vanes in square-throated elbows.

- Avoid projections of ductwork into the air stream.

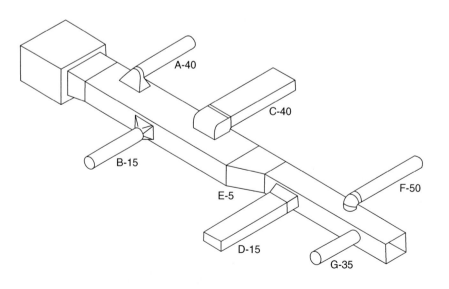

**FIGURE 5-29.** *Typical main duct configuration*

- Place volume dampers of a locking type in each air supply take-off.

- Seal ducts tightly with a mastic tape or duct sealer. Aluminum foil tape works well. It has an excellent vapor barrier and the mastic does not dry out and release the tape. One manufacturer of duct insulation states: "Sheet metal joints must be taped (or otherwise sealed) for insulation to be of any value. Joint leakage heat loss can exceed heat loss through the bare sheet metal, so joints must be tight."

- Avoid splitting a duct near a fan outlet.

- When possible, avoid side outlets at right angles to a main duct.

- Balance the system for proper air distribution.

HVACR and building codes require that ductwork be insulated to conserve the heating or cooling capacity of the system. Insulate any ductwork that is outside the space being conditioned. The thicker the insulation, the greater the heat loss protection (see manufacturer's guidelines). If the insulation is compressed 50% in the installation process, there is a loss of 39% in insulation value. Minimums will usually be established by building codes.

Duct size is determined by:

- the amount of air to be handled

- the maximum permissible air velocity

- the pressure loss of the system.

Total air volume is determined on the basis of the heating/cooling load and temperature change in the air as it passes through the electric furnace or cooling coil. For each conditioned space, the volume of air to the supply outlet depends on the heating/cooling load of the room serviced by the outlet. Design ducts to carry the higher air flow needed during cooling operation. Lower air flow can always be obtained by reducing the fan speed.

Usually, velocity is as high as possible to minimize the required duct size. But there are limitations on air velocity, including fan capacity and maximum sound level requirements. The ideal duct system moves the required quantity of air in the smallest possible duct. It uses a reasonably powered fan with an acceptable noise level. For residential installations, velocities are usually held below 900 ft/min on supply ductwork, and below 700 ft/min on return air ductwork.

There are three basic causes of pressure loss in a duct system. They are *friction* and *turbulence* in straight ductwork, and *eddy flow* in elbows and bends (also referred to as *dynamic loss*). Tables and data on pressure loss in ductwork are readily available from trade associations. These include:

- National Environmental Systems Contractors Association (NESCA)

- Sheet Metal and Air Conditioning Contractors National Association (SMACNA)

- Air Conditioning Contractors of America (ACCA)

- Air Movement and Control Association, Inc. (AMCA).

The ASHRAE Guide and Data Books are also excellent sources of pressure loss data and methods for determining the duct size required for a particular application.

1.      For what purposes are duct heaters used?

2.      Duct heaters operate at voltages ranging from _____ to _____ V.

3.      What type of thermal cut-outs are generally used with duct heaters?

4.      What is *aluminized* steel?

5.      One kilowatt equals _____ Btu.

6.      What is the function of a fan interlock?

7.      What is *staging*?

8.      What does *transition* refer to?

9.      What is *watt density*?

10.     How is watt density generally expressed for duct heaters?

11.     From what direction should a duct heater be installed?

12.     How far should a duct heater be mounted from the heat pump or central air conditioner?

13.     How far must a duct heater be placed from any canvas duct connector?

14.     What protective device should be wired with the duct heater?

15.     What is the maximum watt density per square foot of duct area?

16.     For what wattage rating are duct heaters designed for most applications?

17.     What type of wire is considered suitable for connections to heater terminals or control boxes?

18.     In addition to over-temperature protection, what other protective device is required for duct heaters by UL?

19.     Why do local codes require time delay between stages?

20.     When selecting a transformer for sufficient capacity, how should you compensate for the increased current required to close a contactor?

21.     What is the equation for calculating the temperature rise across a duct heater?

22.     What is the maximum oversizing recommended for electric furnaces by NIEC?

23.     According to NIEC, the best rating for heater stages is _____ per stage.

24.     What type of furnaces use line-voltage controls?

25.     What is the function of the outdoor bulb controller?

26.     What maximum air velocities are permitted for residential installations?

27.     What are the basic causes of pressure loss in a duct system?

28.     Where can you find tables and data on pressure losses in ductwork?

# Baseboard and Unit Heaters

## INTRODUCTION

Electric baseboard heaters are designed for ease of installation. They can be used as the sole heating system in an installation, or as auxiliary units where supplementary heat is required. They can give many homeowners an effective heating system at a low installation cost and a low operating cost. The large number of units per home gives some diversity of demand and will work well with some electric utility suppliers. Low maintenance and installation costs are the big pluses for baseboard heating. There are many applications for which it is the best and only choice. These include small areas, seasonal homes, workshops, new additions, and other locations where heat is desired. In any of these cases, proper insulation is required.

Electric baseboard heaters are usually equipped with a *thermal cut-out*. It protects against overheating by automatically "cutting out" heating elements at a pre-set temperature. This safety device consists of a sensitive thermal element that senses overheated conditions. An automatic reset re-energizes the heaters when the condition causing the overheating is removed and the temperature falls below the pre-set control point.

Baseboard heaters are available in *standard-wattage* or *high-wattage* models. High-wattage heaters should be used only when standard-wattage heating cannot meet heating requirements due to limited available wall space.

Heaters should be centered on an outside wall or walls, under window areas. In these locations, they counteract the downward flow of cool air caused by loss of heat through the glass. Drapes should be kept 6 in. above the top of the baseboard units.

Blank sections can be added to fill out a wall-to-wall installation. These sections are cut with a metal-cutting saw and fastened to the wall in the same manner as the heater sections.

In some cases, it may be difficult to run the thermostat circuit in the existing walls. If so, an integral thermostat section may be installed adjacent to the baseboard heater.

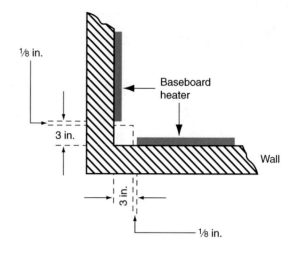

**FIGURE 6-1.** *Inside corner*

### PREPARATION FOR INSTALLATION

First, select the number and length of heating units as required by heat loss calculations. Then decide on the approximate location of the heaters. If wall-to-wall coverage is required, select the number of blank panels (without heating elements) to fill in the balance of the wall length. In determining the length of the units for a complete wall-to-wall installation, note the distance that must be allowed for inside corners, as shown in Figure 6-1.

Electrical wiring can be run through the wall or through the floor. If wiring is run through the wall, which is the usual method, drill a 1½-in. hole through the wall. Locate it as shown in Figure 6-2 for a standard-wattage baseboard, or as shown in Figure 6-3 for a high-wattage baseboard. You may want to connect more than one baseboard to the same branch circuit. If so, two holes are recommended to line up with the two knock-outs at the back of the outlet box.

#### Roughing-in wiring

Run a circuit of the appropriate voltage for the units being used. Run it to the outlet box for the

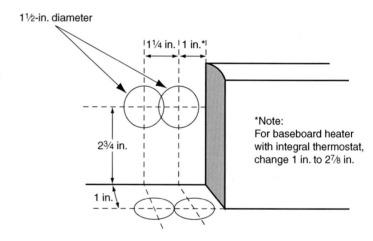

**FIGURE 6-2.** *Standard baseboard without thermostat*

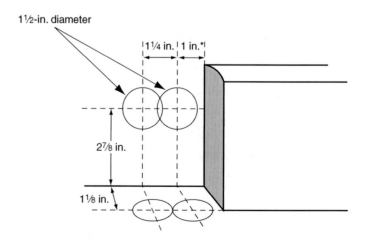

**FIGURE 6-3.** *High-wattage baseboard*

thermostat and then down to the location of the junction box of the nearest heater unit. Provide electrical grounding of the metal housing as required by the applicable electric codes.

Table 6-1 lists some of the more common wire constructions. A more complete listing can be found in current issues of the National Electrical Code (NEC) on good wiring practices. Table 6-2 shows that Types R, T, TW, and THHN wire are satisfactory for supply connections for both wattages. In Table 6-3, the sizes for circuit breakers or fuses are based on 75-ft runs and no motor loads. If the run is more than 75 ft, the wire size should be increased to the next larger size. If there is a motor involved, the full load amperes of the motor (FLA) should be added to the electric heater amperes to determine the wire size. It also may be necessary to increase the wire size one size larger to handle the starting current of the motor. Follow local codes and the 1996 National Electrical Code.

| Maximum conductor operating temperatures | | Wire choice | | |
|---|---|---|---|---|
| | | Line voltages up to 300 V | Line voltages up to 600 V | |
| °C | °F | Wire type | Wire type | Construction |
| 60 | 140 | Use 600-V wire | T<br>TW | Thermoplastic over copper.<br>Moisture-resistant thermoplastic over copper. |
| 75 | 167 | Use 600-V wire | RHW<br>THWN | Moisture- and heat-resistant rubber over copper.<br>Moisture- and heat-resistant thermoplastic over copper. |
| 90 | 194 | Use 600-V wire | RHH<br>THHN | Heat-resistant rubber over copper.<br>Heat-resistant thermoplastic over copper. |
| 200 | 392 | Use 600-V wire | FEP<br>SRG | Teflon over copper.<br>Silicon rubber and glass braid over copper. |
| **Special construction for high-temperature applications** | | | | |
| 250 | 482 | Use 600-V wire | TGT<br><br>TGS | Teflon tape with Teflon-impregnated glass braid over nickel-plated copper.<br>Teflon tape with silicone-impregnated glass braid over nickel-plated copper. |
| 450 | 842 | Use 600-V wire | MGS<br><br>MGT | Mica tape with silicone-impregnated glass braid over nickel-plated copper.<br>Mica tape with Teflon-impregnated glass braid over nickel-plated copper. |
| 594 | 1100 | Bare manganese nickel wire or bus bar with ceramic tube or bead insulation | | |

**TABLE 6-1.** *Common code wire constructions and their temperature capabilities*

## INSTALLING THE HEATER

The heaters and blank panels can be mounted in several ways:

- against the plaster wall

- semi-recessed by mounting directly to wall studs

- mounted to insulation board used in solid masonry construction.

For surface mounting against the plastered wall, complete the roughing-in wiring before lath and plaster are applied, unless wiring is to be run through the floor. Some electrical contractors prefer to wire to an outlet box located directly behind the place where the heater junction box is to be located. However, the use of an outlet box is not required. Wiring can be left temporarily projecting through an opening in the plaster at the proper location.

When units are semi-recessed, wiring and connections may be done before the walls are plastered. In such installations, heaters are fastened directly to the wall studs before plastering. Do not plaster up to the heater enclosure. Leave a space of ⅛ in. for expansion, and use molding for finishing.

When mounted to solid masonry, heaters should be mounted against the insulation board normally used in this type of construction. Use the common mounting methods—such as screws with wood or lead plugs—to secure the heaters to the wall.

Where two or more heaters are joined in one run, the connecting wires are run in the raceway at the bottom of each baseboard section, as shown in Figure 6-4. Where heaters are separated, or not continuous, provide a connecting loop in the roughing-in operation. *Note*: Allow ⅛ in. between adjoining sections for expansion, as shown in Figure 6-5.

| Wire size | Low-wattage RT, T, TW High-wattage RH, RHW, THW | | |
|---|---|---|---|
| | 208 V | 240 V | 277 V |
| Number 14 | 2600 | 3000 | 3500 |
| Number 12 | 3400 | 4000 | 4600 |

**TABLE 6-2.** *Maximum watts for wireway wiring to adjacent units*

| Wire size TW or THHN | Maximum circuit breaker or fuse size |
|---|---|
| Number 14 | 15 amperes |
| Number 12 | 20 amperes |
| Number 10 | 30 amperes |
| Number 8 | 40 amperes |

**TABLE 6-3.** *Maximum circuit breaker or fuse sizes for different wire sizes*

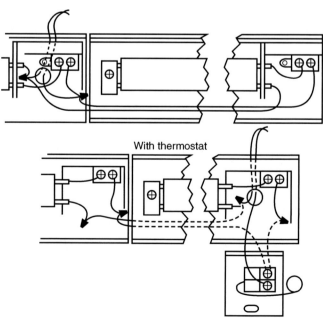

With thermostat

**FIGURE 6-4.** *Connecting wires*

### Mounting and wiring standard-wattage heaters

Remove the front cover of the baseboard heater. Remove the terminal box cover and the knockout or knockouts as required for wiring. There are usually mounting holes in the back panel of heaters, as shown in Figure 6-5. If not, drill holes $\frac{1}{16}$ in. larger than wood screws for mounting. For mounting against a plaster wall, mark the stud positions before placing the heaters in their desired locations. This is not necessary for solid masonry construction.

Before fastening the heater, attach the connector for electrical wiring. Insert the wire through the connector into the junction box on the heater. To prevent warping of the back panel, fasten only at those locations where the panel comes in direct contact with the wall. Washers can be used to fill gaps, if necessary. Use roundhead screws. Draw up firmly first, then back off half a turn to allow for expansion when heated.

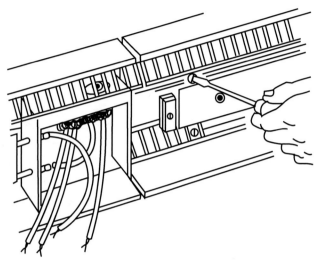

**FIGURE 6-5.** *Allow space between adjoining sections*

For a single heater, run the branch circuit wires to the wall thermostat and then to the two conductors in the junction box. Connect grounding wires as required. Where two or more heaters are coupled together, remove the wiring raceway cover at the bottom. Run extension wiring from the branch circuit in the wiring raceway to the adjoining heaters, as shown in Figure 6-4.

Replace the metal cover for this raceway. Insert the top edge under the lower front panel bracket. Then press along the bottom area to force the bottom edge over the lip. When using baseboard heaters with an integral thermostat or baseboard thermostat section, see Figures 6-4 and 6-6 for typical wiring. Place the cover over the bottom front cover support. Then, while pressing down on the top of the cover support, lift the front cover until it snaps on.

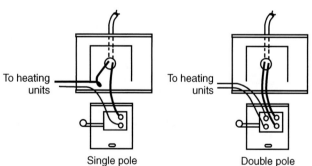

Single pole      Double pole

**FIGURE 6-6.** *Thermostat section*

### Mounting and wiring high-wattage heaters

Lay the baseboard unit on its back and remove the front cover. Remove the terminal box cover. Remove the knockout or knockouts as required for wiring. If units are to be joined in series, remove the appropriate end cap. Position the baseboard heater on the floor at the mounting location.

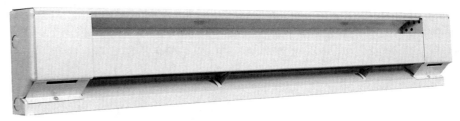

**FIGURE 6-7.** *Baseboard heater*

Install the heater to the wall using mounting holes in the rear of the cabinet. To prevent warping, fasten only at those locations where the panel comes in direct contact with the wall. Washers may be used to fill gaps, if necessary. Use a sealing strip to close off the air flow through any large gaps. Use roundhead screws. Draw up firmly first, then back off half a turn to allow for expansion when heated.

Attach the connectors for electrical wiring. Insert the wires in the junction box on the back panel of the heater. For a single heater, run the branch circuit wire to the wall thermostat and then to the two conductors in the junction box. Connect grounding as required. Where two or more heaters are coupled together, use the wiring raceway.

Normally, installation of an electric wall heater is between $2 \times 4$ studs on 16-in. centers with a ½-in. plaster or drywall finish. Locate the wall box on the wall. Use the box as a guide to nail in the top and bottom framing between 16-in. centers of wall studs. Make sure to allow the proper space for drywall or other wall material between the front flange of the wall box and the face of the $2 \times 4$. Complete the wiring connections in the terminal box. Replace the terminal box cover and front panel. Install splice connectors as required. Figure 6-7 shows a complete baseboard heater.

## ELECTRIC WALL HEATERS

For the installation of compact *electric wall heaters*, it is recommended that horizontal wood headers be used to frame the steel wall box, as shown in Figure 6-8. Then proceed as follows: Place the bottom supporting header approximately 10 to 18 in. from the floor. An exception is a radiant heater, which must be mounted 24 in. from the floor.

Mount the wall box vertically (the long dimension must be vertical). Run approximately 1 ft of electrical wire through the

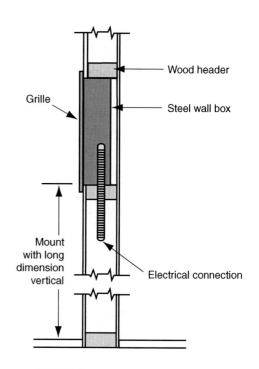

**FIGURE 6-8.** *Electric wall heater installation*

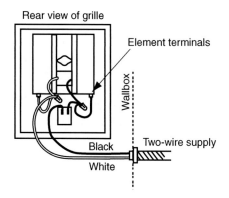

**FIGURE 6-9.** *Typical wiring connection*

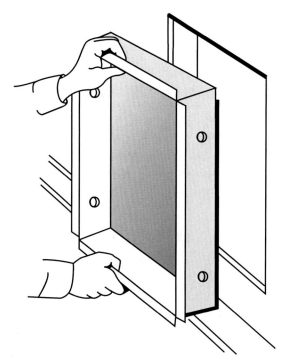

knockout with the appropriate connector. Make sure to use the proper wire size for the unit being connected. Make sure that the wiring is clear of the fan and has adequate clearance from the heating element. A typical wiring connection for a wall heater is shown in Figure 6-9. Make sure that the flange of the box sets flush with the finished tile or plaster wall line, as shown in Figure 6-10. Follow the manufacturer's instructions for installing the wall heater.

**FIGURE 6-10.** *Installing the box*

After finish wall surface has been applied, remove the chassis from the carton and install according to the manufacturer's instructions. Connect the leads to the heater and follow the directions for installing the front cover on the heater. Figures 6-11 shows the front cover of an electric wall heater.

*Register heaters* and *kick-space* (or *toe-space*) *heaters* are similar to wall heaters, and are installed in the same manner. After plastering is finished, complete the wiring to the heater. Fasten the heater to the wall box using the screws provided. Figure 6-12 on the next page shows a typical register cover.

## IN-FLOOR HEATERS

### General instructions

A typical *floor heater* is shown in Figure 6-13 on the next page. When installing a floor heater as a draft barrier below windows, match the heater's capacity to the heat loss of the glass area. Also, the heat spread of each heater is about 5 ft. For continuous draft control, mount heaters 5 ft apart.

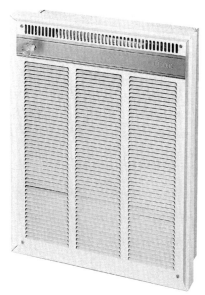

MARLEY ENGINEERED PRODUCTS

**FIGURE 6-11.** *Electric wall heater*

The heaters may be the sole source of heat in the room. If so, match the capacity of the heaters to the heat loss of the room. For good room temperature control, use a wall thermostat mounted on an inside wall. This type of heater is not recommended for use in bathrooms or areas where water may saturate the heater.

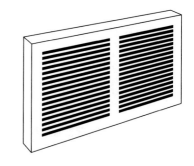

**FIGURE 6-12.** *Register cover*

The heater may be installed as close to a wall or corner as desired. However, take care to prevent discoloration of drapery materials and undue wall discoloration. To do so, the side of the heater should be at least 1 in. from the nearest fold of the drapes. The end of the heater should be no closer than 3 ft to the wall, as shown in Figure 6-14. Do not mount heaters behind doors or in other places where air flow may be obstructed.

### Housing installation in wood floors

Provide a hole in the floor at least 6 in. from the wall. The longest side should be parallel to the wall, as shown in Figure 6-15. Insert the housing into the opening and secure it with four nails or screws. The housing may be installed with flanges flat against the floor and the floor covering between the grille and housing flange. The floor covering should be no thicker than ¾ in., trimmed to prevent any of it extending past the flange and into the housing.

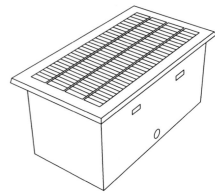

**FIGURE 6-13.** *Drop-in floor heater*

### Wiring the housing

Shut off the electric current to the circuit on which you are working. Make certain that all wiring is in accordance with local codes. Bring the supply wire into the desired knockout. Leave 6 in. of leads extending into the housing. Secure the ground lead to the ground screw on the bottom of the housing.

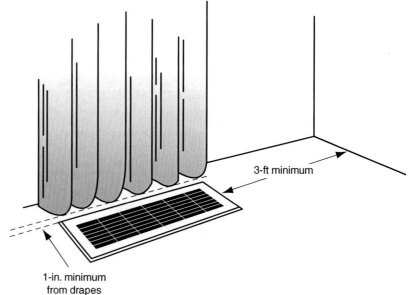

3-ft minimum

1-in. minimum from drapes

### Housing installation in slab floors

Secure two stakes to the diagonally opposite corners of the housing with nuts and bolts. Drive the stakes into

**FIGURE 6-14.** *Recommended distances*

the subgrade to support the housing at the required location (at least 6 in. from wall). The top of the housing should be level with the grade of the finished concrete slab. Bring the conduit into the desired knockout. Wire as for wood floor installation.

Secure the temporary cover pan provided for such applications with screws. Cover the screw threads with the tubing provided. Before pouring concrete, place waterproof paper between the subgrade and the housing to protect it from moisture. After the slab has set and before installing the heater assembly, remove the two screws and cover pan and discard.

### Heater assembly installation

Make sure that the thermostat is placed on the side closest to the outside wall when inserting the floor heater into the floor box. Follow the manufacturer's instructions for wiring the floor heater. Secure the heater assembly to the housing with sheet metal screws.

### Grille installation

Before operating the unit, remove all foreign material from inside the heater. Floor covering may be installed after the housing is installed. Be sure that it does not extend past the edges of the housing. Place the grille over the housing and secure with screws. *Caution*: Do not use the receptacle in the housing as a convenience outlet.

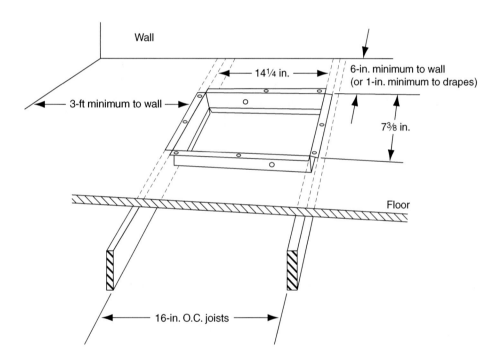

**FIGURE 6-15.** *Installing the housing in a wood floor*

## CEILING HEATERS

### Types of ceiling heaters

Typical *ceiling heaters* can be surface mounted to any 3¼-in. and 4-in. octagon or 3½-in. round electrical box. For recessed heaters, make sure to install a cone to keep insulation away from the heater in the attic. Failure to do so could cause a fire.

*Combination ceiling heaters* for bathrooms include lighting and exhaust fans. Installation is similar to the installation of wall heaters. These units should be installed near the center of the bathroom. Again, make sure to install a cone to keep insulation away from the heater in the attic if the unit is to be recessed. Failure to do so could cause a fire.

Larger-wattage units can be recessed or surface-mounted, or installed in drop ceilings. Installation is similar to wall-mounted heaters. These heaters can be field-adjusted for 50% of heat output. They come in sizes up to 4,800 watts. Figure 6-16 shows a commercial downflow ceiling heater.

### Roughing-in wiring

Mount the box in or on the ceiling, at least 12 in. from any wall. Check the manufacturer's instructions for box installation procedure. Run proper wiring from the switch and/or thermostat, if used, to the box. Check the electrical code or local codes for the proper wiring procedure. For recessed ceiling heaters, make sure to install a cone to keep insulation away from the heater in the attic. Failure to do so could cause a fire.

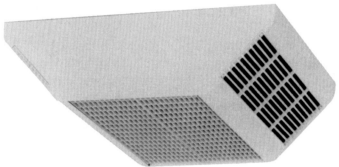

**FIGURE 6-16.** *Commercial downflow ceiling heater*

### Mounting heaters

To mount the heater, remove the cover. Remove the short screws from the outlet box. Replace with the longer screws usually supplied with the heater. Connect the lead wires on the back of the device to the branch circuit wiring. Then fasten the heater—without the cover—to the outlet box. Do so by pushing wires back into the box. Locate the outlet box screws in the appropriate keyholes in the mounting plate and rotate slightly. Complete the installation by tightening these screws and replacing the cover.

### Replacing the fusible link

For protection against overheating, newer ceiling heaters have an automatic reset protector. Some older ceiling heaters have a *fusible link* built into the device. The fuse will open if overheated and shut off the heating element or elements. The fan will still operate so that the element or elements can be cooled. If this occurs, first disconnect the heater from the power supply, and remove the cover. If there is a protective cover over the fusible link, remove the protective cover. Remove one end of the fusible link and check it with an ohmmeter. The fusible link should read close to 0 ohms. If the fusible link is defective, replace it.

## COMMERCIAL/INDUSTRIAL ELECTRIC UNIT HEATERS

### Unit location

A typical *unit heater* is shown in Figure 6-17. In locating such units, consider general space heating requirements of the area. Unit heaters should be located so that they discharge air nearly parallel to exposed walls. In multiple-unit installations, arrange them so that each supports the air stream to the next unit. This will create circulatory air movement in the area. Direct a large portion of the heated air toward the windward side of a building exposed to prevailing winds. Avoid interference of air streams by columns, beams, partitions, or other obstructions as much as possible. To contend with cold air entering at loading dock doors, arrange one or more units to discharge warm air *across* the opening, not toward it. Total cfm capacity of all units should circulate the room air volume several times per hour. Some unit heaters have a built-in thermostat. Others have an option for a summer/winter switch that allows the fan to be operated continuously to circulate air in the summer.

### Special precautions

Maintain separation between units so that the discharge from one is not directed into the inlet of another. Check the manufacturer's instructions for clearance on all sides of the unit. Clearance is needed for ample air supply, service, and to provide adequate distance from combustibles. Do not install the unit above the recommended maximum mounting height or below the minimum height of 7 ft.

Standard unit heaters should not be used in potentially explosive or flammable atmospheres. They should not be used in areas exposed to high humidity, swimming pool areas, marine applications, or packing plants where all equipment is washed down. There are explosion-proof units that can be used in certain types of hazardous areas if they are wired and installed correctly. There are also explosion-proof thermostats available for explosion-proof units. An explosion-proof thermostat is depicted in Figure 6-18. There are stainless steel units that are suitable for high-humidity environments, swimming pool areas, marine applications, and wash-down areas.

Be sure that no obstructions block the air intake or discharge of the unit heater. Do not attach ductwork or poly-tubes to propeller

MARLEY ENGINEERED PRODUCTS

**FIGURE 6-17.** *Typical unit heater*

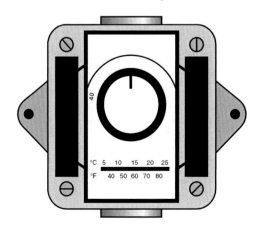

**FIGURE 6-18.** *Explosion-proof thermostat*

units. Consult the electrical and wiring instructions provided before final installation.

### Unit suspension

Provision is made on all units for *suspension*. Suspension can be made with threaded rods, ceiling hangers, or pipes. Some manufacturers have pipe hanger adapter kits available. Some heaters can be installed horizontally, others can be installed vertically. Some can be installed either horizontally or vertically. Consult the manufacturer's instructions for minimum and maximum mounting heights and position.

### Wiring instructions

All wiring must be done according to the 1996 U.S. National Electrical Code or Canadian Electrical Code, whichever has jurisdiction. All applicable local electrical codes must be followed. All internal wiring is completed at the factory. Applicable wiring diagrams are provided with each unit. Some units have fuses for protection in the unit, and others do not. If the unit does not have internal fuses, install a fused disconnect.

The location of a remote thermostat should be determined by heating requirements. It should be mounted on an inside wall about 5 ft above the floor. It must not be located where it would be affected by direct heat from the unit or other sources, or drafts from frequently opened doors or windows. Check the instructions packed with the thermostat.

Some units require a UL-listed line-voltage thermostat, others require a 24-V thermostat. The unit may be controlled by a remote manual ON/OFF switch. If a line-voltage thermostat or a remote manual ON/OFF switch is used, make sure that the device is UL-listed and rated for the current necessary to operate the heater.

To wire the unit:

- Prepare the rough-in conduit and wiring to the heater. Be sure to check unit electrical data for line amperes and minimum wire and conduit sizes. Check the location of openings for power supply and control wiring.

- Connect the power supply and control wiring to the terminal block terminals according to the wiring diagram accompanying the unit. Typical wiring diagrams are shown in Figures 6-19 on the following pages.

Units with factory-installed, unit-mounted thermostats need only power connections to complete installation. No additional external controls are required. The thermostat's range is approximately 40 to 120°F.

### Electrical notes

- All wire must be insulated for 60°C or better.

- 120-V control wiring should be No. 14 AWG (American Wire Gauge), and 24-V control wiring should be thermostat wire with 18 gauge wires. For long runs, 24-V thermostat wire should be replaced with a heavier gauge if voltage drop is excessive.

- Total line amperes includes fan motor current (FLA).

- 208, 240, and 277-V single-phase units over 5 kW in size—as well as 208, 240, and 440-V three-phase units—usually will have built-in transformers.

### Pre-operational checkpoints

- Check the fan clearance. A clearance of ¼ in. is allowed between the fan blade tip and the fan shroud or venturi. Make sure that the fan blade is inserted the proper distance into the fan shroud or venturi.

- Fill the oil cups on the motor, if provided, with SAE 10 motor oil.

- Make sure that fuses are installed in units that require them.

- Check all electrical connections to ensure that they are secure.

- Check the rigidity of the unit mounting. Tighten all fasteners, if necessary.

### Initial start-up procedure

- Set the unit-mounted or remote thermostat to its lowest position.

- Turn on the power supply to the unit.

- Raise the thermostat setting to the desired position.

- Adjust the horizontal louvers for the desired heat distribution.

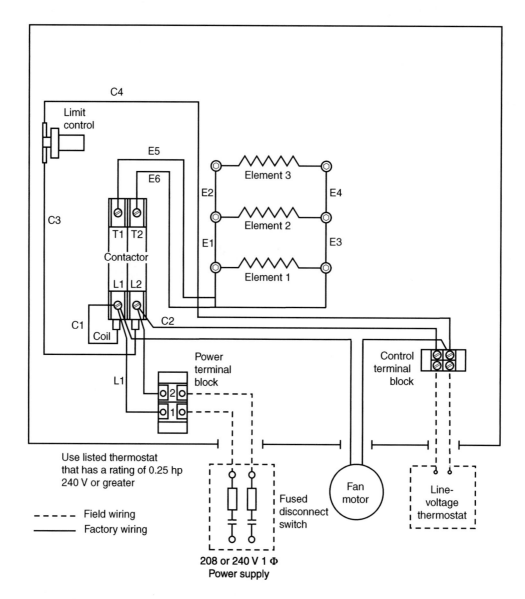

**FIGURE 6-19.** *Wiring diagram for 208/240-V single-phase power supply*

■  To ensure the proper sequence of operation, cycle the unit on and off a
few times by raising and lowering the thermostat setting.

### Overheat control (high-limit switch)

The *overheat control* will interrupt power to the unit contactor in the event of
overheating. It is generally a single-pole, single-throw switch, with a cut-out
setting of 140 to 300°F and an automatic reset of 120 to 270°F. The temperature
settings depend on the manufacturer of the unit. Some manufacturers offer an
optional manual reset limit switch. This switch permits the motor to continue
operation and cool the heater while power to the elements is interrupted.
Overheat control should operate only when something is seriously wrong with

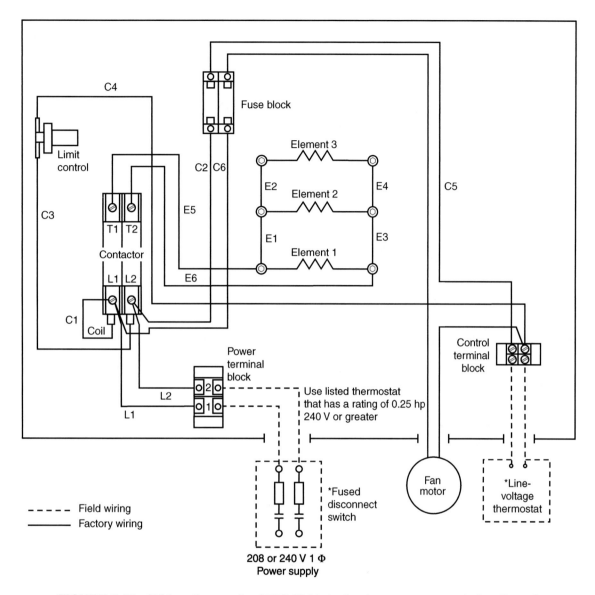

**FIGURE 6-19.** *Wiring diagram for 208/240-V single-phase power supply (continued)*

the unit. When this control operates, correct the difficulty immediately, or serious
and permanent damage may result.

If the overheat control interrupts the power supply during normal operation:

■  Check to make sure that the front louvers are open (not closed more than
   45° from horizontal).

■  Remember to check the actual power input to the unit against the rated
   power input.

■  Check the fan rpm against the motor rpm listed on the nameplate.

- Check the heating elements for accumulation of dirt, grease or foreign materials.

- Replace the limit switch if necessary.

- The fan blades and inside of the casing can be cleaned with compressed air. Use compressed air to clean the heating elements and around the electrical controls.

- Using a good grade of automotive wax will preserve the finish on the outside of the heater.

### Routine maintenance

Unit heaters, like other electrical and mechanical equipment, give lasting, trouble-free service if properly cared for. Observing a few simple periodic procedures will ensure satisfactory operation.

Under average conditions, unit heaters should be inspected before every heating season. Inspect more often in locations where the air is contaminated with corrosive fumes, dust, soot, or oil spray. To perform routine maintenance:

- Disconnect the power supply to the unit.

- Check all components and wiring inside the unit for firm connections and/or wear.

- Tighten the fan guard and motor bracket. Check the fan for proper clearance, free rotation, and firm connection to the motor shaft.

- Lubricate the motor according to the motor manufacturer's instructions.

- Routine cleaning of the unit casing and louvers is recommended for removing dirt, grease, or corrosive substances that may damage the finish. Rusted or corroded spots on the louvers or casing should be sanded and repainted.

- Clean fan blades, elements, and inside of the casing with compressed air. Do not scrape elements.

- When servicing is complete, tag the unit to indicate the date of inspection, lubrication, and cleaning.

1. What safety device is incorporated within a baseboard heater?

2. In what two wattage classifications are baseboard heaters available?

3. Where should baseboard heaters be located, and why?

4. How should the electrical wiring for connecting a baseboard heater be routed?

5. Name three ways of mounting baseboard heaters.

6. How are the wires connecting various units run when two or more heaters are joined together?

7. When fastening the heater, what should you do to prevent the back panel from warping?

8. What should you do prior to installing compact electric wall heaters?

9. How high should radiant heaters be mounted from the floor?

10. When selecting an in-floor heater to be used as a draft barrier below a window, you should match the heater's capacity to the _____.

11. How far apart should in-floor heaters be spaced?

12. What areas are unsuitable for in-floor heaters?

13.     How far should the heater be from the drapes?

14.     How close should the end of the heater be from the wall?

15.     What important task should you remember to do after the installation is completed, but prior to putting the unit into operation?

16.     What device is incorporated within a ceiling heater to protect against overheating?

17.     How should unit heaters be located?

18.     How should the units be arranged for multiple installation?

19.     Where should the air be directed?

20.     What should be done to counteract cold air entering at loading dock doors?

21.     Why is it essential to maintain separation between units?

22.     Why should the manufacturer's recommended clearance be made available at the rear and sides of the unit?

23.     How high should the unit heater be installed?

24.     Where should a room thermostat be located?

25.     What size wire is used for 120-V control wiring?

26.     How often should unit heaters be inspected under average conditions?

# Radiant Heat Installation

## QUARTZ HEATERS

A typical *quartz heater* is designed for ease of installation. These types of heaters may be mounted from ceilings or walls by means of conduit, brackets, or chain. They can be used as the sole heating system, or as auxiliary units where supplementary heat is required. Properly installed, they give highly efficient performance in production of radiant heat energy. Common applications include basements, workshops, garages, bowling alleys, and similar indoor uses. They also can be used for heating patios, loading docks, swimming pools, and similar locations. For most fixtures, there is a choice of three types of heating elements—clear quartz lamps, quartz tubes, and metal sheath elements.

*Clear quartz lamps* have a color temperature of about 4,100°F. They provide 6 to 8 lumens of output per watt. Quartz lamps heat up and cool down almost instantaneously. They have the highest moisture resistance of the three types of lamps, and a radiant efficiency of approximately 96% . Mechanical ruggedness is average.

*Quartz tubes* have a color temperature of about 1,800°F. A quartz tube also heats up and cools down quickly. Moisture resistance is high for quartz tubes. Quartz tubes have a radiant efficiency of approximately 60%. Mechanical ruggedness is good. Figure 7-1 on the next page shows a quartz tube.

*Metal sheath elements* have a color temperature of about 1,600°F. A metal sheath element heats up and cools down slowly. Moisture resistance is low for metal sheath elements. Metal sheath elements have a radiant efficiency of approximately 50%. Mechanical ruggedness is excellent.

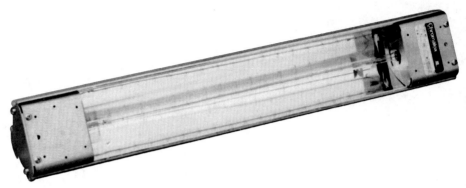

**FIGURE 7-1.** *Quartz tube radiant heater*

When installing these types of heaters, you first must determine the method of mounting. If bracket mounting is desired, an accessory mounting kit is needed for each fixture.

### Minimum spacing

Heating units should be mounted out of reach of the people for whom the heat is being provided. Any surface should be at least 25 in. from the direct heat of the unit. Mount the unit a minimum of 3 in. from the ceiling. The units should be mounted a minimum of 36 in. apart, and a minimum of 24 in. from a vertical surface. These are general guidelines. Always read and follow the instructions from the manufacturer.

*Important*: Fixtures should be mounted to keep heating lamps in a horizontal position. At final assembly, take care to wipe the lamps clean of all foreign contamination, including fingerprints.

### Roughing-in wiring

Run the branch circuit to the device mounting box that will house the control unit, switch, thermostat, timer, etc. Then run cable to the location of the nearest heater. Leave enough excess to make connections.

## MOUNTING HEATERS

### Chain mounting

Secure chains—two or more for each heater, depending on heater size. Chains should be cut to length to achieve the desired mounting height above the floor. Follow the manufacturer's instructions for mounting and wiring the units.

### Conduit mounting

Locate conduits to correspond with the knockout openings in the raceway cover. To prevent the fixture from turning, two conduits are required in all cases. Attach the raceway cover to the conduits. Install supply conductors, leaving a minimum of 6 in. extending through the access cover opening. Attach the raceway cover to the heating unit. Follow the manufacturer's instructions.

### Bracket mounting

Attach brackets to the ceiling or wall with the correct spacing for the heating unit. Locate the brackets so that the heater will meet the minimum spacing requirements. Follow the manufacturer's instructions for the installation of all quartz lamps, tubes, or metal sheath elements. It is very important to keep quartz tubes clean. Quartz lamps should be handled with clean cotton gloves or clean paper towels, etc. If the tube is dirty, it should be cleaned with alcohol and a clean cloth. Be careful, or you can break the lamp. Quartz tubes and metal sheath elements are not as critical as quartz lamps. However, care should be used to keep these elements clean as well.

### Finish wiring

Complete the wiring connections by the approved means. Push the wires back into the fixture, and replace the wiring access cover.

## NATURAL CONVECTION HEATERS

### Application

Figure 7-2 shows a *natural convection* utility heater. Such heaters are ideal for heating out-of-the-way places that can be a problem in cold weather. They are especially suited for small areas where natural convection is enough to maintain an even temperature.

### Installation

The preferred location for a natural convection utility heater is near cold air inlets, such as under windows. Remove the front cover screws and remove the cover. Mount the heater on the wall at the desired location. Use four screws through the mounting tabs. Mount the heaters at least 2 ft above floor level.

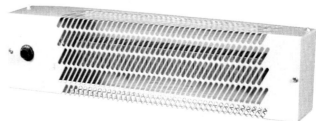

FIGURE 7-2. *Electric utility heater*

MARLEY ENGINEERED PRODUCTS

Run wiring from the wall switch or thermostat to the base of the heater. Pass cable through the cable opening in the base of the heater. Secure with a cable clamp (not provided). Fasten the incoming leads to the cable terminals in the conventional manner. Replace the front cover.

## INSTALLING RADIANT CEILING PANELS

*Radiant ceiling panels* are designed to be surface-mounted or flush-mounted on ceilings. They provide auxiliary heating for areas of greatest heat loss.

### Location

Areas of greatest heat loss usually appear at windows and doors. For maximum comfort, mount panels end-to-end along the outside wall. When locating panels, observe the following guidelines:

- Maintain a minimum space between the panel and vertical surfaces. Plan 6 in. for surface mounting, and 9 in. for flush mounting.

- Maintain a minimum space between adjacent panels. Plan 2 in. for surface mounting, and 4 in. for flush mounting.

- Maintain a minimum space of 2 in. between a panel and metal objects that are not part of the panel. Maintain a minimum space of 8 in. between a panel and light fixtures.

Panels are best handled by at least two persons during the installation process.

### Mounting

Radiant ceiling panels are available for T-bar, surface, or recess mounting. Follow the manufacturer's instructions for mounting the panels. Make sure that the ceiling will support the weight of the panels. Radiant ceiling panels are available with seal-tight flexible conduit connectors. They can be purchased with stainless steel construction for chlorine storage areas. Radiant ceiling panels are also available in silk screen or custom colors to blend with the ceiling. Follow the manufacturer's instructions for mounting and wiring the panels.

### Wiring

Areas directly above the ceiling panels must be free of all junction boxes, conduit, and wiring, except as required to supply current to the panel. All wiring to the panels must conform to applicable provisions of the Canadian or U.S.

National Electrical Code, and to applicable local codes. Do not splice the supply cable, remove the junction box, or disassemble the cable from the panel terminal housing.

## ELECTRIC HEATING CONTROLS

### Thermostats

Perhaps the most important advantage of electric heat is that of room-by-room control. Give careful consideration to the selection and placement of thermostats in every room. This will ensure proper operation of the electric heating system.

Thermostats should be located 52 to 60 in. above the floor on inside walls. They should be in locations not subject to abnormal temperatures. For example, they should not be mounted near doors, windows, on or adjacent to cold walls, or in drafts. Neither should they be mounted near heat sources, such as ranges, refrigerators, televisions, lamps, hot water pipes, or where they are exposed to direct rays of the sun. Do not mount the thermostat on a wall with a heat source on the adjacent or reverse side—for example, a dining room wall that is backed up by a kitchen oven.

For optimum comfort level control, a thermostat must sense the average room temperature. For this reason, a wall-mounted thermostat is recommended. Thermostats built into baseboard or wall heater units are subjected to the heat from these units. This can cause wide variances in room temperatures.

Line-voltage thermostats should be of the type designed especially for electric heating. Their high electrical ratings permit direct control of heating units, with no need for relays. They may be of the single-pole or double-pole type.

### Combination switch-thermostat

A line-voltage thermostat may be combined under a common wallplate with a switch, outlet, and/or pilot light. This provides for stylized control of heating and lighting. The unit mounts on a two-gang box. Wiring of the thermostat is the same as shown for line-voltage controls in Figure 7-3. A special metal insert marked "Heat-Cool" is usually available. This satisfies the desire to use a system selector

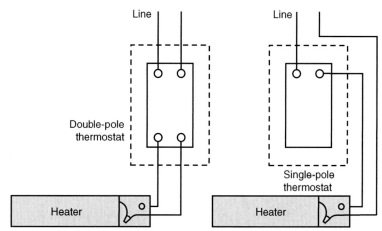

**FIGURE 7-3.** *Thermostat wiring*

switch in conjunction with the thermostat. A typical wiring diagram for this connection is shown in Figure 7-4. The thermostat built into the air conditioner is used for control of the air conditioning unit.

## IN-FLOOR ELECTRIC HEATING SYSTEMS

### Description

The following pages discuss Infloor® electric heating systems. The purpose of this section is not to endorse a particular product, but to introduce you to the operation principles of heating a space by means of electric in-floor heating cables. Infloor electric cable is embedded in 1¼ in. of Therma-Floor® underlayment to provide a complete radiant floor heating system, or it can be used to provide temperature-controlled (warm) floors in selected areas.

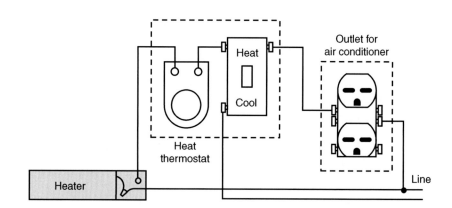

**FIGURE 7-4.** *Wiring a thermostat with a system selector switch*

The shielded heating cable comes in various lengths with a 10-ft cold lead on each end. A combination of one or more cables wired in parallel to a thermostat provide the flexibility of adapting to various zone sizes.

When installed as the primary heating system, an air-sensing thermostat is used in conjunction with a temperature high-limit device that is attached to the cable and embedded in the underlayment. When installed to provide warm floors, a remote-sensing thermostat is used to control the temperature of the underlayment.

Electric Infloor heating systems are capable of producing more than 13 watts per square foot of floor space. Actual output is governed by the floor covering, desired surface temperatures, and cable spacing.

### Application

Infloor electric cable heating systems are applied directly to suspended wood floor structures. When applied to concrete plank or slab, at least 1 in. of board insulation is recommended between the concrete and the Infloor system to eliminate excessive lag time.

®Infloor and ®Therma-Floor are registered trademarks of the Maxxon Corporation. Material used with permission.

Before the drywall is installed, rough in the wiring for the thermostat. Actual cable installation is done following the drywall, as shown in Figure 7-5. The builder should be aware of the preparations required for the Therma-Floor underlayment. This is the only cementitious thermal mass approved for use when the electric Infloor heating system is installed over suspended wood subfloors.

## SYSTEM SIZING

### Heat loss calculations

Good insulating techniques are a major factor contributing to the success of a radiant floor heating system. Use a NEMA publication or similar heat loss calculation guide to calculate room-by-room heat loss. Pay special attention to rooms with high heat loss potentials. When slab-on-grade applications are properly insulated, heat loss at the edge of the slab is not significant.

### Required floor output

The heat lost from a room must be replaced by heat from the floor. The total heat loss divided by the *adjusted gross floor area* (do not include cabinet areas or other areas that do not generate heat) will produce the required floor output in Btu per square foot. Remember that 1 watt = 3.414 Btu/ft$^2$.

### Cable coverage area

Once the heat loss of an area is determined, the cable coverage area used for radiant heat must be calculated. Subtract the area 6 in. from the walls and cabinets from the total floor area, as shown in Figure 7-6 on the next page. Also subtract closet areas, stairs, and any other area that does not receive cable.

### Floor coverings

Floor coverings have a pronounced effect on the performance of radiant floors due

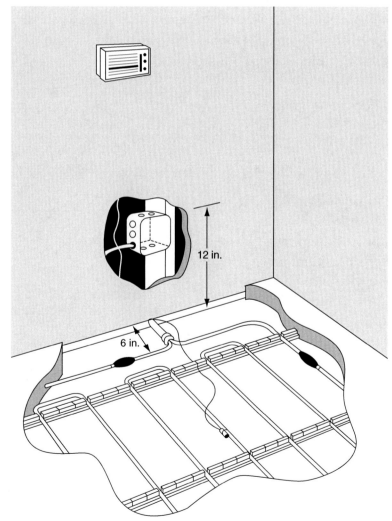

**FIGURE 7-5.** *In-floor electric heating cable installation*

163

to their insulative qualities. Add the "R" value of the desired floor covering to that of the pad (if used). The lower the R value, the better-suited the covering is for radiant floors. Floor coverings help determine the actual floor output. Table 7-1 on page 171 shows how to calculate the R value of various floor coverings.

**Actual floor output**

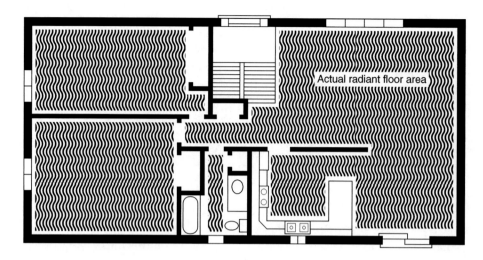

**FIGURE 7-6.** *Subtract 6 in. from walls and cabinets to figure cable coverage area (electric cable may not be installed in closets)*

Infloor cable temperature is limited to 140°F. Generally, 85°F is accepted as the maximum surface temperature for comfort where there is prolonged foot contact with the floor. Perimeter areas outside normal traffic areas can operate at higher surface temperatures.

With these limits in mind, find the actual floor output from the information shown in Figure 7-7. If needed, supplemental heat may be used to make up the difference between the required floor output and the actual floor output.

Varying floor outputs can be averaged in a room to achieve a higher overall Btu/ft² output. High-output tile floors under windows may be used to compensate for low-output carpeted floor areas.

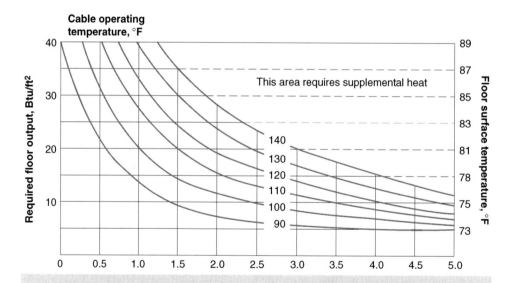

1. Find the required floor output on the left side of the graph and extend a line to the right to read the floor surface temperature.

2. Locate your selected floor covering R value along the bottom of the graph. Extend a line up to cross your first line and read the cable operating temperature at this intersection.

3. If the lines intersect beyond the 140° arc, do one or more of the following:
   a. Select a different floor covering.
   b. Reduce room heat loss.
   c. Calculate supplemental heating.

**FIGURE 7-7.** *Output based on 70°F inside air temperature*

### Cable selection

As shown in Figure 7-8, cable selection is a function of the size of the zone to be heated and the spacing of the cables. In most cases, cables spaced 6 in. apart will provide adequate heating. For rooms with large windows, space cables closer together. For basements, space cables farther apart.

Select the proper cable combination for each zone to be heated using the cable coverage area. A "zone" consists of a room or rooms to be serviced by one thermostat. The amount of cable required for a zone is calculated by multiplying the cable coverage area by the "factor" listed in Table 7-2 on page 172. (*Note*: Cables must not be spaced closer than 2½ in., according to the National Electrical Code.)

### INSTALLATION

#### Installing electrical boxes

A *heating system application* is controlled by an air-sensing thermostat, a high-limit temperature sensor, and a switching control (relay/transformer).

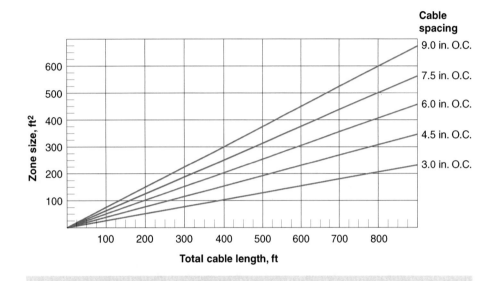

1. Locate your zone size on the left of the graph and extend a line to the right until it intersects the diagonal line representing your chosen cable spacing.

2. From that intersection, draw a line down vertically to the bottom of the graph. This will tell you the length of cable needed.

3. Locate the length of cable from Table 7-2. Use combinations as necessary to achieve the length required.

4. Multiple cable combinations should be wired in parallel only.

5. When using multiple cable combinations, the total amperage of the combinations must not exceed the relay rating (25 A resistive).

**FIGURE 7-8.** *Radiant cable sizing based on 4.4 watts/linear foot*

As shown in Figure 7-9A on the next page, a standard junction box should be mounted near the termination of the heating cable, generally about 12 in. from the floor. Conduit is run from the junction box to the floor with a 90° turn at the bottom. The 10-ft cold leads are long enough to reach from the floor to the junction box.

Mount another junction box with a mud ring approximately 5 ft above the floor (thermostat height). Run conduit from the junction box to the floor with a standard 90° turn at the bottom. The leads from the high-limit sensor are run

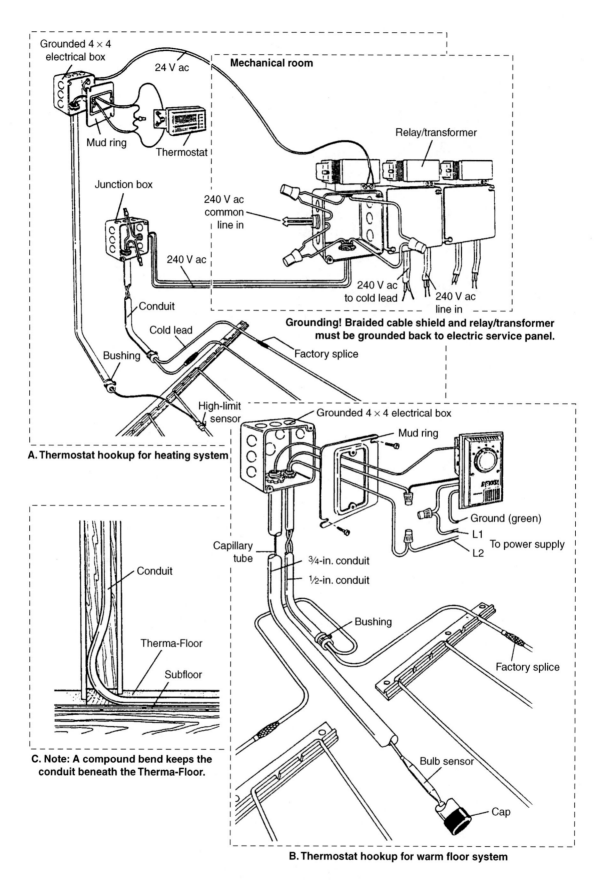

**A.** Thermostat hookup for heating system

**C.** Note: A compound bend keeps the conduit beneath the Therma-Floor.

**B.** Thermostat hookup for warm floor system

**FIGURE 7-9.** *Installation techniques and procedures*

through this conduit. The high-limit sensor is a low-voltage device. The conduit allows easy installation of the high-limit sensor after the drywall is installed.

Multiple cables may require additional junction boxes and must be wired in parallel only. Do not exceed the amperage rating of the controls with the amperage draw of the cables.

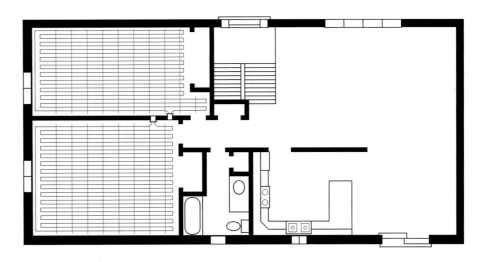

**FIGURE 7-10.** *Cable is laid out in a grid pattern using cable spacer strips*

The recommended location for the switching control is in the mechanical room or next to the electrical service. The switching controls are mounted to gang boxes and wired to the electrical service and the electric cables.

Low-voltage thermostat wire (18/2) is run from the thermostat terminals of the switching control to the thermostat location, and wired in series to the thermostat and high-limit sensor.

A *warm floor application* is controlled by a remote-sensing thermostat. As shown in Figure 7-9B, a standard junction box with a mud ring should be mounted approximately 5 ft above the floor (thermostat height). A ¾-in. conduit and a ½-in. conduit are run from the junction box to the floor. A compound bend in each conduit will keep them beneath the surface of the underlayment, as shown in Figure 7-9C.

When facing the wall, the conduit on the right (½ in.) will contain the cold leads from the heating cable. Place a bushing on this conduit. The 10-ft cold leads are long enough to reach from the floor to the junction box. Multiple cables may require additional junction boxes and must be wired in parallel only. Do not exceed the amperage rating of the controls with the amperage draw of the cables. The conduit on the left (¾ in.) will contain the capillary tube from the remote-sensing thermostat.

### Cable spacer strips

Once the drywall has been installed and the floor prepared for the Therma-Floor underlayment, lay out the cable spacer strips as shown in Figure 7-10. These

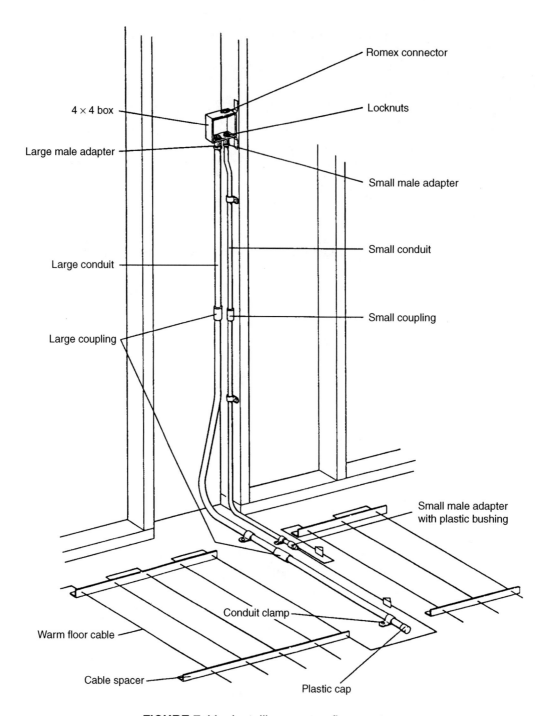

**FIGURE 7-11.** *Installing a warm floor system*

plastic spacer strips have a notch every 1½ in. to hold the cable at the proper spacing. They also have a flange for stapling or gluing to the floor. The spacer strips must be placed at 2-ft intervals. Make sure that the lip on the top of the strip is facing away from the cable at the ends of the room. Figure 7-11 above shows the electrical rough-in and the cable spacers laid out for a warm floor application.

### Cable layout

Electrical continuity checks should be made at three times:

■ when the cable is first taken from the carton

■ after the cable has been strung in position

■ after the Therma-Floor has been poured.

Cable should be laid out in a grid pattern, starting with an outside wall or the wall farthest from the thermostat. Cables do not need to be strung taut, because the Therma-Floor will flow under the cable and support it off the subfloor. The cable must not cross or touch.

For warm floor applications, conduit from the thermostat will extend out away from the wall. Route the cable parallel to the conduit with a distance of 2 in. between the conduit and the cable.

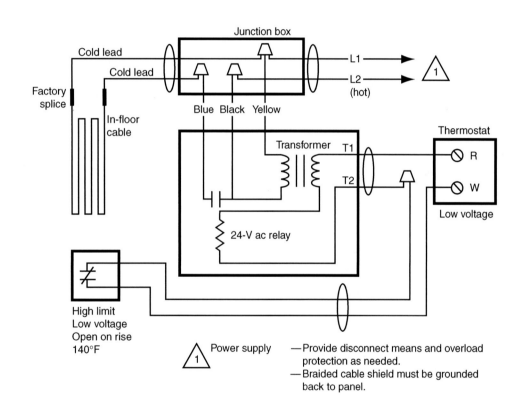

**FIGURE 7-12.** *Thermostat hookup for a heating system*

The cold leads must be protected by bushed conduit at the point where it emerges from the slab. Be sure that the hot-to-cold connection is embedded in the Therma-Floor. *In no case should the length of the heating section be altered.*

### Thermostat hookup

Do *not* operate the system until the Therma-Floor has been poured. For heating system applications, a low-voltage room air-sensing thermostat is used in conjunction with a high-limit device. As shown in Figure 7-12, this device opens the 24-V ac relay if the cable temperature exceeds 140°F. It should extend toward the center of the room and be in contact with the cable. Use the detailed instructions supplied with the thermostat controls for actual wiring.

For warm floor applications, a line-voltage remote-sensing thermostat is used, as shown in Figure 7-13. First, run the remote sensor to the end of the ¾-in. conduit. Fill the conduit with heat-conducting grease, completely surrounding the sensor, and cap the conduit. Then use the detailed instructions supplied with the thermostat controls for actual wiring.

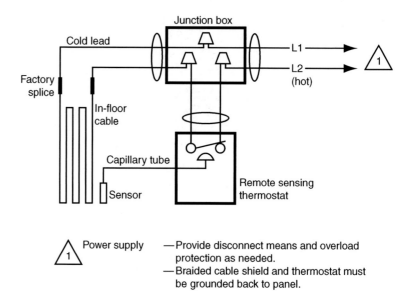

**FIGURE 7-13.** *Thermostat hookup for a warm floor system*

For all applications, multiple cables may be wired to one control, provided they are wired only in parallel and do not exceed the rated capacity of the control. The braided cable shield must be grounded back to the main panel. Figure 7-14 shows multi-cable control wiring.

All wiring connections and installation functions should conform to the latest National Electrical Code and be inspected and approved before covering.

**Therma-Floor**

The Therma-Floor underlayment becomes the thermal mass radiating heat generated by the electric cable. It is to be poured in place by an authorized applicator to a recommended depth of ¼ in. Special rubber finishing platform shoes must be worn to protect the electric cables during the pour. Dragging the hose, tools or feet should be avoided to prevent displacing or damaging the cable.

Once the Therma-Floor has become hard, the Infloor system can be turned on to assist in the drying process. Apply all

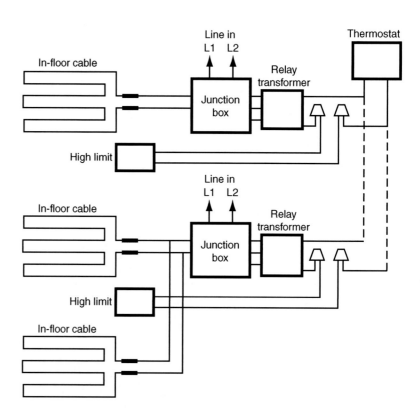

**FIGURE 7-14.** *Multi-cable control*

170

floor coverings according to instructions provided by the manufacturer. Table 7-3 on the next page shows various specifications for the Infloor system.

| R value | Floor covering | Tufts per in² | Depth (in.) |
|---|---|---|---|
| 0.20 | Bare floor | — | — |
| 0.21 | Linoleum or vinyl sheet goods | — | — |
| 0.22 | Ceramic tile | — | — |
| 0.54 | Hardwood | — | ³⁄₈ |
| 0.55 | Nylon level loop | 86 | ¹⁄₈ |
| 0.65 | Nylon level loop | 48 | ¹⁄₈ |
| 0.67 | Nylon level loop | 67 | ³⁄₁₆ |
| 0.68 | Nylon level loop | 80 | ¹⁄₈ |
| 0.78 | Acrylic level loop | 80 | ³⁄₁₆ |
| 0.93 | Hardwood | — | ³⁄₄ |
| 0.95 | Polyester plush | 54 | ¹⁄₄ |
| 1.03 | Acrylic level loop with foam back | 80 | ¹⁄₄ |
| 1.12 | Nylon plush | 88 | ¹⁄₄ |
| 1.33 | Nylon high low tip sheared | 55 | varies |
| 1.51 | Nylon shag | 28 | 1 |
| 1.66 | Polyester high low tip sheared | 54 | varies |
| 1.71 | Acrylic plush | 44 | ¹⁄₂ |
| 1.83 | Nylon plush | 80 | ⁷⁄₈ |
| 1 90 | Acrylic plush | 58 | ¹¹⁄₁₆ |
| 1.96 | Nylon saxony | 29 | ⁹⁄₁₆ |
| 2.19 | Wool plush | 45 | ¹⁄₂ |
| 2.46 | Nylon shag | 22 | 1¹⁄₄ |

| R value | Carpet pad underlayments | Depth (in.) |
|---|---|---|
| 0.49 | Therma-Pad® carpet cushion | ¼ |
| 0.78 | Waffled sponge rubber 48 oz | — |
| 1.61 | Prime urethane 2.2 lb density | ³⁄₈ |
| 1.71 | Coated combined hair and jute 56 oz | — |
| 2.09 | Bonded urethane 4 lb density | ¹⁄₂ |
| 2.15 | Prime urethane 2.2 lb density | ¹⁄₂ |

**Total R value**

**TABLE 7-1.** *Determining R values*

| Cable | Length, ft | Amps* |
|-------|-----------|-------|
| IF 31 | 31 | 0.6 |
| IF 64 | 64 | 1.1 |
| IF 88 | 88 | 1.7 |
| IF 136 | 136 | 2.5 |
| IF 182 | 182 | 3.3 |
| IF 318 | 318 | 5.8 |
| IF 409 | 409 | 7.5 |
| IF 557 | 557 | 9.2 |
| IF 682 | 682 | 12.5 |
| IF 909 | 909 | 16.7 |
| IF 1188 | 1,188 | 20.0 |

| | | | |
|-------|-----|-----|-----|
| Spacing, in. | 7.5 | 6.0 | 4.5 |
| Watts/ft$^2$ | 7.0 | 8.8 | 11.4 |
| Btu/ft$^2$ | 24.0 | 30.0 | 39.0 |
| Spacing factor | 1.6 | 2.0 | 2.6 |

*Amps at 240 V ac

**TABLE 7-2.** *Maximum output based on cable spacing*

## Control system specifications
### (for heating system applications)

*Thermostat*
    Room air-sensing
    Temperature range:   50 to 90°F
    Voltage:   24 V ac
*Switching control*
    Line-in voltage:   240 V ac
    Line-out voltage:   24 V ac
    Contact rating:   25 amperes resistive
*Cable limit control*
    Cut-out temperature:   140°F

## Remote-sensing thermostat specifications
### (for warm floor applications)

Electrical rating:
    20 amperes resistive   120 V ac
    20 amperes resistive   240 V ac
Temperature differential:   2°F
Lead wires:   12 gauge
Bulb size:   3/8-in. diameter by 3 1/4-in. length, with tapered ends

## Cable specifications
### (240-V operation*)

| Cable | Length, ft | Watts | Amps | Ohms |
|-------|-----------|-------|------|------|
| IF 31 | 31 (9 m) | 150 | 0.6 | 384.0 |
| IF 64 | 64 (19 m) | 275 | 1.1 | 209.5 |
| IF 88 | 88 (27 m) | 400 | 1.7 | 144.0 |
| IF 136 | 136 (41 m) | 600 | 2.5 | 96.0 |
| IF 182 | 182 (55 m) | 800 | 3.3 | 72.0 |
| IF 318 | 318 (97 m) | 1,400 | 5.8 | 41.4 |
| IF 409 | 409 (124 m) | 1,800 | 7.5 | 32.0 |
| IF 557 | 557 (170 m) | 2,200 | 9.2 | 26.2 |
| IF 682 | 682 (208 m) | 3,000 | 12.5 | 19.2 |
| IF 909 | 909 (277 m) | 4,000 | 16.7 | 14.4 |
| IF 1188 | 1,188 (362 m) | 4,800 | 20.0 | 12.0 |

*Multiply watts times 0.75 for 208-V operation.

**TABLE 7-3.** *Infloor electric heating system specifications*

1. Name some of the applications of quartz heaters.

2. For what purpose are natural convection heaters ideally suited?

3. What is the preferred location for a natural convection heater?

4. What is the purpose of radiant ceiling panels?

5. At what height should thermostats be located?

6. In-floor electric heating cable is imbedded in _____ in. of underlayment.

7. In-floor electric heating systems are capable of producing more than _____ watts per square foot.

8. One watt is equivalent to _____ Btu/ft$^2$.

9. Which is a more desirable floor covering, one with a high R value or one with a low R value?

10. What is the generally accepted maximum floor surface temperature for comfort?

11. If the required floor output is 25 Btu/ft$^2$, what is the maximum R value of the floor covering?

12. Cables must not be spaced closer than _____.

13. If you have a 200-ft² room and want to use 6-in. spacing, what is the length of the needed cable?

14. How many junction boxes are required for wiring an in-floor heating system?

15. Multiple cables must be wired in _____.

16. What type of thermostat wire should be used to connect the thermostat and the high-limit sensor?

17. The high-limit device opens a 24-V relay if the cable temperature exceeds _____.

18. All wiring connections and installation functions must conform to the _____.

# System Control Devices

## TYPES OF HEATING SYSTEMS

Electric resistance heating systems are divided into two basic types. They are *central heating systems* and *decentralized heating units*. Decentralized electric heating units include electric baseboard heaters, radiant heating panels that serve individual rooms, and so on. Central electric heating systems fall into four categories:

- electric furnaces

- electric boilers

- heat pump supplementary elements

- a central system with duct heaters.

All of these central heating systems use ducts or piping to distribute heat to occupied areas. They all require a central blower or pump to move the heating medium through ductwork or piping. Therefore, the control devices that are needed are very similar. They differ only in their design, according to the type of system in which they are to be used. Some devices are designed for use with warm air systems, for example. Others are for use with hydronic heating systems.

175

## CENTRAL ELECTRIC HEATING SYSTEM CONTROL FUNCTIONS

Figure 8-1 shows a typical central electric heating system. The control system must perform the following functions:

- room temperature sensing (and signaling)

- load switching (in response to room temperature)

- fan switching (in warm air systems)

- limit protection.

These functions are common to central electric heating systems. Nearly all use low-voltage thermostats. However, the type of load switching device—relay or sequence—and limit control will vary. The most common control systems will be covered in more detail later.

### Room temperature sensing

Typically, central electric heating systems use *low-voltage* controls. Room temperature sensing is usually done by a low-voltage thermostat. The heavy loads used in a central electric heating system require heavy-duty switching devices. A *line-voltage* thermostat would be capable of handling such loads (up to approximately 5 kW). However, line-voltage thermostats generally respond more slowly to temperature changes than do low-voltage thermostats. This is because they have sensing elements of greater mass. They are, therefore, best suited to control of high-mass, slow-response loads. The lighter, more sensitive element of the low-voltage thermostat permits a faster cycling rate. The cycling rate also can be varied (by using a heat anticipator) to better match the response rate of the heating equipment.

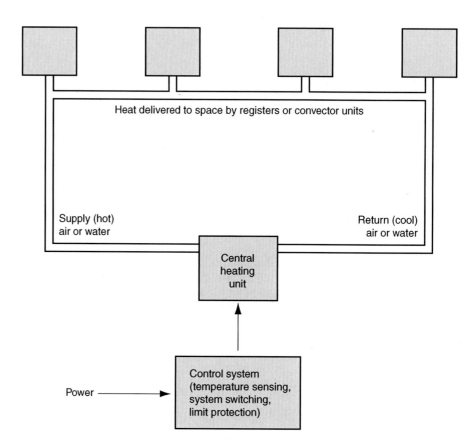

FIGURE 8-1. *Central electric heating system*

176

Low-voltage thermostats handle the heavy electrical loads of central heating systems by using intermediate switching relays to switch the load. There are several things to consider when selecting either a line-voltage or low-voltage control system, including:

- type of application

- comfort level desired

- electrical load

- any special features desired.

Low-voltage thermostats can control any size load up to the rating of the switching relay used. In addition, they offer features that are desirable in central systems that are not available with line-voltage thermostats, including:

- night setback

- multistage control capability

- integral system switching

- single-thermostat heating/cooling control.

Low-voltage (24 V) wiring is usually easier to run and is less expensive. It is especially advantageous in conversion work.

### Low-voltage thermostat installation

Select a location about 5 ft above the floor on an inside wall. It should have good natural air circulation at average room temperatures. Avoid hot spots caused by concealed pipes, warm air ducts, radiators, fireplace, appliances, televisions, or exposure to sunlight. Avoid cold spots caused by the location on an outside wall, an unheated room on the other side of the partition, or drafts from stairwells and doors. Avoid dead spots caused by lack of circulation behind doors, and in alcoves or corners.

Run low-voltage thermostat cable with enough conductors for the specific application—heating or heating/cooling. Connect the thermostat heating circuit in series with one side of the 24-V secondary of the low-voltage transformer and one side of the low-voltage actuator in the central heating system switching relay. To complete the circuit wiring, connect the remaining transformer

secondary lead to the other side of the low-voltage
holding coil, or warp switch heater.

### Heat anticipators

Most low-voltage thermostats have adjustable
*anticipation heaters*, as shown in Figure 8-2. They permit
the heater to be matched to the exact current draw of the
controlled component. Figure 8-3 shows the method of
adjustment on a typical thermostat.

The heat added to the inside of the thermostat by the
anticipator has several effects:

- It compensates for *overshoot*. It shuts off the
  heating equipment before the actual room
  temperature reaches the shutoff point. Residual heat
  from the system raises the room temperature to the
  shutoff point.

- It has the effect of increasing the cycling rate.
  Heating equipment ON time is reduced.

- It compensates for the thermostat's mechanical lag.
  It moves the temperature of the bimetal element
  through its operating range at a faster rate.

In the typical low-voltage thermostat, the heat anticipator is
in series with the thermostat switch. It is heated by the entire
current draw of the controlled component. For consistent
performance, the value of the anticipator heater
must be matched to the current draw of the
controlled component. In this way, the internal
heat produced is constant. This is done by
applying a mathematical formula. Heat produced
in watts equals current draw squared times
resistance. The equation is written as follows:

$$W = I^2R$$

Generally, an identification label or attached plate
shows the current draw of the controlled
component. If not, there are ways to measure

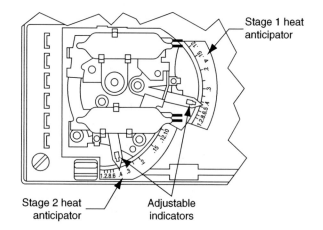

**FIGURE 8-2.** *Heat anticipator*

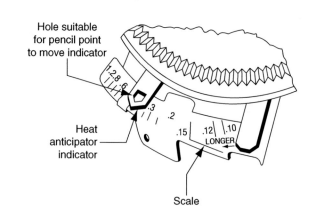

**FIGURE 8-3.** *Heater adjustment*

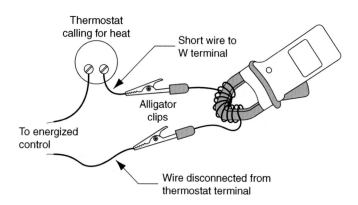

**FIGURE 8-4.** *Measuring current in a thermostat circuit*

current draw in the thermostat circuit. One method is to wrap ten turns of No. 18 or No. 16 stranded wire around the jaws of a clamp-on ammeter. This is shown in Figure 8-4. Set the selector switch to the lowest scale on the ammeter and divide by 10. In other words, assume that the full-scale reading on the ammeter is 6 amperes (A). The ten loops of wire have increased the sensitivity by a factor of 10. The full-scale reading is now 0.6 A instead of 6 A.

On many new thermostats, you cannot attach an alligator clip to the thermostat terminal itself. Use a short piece of wire, as shown. Or, if a sub-base is used, terminals R and W may be jumpered. The amperage reading is taken with the thermostat itself removed.

There are digital ammeters, such as the clamp meter shown in Figure 8-5, that will read as low as 0.2 A with good accuracy. Other ammeters are capable of measuring current from 0.1 to 1.2 A.

Adjusting the heat anticipator for two-stage thermostats, such as the Honeywell T874 shown in Figure 8-6, is done in the same manner as for single-stage thermostats. An *electronic programmable thermostat* is shown in Figure 8-7. Electronic programmable thermostats do not have heat anticipator adjustments. There are controls that adjust the number of cycles per hour. The thermostat is pre-set for 6 cycles per hour for heat. Electric warm air systems are generally set for 9 cycles per hour.

The electronic programmable thermostat shown in Figure 8-8 on the next page can be programmed over the telephone. The heating cycles per hour are adjusted in the same way as for the model shown in Figure 8-7.

THE FLUKE CORPORATION

**FIGURE 8-5.** *Clamp meter*

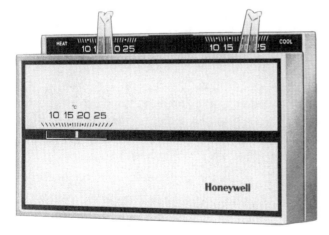

HONEYWELL INC.

**FIGURE 8-6.** *Multistage thermostat*

HONEYWELL INC.

**FIGURE 8-7.** *Electronic programmable thermostat*

Other kinds of thermostats, such as the thermostat and transmitter shown in Figure 8-9, and the logic panel shown in Figure 8-10, do not have heat anticipator adjustments. The reason is that the system *modulates*. The system can have up to ten stages of heat. Line-voltage thermostats do not have heat anticipators, either. A typical line-voltage thermostat is shown in Figure 8-11.

A slightly higher setting will give longer heating system ON times (and thus fewer cycles per hour). This may be desirable with some types of systems, such as a one-pipe steam system.

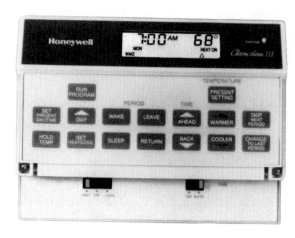

HONEYWELL INC.

**FIGURE 8-8.** *Communicating thermostat*

**Example**. If heating system ON time is too short, proceed as follows. If the nominal anticipator setting is 0.4, adjust to a 0.45 setting and check system operation. Then adjust to a 0.5 setting and recheck, etc. Continue until you get the desired heating system ON time. If the room temperature overshoots the thermostat setting excessively, decreasing ON time may produce a more constant temperature. To do this, adjust the anticipator setting to a lower value gradually. Recheck operation until the desired results are obtained.

### Line-voltage thermostat installation

Figure 8-11 shows a typical *line-voltage thermostat*. It has the same mounting requirements as a low-voltage thermostat. However, since it carries full load directly (up to 5 kW), mount it on a vertical wall outlet box. Then connect it in series with one side of the electrical supply to the resistance heater. The maximum rating is 5 kW in a single-phase system, or in series with one side of the line-voltage holding coil in an appropriate size contactor in a three-phase system, or when the resistance heater load exceeds 5 kW in a single-phase system.

### Thermostat setting and operation

After the thermostat has been installed and wired, simulate normal operation:

- Turn the setting dial all the way clockwise. The electric heater should begin operation.

- Turn the dial all the way counterclockwise. The power circuit should be broken and the electric heater should shut off.

HONEYWELL INC.

**FIGURE 8-9.** *Thermostat and transmitter*

For final setting, begin by setting the indicator at 4 or 70 on the scale. If this is not satisfactory after at least two hours of operation, make an adjustment. Turn the setting indicator upscale to raise the temperature or downscale to lower the temperature. Move the indicator only a few degrees for each adjustment.

### Calibration

Thermostats are calibrated at the factory with precision instruments. Normally, no recalibration is needed. Before you assume that it needs calibration, check to see that the thermostat is properly located. It should be in an area with natural air circulation. There should be no sources of heat or cold affecting it. Such sources include a television, heating or cooling ducts, or radiation from a fireplace. If recalibration is required, make sure that the thermostat is level if it contains a mercury bulb. Make sure that there is no draft inside the wall before attempting recalibration of any thermostat.

**FIGURE 8-10.** *Logic panel*

Let the system operate for several hours. If the thermostat maintains room temperature consistently above or below its setting, check the calibration:

- Place an accurate thermometer near the thermostat.

- Turn the setting knob up until the heater turns on. (Listen for an audible snap of the thermostat switch.)

- When the thermostat switch makes contact, note the temperature on the test thermometer. If the thermostat setting is about the same, recalibration is not needed.

- If the thermostat setting differs from the thermometer reading, record the degrees of difference above or below the actual temperature. Then recalibrate.

To recalibrate, perform the following nine steps:

1. Rotate the setting knob clockwise to its highest setting (80°F or No. 5). Wait 10 minutes.

2. Remove the thermostat cover.

**FIGURE 8-11.** *Light-duty line-voltage thermostat*

3. Slip the calibration wrench onto the hex-head screw. Rest the wrench flush against the bimetal element.

4.  Rotate the hex-head screw a quarter turn (90°) at a time. Each quarter turn changes the calibration 1½°. If the thermostat makes contact at a setting above the room temperature, rotate the screw clockwise. If the thermostat makes contact at a setting below the room temperature, rotate the screw counterclockwise.

5.  Replace the thermostat cover. Set the knob to normal room temperature for 10 minutes to stabilize the bimetal temperature.

6.  Manually rotate the knob until the thermostat makes contact. Then check the setting against the temperature shown on the thermometer.

7.  If additional adjustment is necessary, repeat the calibration procedure.

8.  When the switch makes contact at about room temperature, cycle the thermostat three or four times to check for proper operation.

9.  Reseal the calibration screw to the bracket. Use Duco cement or a similar sealant.

### Cover thermometer recalibration

The cover thermometer also may be adjusted. Insert the hex-head wrench or Allen wrench (included with the thermostat) into the hole in the bimetal hub and turn. Set the thermometer 2° below actual room temperature. This allows for normal internal heat of the thermostat. Other thermostats may have slightly different procedures for calibration. Read and follow the manufacturer's instructions.

## LOAD SWITCHING RELAYS

*Load switching relays* or *contactors* allow a relatively light-duty (low-voltage) thermostat to control a heavy-duty electric resistance heater. Relays also serve other important purposes:

- reversing or changeover control action

- providing control in stages

- instituting delaying actions.

Relays may be used with line-voltage as well as low-voltage thermostats. Low-voltage temperature controls are more widely used because of their faster cycling rates and minimum droop characteristics.

Relays also make it possible to include many special automatic features available only in low-voltage thermostats. An example is automatic day/night control. Relays with low-voltage holding coils or snap-action bimetal-actuated low-voltage warp switches simplify installations. There is no need for line-voltage wiring between the thermostat location and the controlled equipment location. Relays also permit the use of simple central wiring panels at the most convenient locations.

Load switching relays also serve other important functions. These include heater bank sequencing and staging, and switching of fans, damper motors, air conditioning, and other types of related system equipment.

### Typical relay operation

The operational pattern of a typical load switching relay depends on its degree of sophistication. Its simplest action is described schematically in Figure 8-12. It is the ON and OFF switching of one resistance heating element in response to a signal from one low-voltage thermostat, opening or closing one SPST switch. Two or more of this basic type can be connected to one low-voltage thermostat. They can switch on a number of electric heaters in sequence about one minute apart, as shown in the schematic in Figure 8-13 on the next page. The result is a reduced initial line load on large-kilowatt systems. Note, for later comparison, that in Figure 8-13 the recommended thermostat heat anticipator setting is 0.2 A. This is because the thermostat directly controls only one relay.

The basic load switching relay just described is usually available either with a built-in low-voltage transformer or for use with a remotely located transformer. Figure 8-14 on page 185 shows wiring details of the latter type. It is for a one-to-one application (one thermostat, one relay, one electric heater).

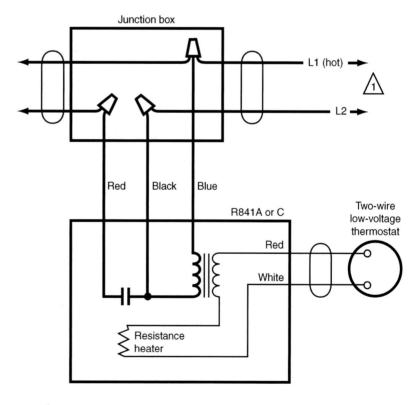

1. Power supply. Provide disconnect means and overload protection as required.

**FIGURE 8-12.** *Internal schematic and connection diagram for one relay with built-in transformer*

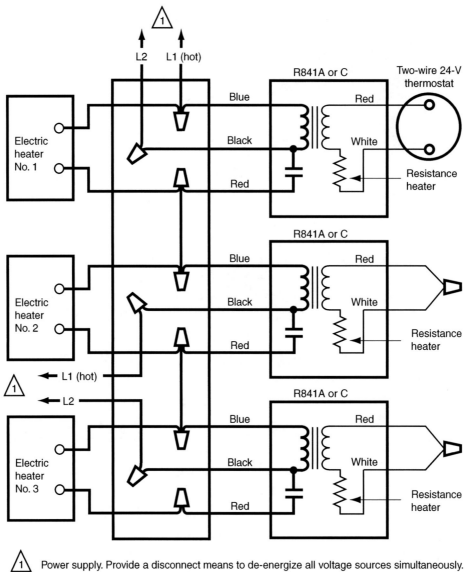

Power supply. Provide a disconnect means to de-energize all voltage sources simultaneously. Provide overload protection as required.

**FIGURE 8-13.** *Two or more relays connected to one thermostat*

Figure 8-15 shows connections when one low-voltage thermostat controls two electric heaters through two relays, using one remote low-voltage transformer. In this type of application, one thermostat handles the current draw of two warp switch heaters. Accordingly, the heat anticipator setting recommended is 0.4 A. This is double that of the setting shown in Figure 8-13.

Figure 8-16 on page 186 shows another variation using the single switching action relay. Four relays are used for switching four separate electric heating elements. Each is controlled by its own thermostat, but they use one low-voltage transformer as total control circuit power supply. Remember this most important point when selecting an externally mounted low-voltage transformer to provide

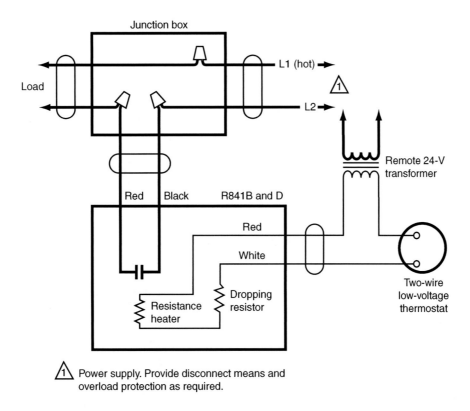

FIGURE 8-14. *Internal schematic and connection diagram for typical relay using remote transformer*

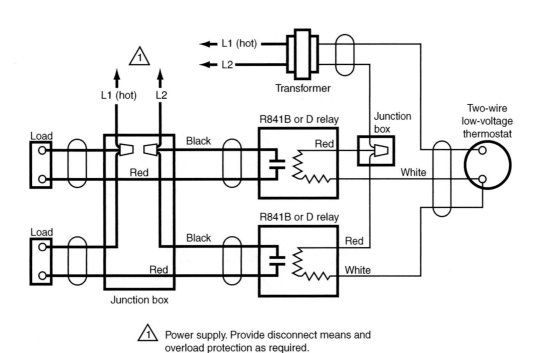

FIGURE 8-15. *Connections for two load relays used with one transformer and thermostat*

185

power for a number of components. Select one with sufficient capacity to handle the total number of components at one time, if necessary.

Figures 8-17 and 8-18 show typical wiring hookups for a more sophisticated type of load switching relay. It contains a built-in low-voltage transformer and two independently operated switching devices (snap-acting warp switches). The application in Figure 8-17 on the opposite page includes two thermostats, each with its own load. In Figure 8-18 on page 188, one thermostat is connected to one load so that both sides of the single-phase supply are switched.

The cycling pattern of a typical dual warp switch relay is determined by the thermostat. On a call for heat, the thermostat activates the low-voltage

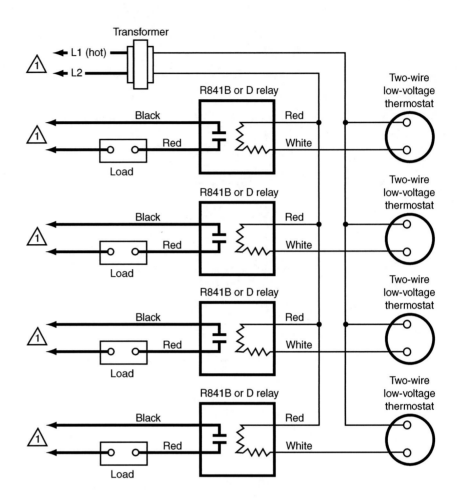

FIGURE 8-16. *Connections for four relays and thermostats used with one transformer*

resistance heater in the relay. The heater drives the bimetal strip to actuate a SPST snap-acting switch or switches. The bimetal strip is ambient temperature compensated within the specified ambient range. As an example of this type of operation, at rated voltage and frequency, switch contacts in a Honeywell R481 load switching relay close approximately 75 seconds (from a cold start) after the thermostat calls for heat. The top switch on a special relay with optional specification is adjusted to about 55 seconds, the bottom switch to about 75 seconds. This variation, in effect, represents sequencing by allowing, at the very minimum, 10 seconds of time between contact action in both opening and closing sequence. For typical wiring hookups for this type of relay, see Figures 8-17, 8-18, and 8-19. They show various application options relating to its use.

Understanding the function, operation, and electrical circuitry of electric heating load relays is basic to the successful troubleshooting of problems with these components. Equally important is the automatic check-out of equipment after

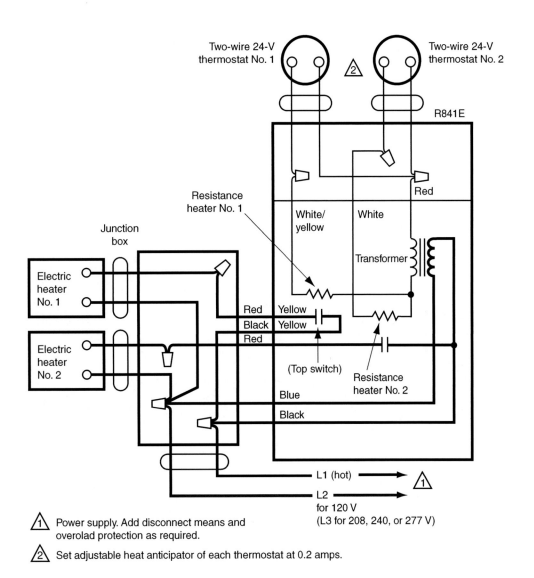

FIGURE 8-17. *Typical wiring hookup of dual-switch relay with two thermostats, each with its own load*

correcting a malfunction. Set the thermostat above the existing room temperature so that it switches on the heating elements involved. Let the system operate long enough to confirm its proper function. Then reset the thermostat to the desired room temperature. Only now can you consider the service call complete.

## LIMIT PROTECTION

There are two ways to provide limit protection for a central electric heating system:

- overcurrent protection

- high-temperature protection.

187

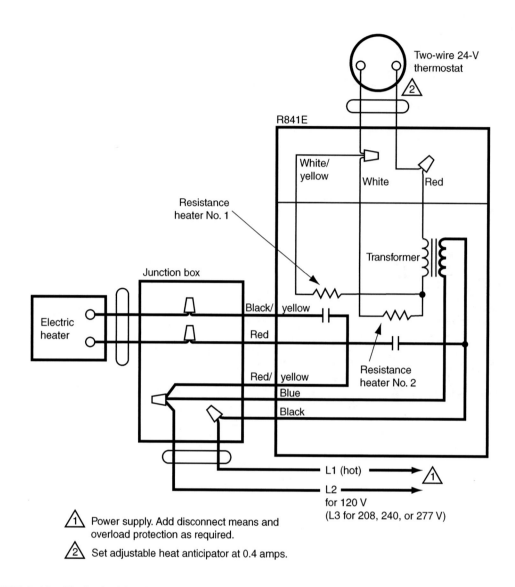

**FIGURE 8-18.** *Typical wiring hookup of dual-switch relay with one thermostat connected to one load*

*Overcurrent protection* is specified by electrical codes for an entire system. In addition, most electric furnaces and boilers have *fusible links* in each heater element. Most codes require them. These fusible links, or backup limits, lock out under extreme overheating conditions. They are calibrated to open the circuit to the heating element in which they are installed at a higher temperature than that set for the regular limit control.

*Temperature protection* in an electric furnace can use a disk-type limit switch for each heater element. Spot limit controls of this type are usually used instead of the standard warm air limit controls. This is because spot limit controls are not affected by the position of the furnace. The furnace remains completely multi-positional. It would be very difficult to install a conventional plenum control so that it would function in any position.

Like its oil or gas system counterpart, the electric heating system limit control is wired in series with one leg of the line-voltage supply circuit. This is the case whether the disk-type limit control or the fusible link is used. A typical location example is shown in the control system configuration in Figure 8-20 on the next page.

## TYPICAL CONTROL SYSTEMS

The rest of this Lesson explores many facets of the typical complete electric heating furnace control system configuration. You will see that heating element sequencing and multistage control are common refinements.

### Electric heat sequencer circuit wiring

A *sequencer* is designed to sequence heating elements and the system fan on and off. A typical example is the Honeywell R8330. The control switches the fan on when the first element is switched on. It switches the fan off when the last element is

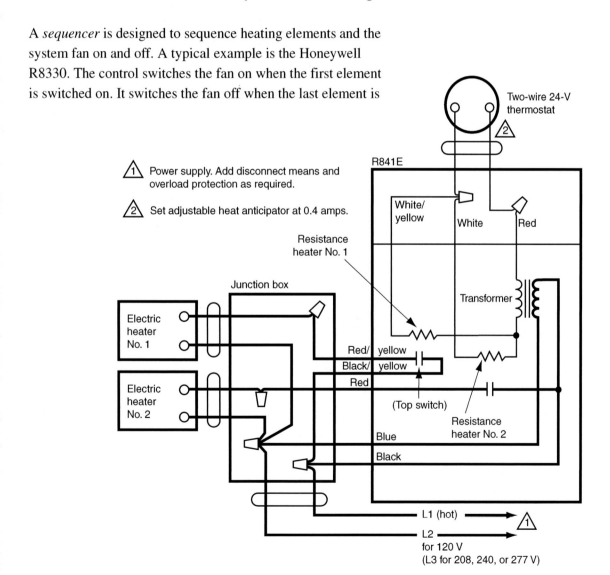

FIGURE 8-19. *Typical wiring hookup of dual-switch relay with one thermostat connected to one load*

189

switched off. A ten-second minimum time delay is provided between stages. This is in accordance with AR1280 and the EEI-NEMA Standard.

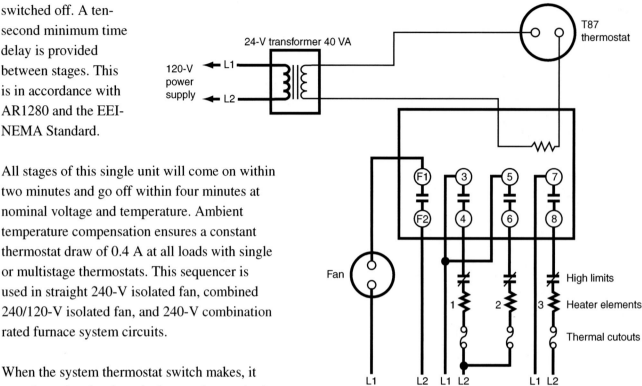

**FIGURE 8-20.** *Three-element 240/120-V system with isolated fan*

All stages of this single unit will come on within two minutes and go off within four minutes at nominal voltage and temperature. Ambient temperature compensation ensures a constant thermostat draw of 0.4 A at all loads with single or multistage thermostats. This sequencer is used in straight 240-V isolated fan, combined 240/120-V isolated fan, and 240-V combination rated furnace system circuits.

When the system thermostat switch makes, it completes the circuit to the heater element in the sequencer. The heater is wrapped around a bimetal. It provides the force to operate the switches. As the bimetal moves, the fan and first element switches make at the same time. Successive switches make in sequence.

When the thermostat switch breaks, the current flow to the sequencer heater element stops. The bimetal starts to cool. As it cools, it moves in the opposite direction. It causes each element switch to break in sequence, starting with the last element on. The sequence ends with the simultaneous turning off of fan and first element. Figure 8-20 shows wiring for sequence control of a three-element 240/120-V system with isolated fan.

Some sequencers have an auxiliary switch that closes when the last element is energized (contacts 7 and 8 make). It opens when the element switch that controls the first element of the control is de-energized (contacts 3 and 4 break). Figure 8-21 shows the typical sequence of operation of a six-element system.

When thermostat contacts make, the heater element of the first control is powered. The fan, first, second, and third heating elements sequence on. When the third element contacts (7 and 8) make, the auxiliary switch closes. The heater element of the second R8330 is then powered. The fourth, fifth, and sixth heating elements sequence on. When the thermostat is satisfied, its contacts break the circuit to the heater element of the first sequencer. The third, second, and first heating elements sequence off. (The fan remains powered through the fan contacts of the second R8330.) When the first element contacts (3 and 4) open, the auxiliary switch opens. The heater element of the second sequencer is de-energized. The sixth, fifth, and fourth heating elements then sequence off, ending with the simultaneous switching off of the fan and fourth element. Figure 8-22 on the next page is an easily followed step-by-step sequence chart covering the control system.

## MULTISTAGE CONTROL

With a switching device like the sequencer for each heating element, an electric heat furnace can be adapted very easily to *multistage* operation. Multistage control is common in central electric heating applications. It is a way to decrease the output of the furnace when full capacity is not required. The maximum output of any heating system must meet the heaviest expected heating loads. Therefore, at less than maximum load conditions, the system is actually oversized. Under very light load conditions, this may cause large temperature swings in heated areas. This is especially true of electric heating systems. They have the ability to deliver heat at near maximum capacity almost as soon as all elements are energized.

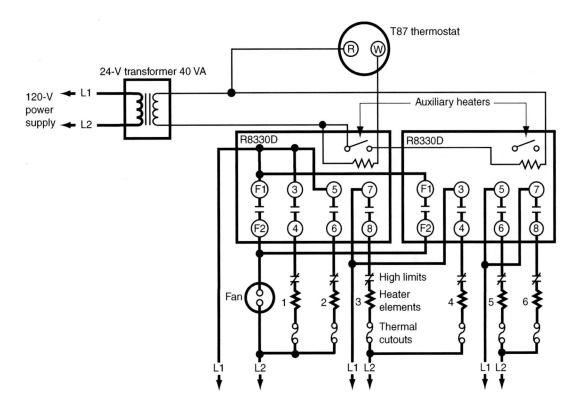

**FIGURE 8-21.** *Single-stage six-element 240/120-V system with isolated fan*

There are two ways in which multistage control can be applied to an electric furnace. The first method is to use a multistage indoor thermostat. It prevents operation of part of the heating system unless the first stage cannot restore the desired setpoint without help. This is true two-stage control. Each stage is controlled by a separate thermostat signal.

The second method uses an outdoor thermostat. It prevents operation of part of the system until outdoor temperature falls below a preset level. This is actually a single-stage system with a variable capacity that depends on outdoor temperature. Either of these methods provides improved temperature control.

The Honeywell old style T872 or new style T874 is a typical example of a two-stage heating thermostat. It contains a separate mercury switch for each stage. Both switches are connected to the same bimetal. It produces a constant set point difference between the stages. Each switch also has a separate heat anticipator. Figure 8-23 shows typical operation of a six-element system controlled by a two-stage heating thermostat.

It is also possible to use an outdoor thermostat with a two-stage wall-mounted thermostat. This can more effectively match the heating load to the heat output of the electric heaters. A system with two or more stages can be particularly helpful if there is a demand rate involved. Some electric companies have a demand rate for residential customers as well as commercial customers.

It is recommended that a diaphragm-type air flow switch be wired in series with the R side of the transformer. Then, the electric heat cannot come on unless there is sufficient air flow.

As Figure 8-23 shows, a two-stage heating thermostat controls a system by using a sequencing relay to switch the heating loads. This hookup shows three heating elements energized by the first stage, and three by the second stage. The proportion could be whatever circumstances might require.

Assume that the thermostat is set to close the first stage switch at 68°F. When room temperature drops to 68°, the first-stage thermostat switch energizes the resistive heater in the first sequence relay. After a time delay, F1-F2 and the 3-4 contacts close. This energizes the fan and the first furnace heating element. Another 10 to 30 seconds pass,

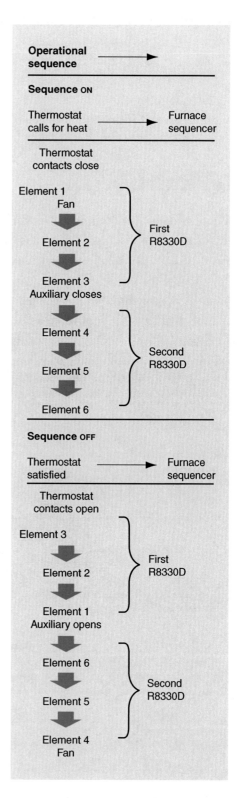

**FIGURE 8-22.** *Typical operational sequence chart*

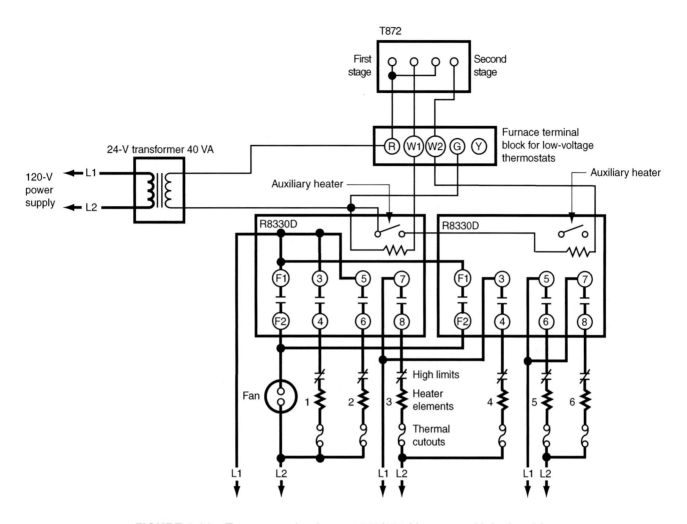

**FIGURE 8-23.** *Two-stage six-element 240/120-V system with isolated fan*

and the 5-6 contacts close. This energizes the second heating element. After another time delay, the 7-8 contacts and the auxiliary contact make at the same time to power the third heating element.

If the temperature continues to drop, it means that the first-stage heaters cannot satisfy the demand for heat. Then the second-stage thermostat switch closes. This powers the resistive heater in the second sequence relay through auxiliary contacts in the first sequencer. With proper delays, the fourth, fifth, and sixth elements sequence on, as did the first, second, and third elements through the first relay. Under light heating loads, elements 1, 2, and 3 will prevent the temperature from falling far enough to bring on the second heating stage. This results in smaller heat output to match smaller demand.

The second method for two-stage control is to add an outdoor thermostat. The entire system can be energized only if the temperature drops below a preset level. This system has some advantages. It is easily applied, inexpensive, and easily modified even after it is installed. It does not, however, give the degree of comfort control provided by a two-stage thermostat.

Figure 8-24 shows a low-voltage outdoor thermostat on a six-element heating system. This is the same size control system as the one shown in Figure 8-23, with the simple addition of the outdoor thermostat. In this arrangement, the fan and three heating elements are energized under light heating load conditions. The last three heating elements cannot be powered unless the outdoor thermostat contacts close.

## DELAYED FAN OPERATION

Among the many facets of central electric heating system control configurations is the provision for electric warm air furnace fan operation partially or completely comparable to that available with oil or gas-fired furnaces. This is done by adding a separate fan control. It applies regardless of the number of heating elements involved, or their sequencing.

Figure 8-25 shows a fan control wired into an existing heating system control circuit. This arrangement provides partial delayed fan

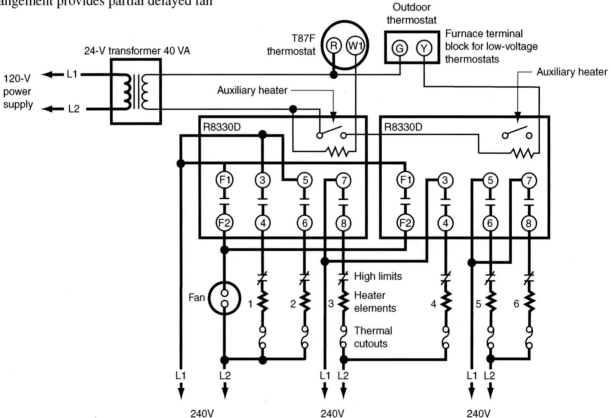

**FIGURE 8-24.** *240-V system with isolated fan*

operation. The fan is energized when the first heating element is switched on. It remains in operation after the last element is switched off, and continues to operate until the actual furnace temperature cools down to the fan control setpoint.

Completely automatic fan operation can use the separate fan control instead of the sequencing relay. This is done by wiring the fan control as shown in Figure 8-26 on the next page. It delays start-up of the fan until actual furnace temperature reaches the fan control setpoint. Fan operation continues until the furnace temperature cools down to the fan control setpoint. This, of course, is after all the heating elements have been switched off by the sequencing relay.

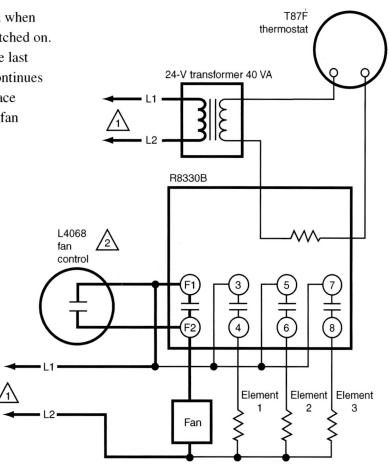

△1 Provide disconnect means and overload protection as required.

△2 Fan on with first element and remains on until furnace cools to fan control setpoint (delayed fan off).

**FIGURE 8-25.** *Wiring schematic for fan delayed OFF*

## CONTROL SYSTEM CHECKOUT

Set the system thermostat to call for heat. Make sure that all elements sequence on and off properly. Check that the fan starts with first element on. It should stay on until all the elements are off. Remember that this is a time delay device. Allow time for the elements to sequence on and off.

The sequencing relay is not field-repairable. If any component fails, it should be replaced. No adjustment or periodic service is required on these controls. Since all R8330 models are very similar, the R8330D may be used to replace the R8330A-H or J.

## HEATING

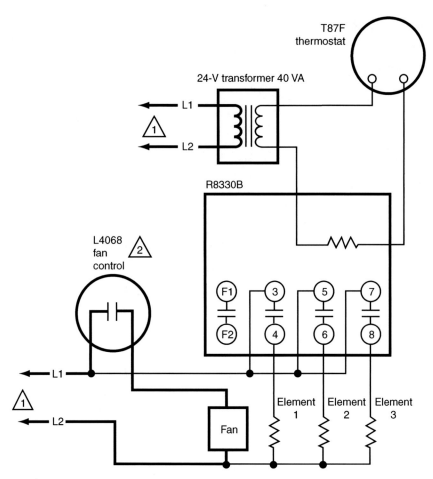

**TROUBLESHOOTING**

**Preliminary system checkout**

1. Check the wiring system for any loose or broken connections.

2. Make sure that the unit has proper power (230 V for most units). Measure across the lines, not to ground, to check voltage.

3. Make sure that the transformer has the proper voltage on the input side.

4. Make sure that the fan and all heating elements are operating properly.

**Transformer checkout**

① Provide disconnect means and overload protection as required.

② Fan on when furnace warms to fan control setpoint and operates until furnace cools to setpoint (delayed fan on and off).

**FIGURE 8-26.** *Wiring schematic for fan delayed ON and OFF*

1. Use an ac voltmeter to measure the voltage across the secondary terminals. If the voltage is 24 V ac ±10%, proceed to check the sequencing relay. If incorrect, proceed to Step 2.

2. Check that the voltage across the transformer primary is within ±10% of the rated voltage. If correct, replace the transformer. If the primary voltage is incorrect, correct the source problems.

**R8330 system checkout**

Refer to the wiring diagrams provided by the manufacturer. Note that if sequencers are used in combination, troubleshooting procedures must be adapted for the individual system.

1. Move the thermostat setpoint above the room temperature so that the thermostat calls for heat.

   a. If the system does not start (after a time delay), proceed to Step 2.

   b. If the fan and/or some (but not all) heating elements start, proceed to Step 3.

   c. If the fan and heating elements all sequence on properly, proceed to Step 4.

2. Jumper RH to W1 at the thermostat.

   a. Make sure that there is 24 V across the RH and W1 terminals at the thermostat before you jumper RH to W1. If there is 24 V across the RH and the W1 terminals, jump out the thermostat terminals. The fan and heating elements should begin operating after a delay.

   If there is not 24 V at the thermostat terminals, check the thermostat wire to see if it is defective. Check the low-voltage wire from the transformer to the sequencer to make sure that the wiring and connections are good.

   You may jump out the air flow switch contacts temporarily to see of the heaters come on. As soon as the heaters come on and you find that there is a problem with the air flow switch or the air flow, remove the jumper immediately.

   If there is an air flow switch, it is imperative that you have either a *slope gauge* or a *magnehelic differential pressure gauge*. It should read pressures between 0.05 and 0.25 inches of water column, with minor divisions of 0.01 inches of water column.

   If the tube on the pressure switch has an elbow, the tube on the slope gauge or magnehelic gauge must be the same. You will need information from the manufacturer on pressure switch settings so that you can measure the pressure and determine if the problem is an air flow problem or a pressure switch problem.

   If the pressure reading on the manometer or magnehelic gauge is below the setpoint on the pressure switch, there is an air flow problem. If the pressure reading is above the setpoint on the pressure switch, then the air switch is defective.

b.  If the fan and heating elements now begin operating (after a time delay), check the thermostat and wiring. Replace the thermostat if necessary. Proceed to Step 4.

c.  If neither the fan nor heating elements operate (and the system wiring has been checked), replace the sequencing relay.

3.  Jumper across the terminals of an inoperative fan or heating element. If the fan or element now starts, the contacts are not conducting. Replace the sequencing relay.

4.  When all elements and the fan are on, break the power supply to the sequencing relays by lowering the thermostat setpoint (or removing jumper RH-W1) so that the switch breaks. Check to make sure that all heating stages sequence off, beginning with the last element on. The fan should operate until all stages are off, turning off with the last stage unless controlled by a separate fan control. Again, remember that this is a time delay device. Allow time for all elements to sequence off.

1.  What does a central heating system use to distribute heat to the occupied areas?

2.  What is the maximum electrical load normally controlled by a line-voltage thermostat?

3.  Which instrument is more sensitive, the line-voltage thermostat or the low-voltage thermostat?

4.  How does a low-voltage thermostat control heavy electrical loads?

5.  A low-voltage thermostat operates on a voltage of _____.

6.  Which type of control wiring is more expensive, low-voltage or high-voltage?

7.  A control thermostat should be located at a height of _____.

8.  On what wall of a house should a low-voltage thermostat be located?

9.  Why do most low-voltage thermostats have adjustable anticipation heaters?

10. Does a heat anticipator increase or decrease the cycling rate?

11. You can measure current draw in a low-voltage thermostat circuit by using a(n) _____.

12.  What can be done to adjust the heat anticipator to a longer ON period if the nominal setting is 0.4?

13.  Are thermostats normally factory-calibrated?

14.  Load switching relays allow for control to be provided in _____.

15.  How do relays with low-voltage holding coils simplify installations?

16.  How long after the R841 load switching relay is activated do switching contacts close?

17.  What is required for troubleshooting component problems on electric heating systems?

18.  In what two ways can limit protection be provided for central electric heating systems?

19.  Fusible links provide protection against _____.

20.  What type of temperature protection is provided on an electric furnace?

21.  Is delayed fan operation available on electric furnaces?

22.  In Figure 8-13, what happens to heater No. 3 if the resistance heater in the No. 2 control relay opens?

23.  In Figure 8-15, what happens to the lower load if the low-voltage heater in the top control relay opens?

24.     In Figure 8-17, which heater does thermostat No. 2 control?

25.     What happens to fan operation if the switch to the second heater control opens?

26.     In Figure 8-23, which heaters are controlled by the first thermostat stage?

27.     In Figure 8-24, if the indoor thermostat fails to open, will heaters 4, 5, and 6 operate?

28.     In Figure 8-24, if the outdoor thermostat fails, will heaters 1, 2, and 3 operate?

# Electric Furnaces

## GENERAL CHARACTERISTICS OF ELECTRIC FURNACES

Electric furnace heating elements are controlled by *sequencing* switches. These switches close and open power circuits to the heating elements at predetermined time intervals. The intervals are usually between 15 and 90 seconds to close and between 25 and 90 seconds to open.

Sequencer contacts are closed by the heating effect of an integral heater (or *warp switch*). On Therm-O-Disc controls, the 24-V integral heater is identified as H1 and H2. Terminals of main contacts, which complete the power circuit of the furnace heating elements, are identified as M1 and M2.

Each individual heating element is equipped with an automatic reset *temperature limit switch*. It will open the power circuit to the element if an unusual operating condition should occur—a blower motor failure, for example, or a blocked air inlet or outlet, which would cause excessively high temperatures in the area of the elements. In addition, each heating element has a supplementary safety device called a *fusible link*. It is designed to rupture under extreme operating conditions, opening the power circuit to the protected element.

**SEQUENCER OPERATION**

Figure 9-1 is a diagram that shows sequencer operation during the start-up phase of a typical electric furnace:

1. The low-voltage operating control (room thermostat, or other temperature or pressure control) calls for heat. A low-voltage circuit is completed to sequencer No. 1.

2. In about 18 seconds, the blower motor contacts and the contacts for heater No. 1 close. This energizes the blower motor and the No. 1 (5-kW) heater at the same time.

3. About 35 seconds after the low-voltage circuit is completed to sequencer No. 1, the contacts for heater No. 2 close. This energizes the No. 2 (5-kW) heater.

4. About 60 seconds after the low-voltage circuit is completed to sequencer No. 1, the contacts for heater No. 3 close. This energizes the No. 3 (5-kW) heater.

5. About 60 seconds after the low-voltage circuit is completed to sequencer No. 1, the auxiliary contacts for sequencer No. 1 close. They close at the same time as the contacts for heater No. 3. These contacts supply power for sequencer No. 2.

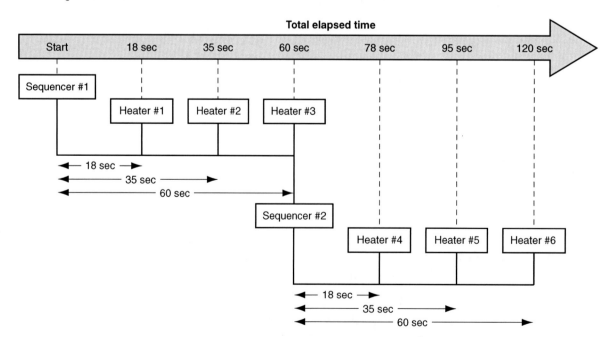

**FIGURE 9-1.** *Sequencer operation steps during start-up of a typical electric furnace*

6. Sequencer No. 2 energizes the next three heating elements in the same manner that sequencer No. 1 did. Sequencer No. 2 may also have auxiliary contacts to energize a third sequencer.

The total time required to energize all the heating elements in an electric furnace will depend on the number of sequencers and elements. As you can see, it takes about 120 seconds, or two minutes, for the example furnace with two sequencers and six heating elements.

With the system described, furnace shutdown is basically the reverse sequence of furnace start-up operation:

1. The operating control (thermostat) is satisfied. It opens the low-voltage circuit to the sequencer's warp switch heaters and they begin to cool. In about 60 seconds, all sequencer contacts, except those for the blower and heater No. 1, will be open. The heating elements powered through these contacts will become inoperative.

2. The sequencer No. 1 fan and the No. 1 heater contacts will remain closed for about 90 seconds. Thus, heater No. 1 and the furnace blower operate long enough to ensure that all other sequencer contacts are open.

The total time for complete shutdown is about 90 seconds for most electric furnaces.

*Note*: If you replace a sequencer that is operated off the primary sequencer, be sure that the timing for all contacts is less than 90 seconds. In other words, make sure that all contacts on the secondary sequencer are open before the furnace blower shuts off.

Figure 9-2 on the next page shows a typical electric furnace. Many electric furnaces are actually *evaporator blower coils* with electric heat controls and heaters added. The Lennox CB29M series blower coil units operate similarly to the description above. The sequencers in most electric heat controls are manufactured by White Rodgers, Therm-O-Disc, and Honeywell. Figure 9-3 on the next page shows a Honeywell sequencer. Figure 9-4 on page 207 is an example of a wiring diagram for a typical blower coil with electric heat.

On Carrier FB4A series units and similar Bryant units, there is an ac-to-dc voltage converter. The dc voltage supplies power to the time delay circuits for the fan relay coil circuit for the fan relay. In the air conditioning mode, the fan relay turns on the blower with the outside condensing unit. The blower turns off 90 seconds after the air conditioning unit is turned off.

In the heating mode, the fan or blower has a time delay that closely matches the time delay on the first-stage electric heat element. The blower shuts off 90 seconds after the first stage of electric heat shuts off. The electric heat coil is energized through a standard electric heat sequencer with a time delay. The delay is accomplished by a small heater and a bimetal switch.

On Trane TWE series units, a printed circuit board controls the blower. In the cooling mode, the blower motor turns on when there is a call for cooling. It shuts off when the thermostat is satisfied. In the heating mode, the blower motor turns on when there is a call for heat. It shuts off about 20 seconds after the last heating element is turned off. Again, the electric heat coil is energized through a standard electric heat sequencer with a time delay. The delay is accomplished by a small heater and a bimetal switch.

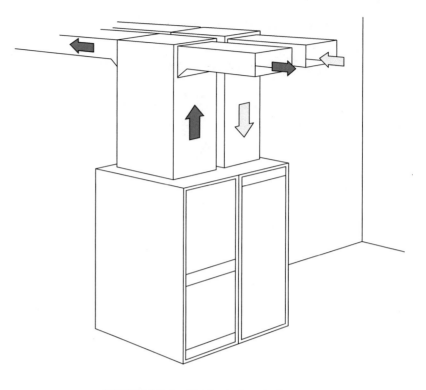

**FIGURE 9-2.** *Typical electric furnace*

### CHECKING HEATER OPERATION

1. Remove the vest panel to expose the wiring area.

2. Turn the thermostat above room temperature to energize the elements. If an outdoor thermostat is used, turn it above the outside temperature to energize the second stage of heat. The second stage of heat may be energized by jumping out the outdoor thermostat.

3. Check the amperage draw of each wiring lead to the heater elements with a clamp-on ammeter, shown in Figure 9-5 on page 208. All leads should measure about the same amount of current. The elements can be checked by multiplying the amperes times the volts on single-phase coils. The watt rating of the coil should be about the same as the volts times the amperes. If the coil is a three-phase coil, multiply

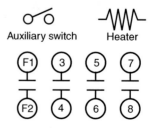

**FIGURE 9-3.** *Electric furnace sequencer and internal schematic*

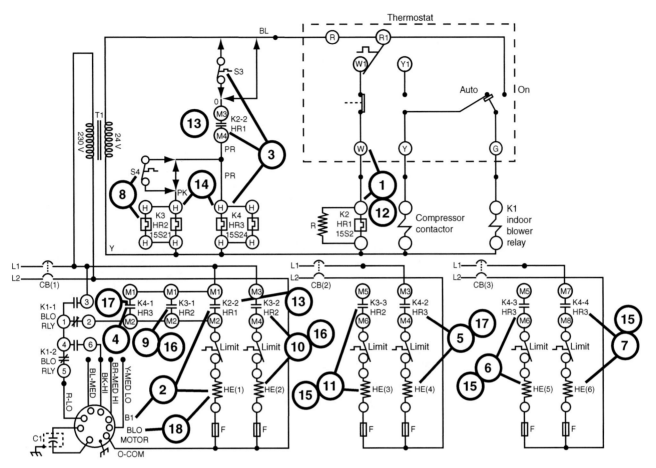

1. On a heating demand, K2 heat relay No. 1 (15S2) is energized. Within 1 to 60 seconds, K2-1 and K2-2 switches make together.
2. K2-1 contacts close to energize the blower motor on heating speed through N.C. K1 contacts. K2-1 also powers the first heating element
3. If the optional outdoor thermostat (S3) is made, K2-2 energizes K4 heat relay No. 3 (15S24). Both K4 heaters are energized simultaneously. K4-1 (terminals M1-M2) and K4-2 (terminals M3-M4) switches are the first to make.
4. K4-1 locks in blower operation to element demand.
5. K4-2 powers element No. 4.
6. K4-3 (terminals M5-M6) contacts next make to power element No. 5.
7. K4-4 (terminals M7-M8) contacts next make to power element No. 6.

*Note*: All K4 switching is accomplished within 1 to 110 seconds.

8. If the optional outdoor thermostat (S4) is made, K2-2 also energizes K3 heat relay No. 2 (15S21) in step 3. Both K3 heaters are energized simultaneously. K3-1 (terminals M1-M2) and K3-2 (terminals M3-M4) switches are the first to make.

9. K3-1 locks in blower operation to element demand.
10. K3-2 powers element No. 2.
11. K3-3 (terminals M5-M6) contacts next make to power element No. 3.

*Note*: All K3 switching is accomplished within 1 to 110 seconds.

12. When the heating demand is satisfied, the thermostat opens to de-energize K2.
13. Within 45 seconds, K2-1 and K2-2 switches open together. Element No. 1 remains energized through K4-1 and K3-1.
14. When K2-2 opens, both K4 and K3 heaters are de-energized simultaneously.
15. K3-3, K4-3, and K4-4 switches open at random to de-energize elements No. 3, 5, and 6.
16. Switches K3-1 and K3-2 break together. Element No. 2 is de-energized.
17. Switches K4-1 and K4-2 break together. Element No. 4 is de-energized.

*Note*: All K3 and K4 switches open within 1 to 110 seconds.

18. When K3-1 and K4-1 contacts are both closed, the blower motor and element No. 1 are de-energized.

**FIGURE 9-4.** *Electric furnace wiring diagram*

THE FLUKE CORPORATION

the volts times the amperes times 1.73 to determine the watt rating for the coil. *Caution*: Use extreme care. This is a high-voltage area!

4.  If an element does not register a proper reading, check for a shorted element, an open element, or a blown fuse. Check to see if there is proper voltage across the heating coil. The best way to check voltage at the heating coils is with all the coils operating. It may be necessary to jump out thermostats or other controls to get all of them operating. This places the greatest load on the electric circuits, and shows up any deficiencies in the power to the elements. A digital meter will give a more accurate reading of the voltage to the electric heat coils. If there is proper voltage at the coil, then the coil is bad. If not, then the wiring should be traced back to the heat relays and limits. Check to see if the heat sequencer heaters in the control circuit have 24 V at the terminals.

5.  Another way of checking an electric heat coil is with an ohmmeter and a megohm meter. First, shut off all power to the electric furnace. Second, remove the wires from the electric heat coil. A 230-V, 5000-W coil should measure about 10 to 12 ohms of resistance. The coil should measure at least 20 megohms to ground with a test voltage of 250 V.

**FIGURE 9-5.** *Clamp-on ammeter*

## CHECKING CONTROL CIRCUIT OPERATION

1.  Check the voltage on the primary or input to the control transformer. Most transformers can be used with more than one voltage. Many transformers have two voltage taps. The transformer can be connected for 230 V or 208 V. Make sure that the transformer is connected for the proper voltage.

2.  Check the heater terminals at the first sequencer. Make sure that there is 24 V across the heater for the warp switch.

## AIR CIRCULATION (BLOWER MOTOR) CIRCUIT

The air circulation system is a special feature of the blower coil (electric furnace). Generally, the blower is a direct-drive blower with a three-speed or four-speed motor. Any speed can be connected for heat or cool. The system is designed to ensure that warm air is delivered to the registers at all times. However, on initial start-up, it is impossible to prevent some cold air from being felt at the registers. The blower needs time to recirculate and temper the cold air that accumulated in the duct system while the furnace was off.

1. What closes sequencer contacts?

2. Which switch opens the power circuit if the temperature is excessive?

3. How long after the low-voltage circuit to the sequencer is completed does the first heater become energized?

4. What is the total time for complete shutdown for most electric furnaces?

5. Are the contacts on limit switches normally open or closed?

6. How can you check to see if a heating coil is good?

7. You can determine the watt rating of a three-phase coil by multiplying volts times amperes times _____.

8. When you check for proper voltage across a heating coil, how many coils should be operating?

9. Can most transformers be used with more than one voltage?

10. What should you do before checking heating elements with an ohmmeter?

11. What should the resistance of a 5-kW heater read?

# Duct Heaters

## GLOSSARY OF TERMS AND DEFINITIONS

The first section of this Lesson presents some of the key technical terms, and a definition of each, that are commonly used in discussing the installation and maintenance of electric duct heaters. You should be familiar with these words and phrases. Part of being a good service technician is understanding and using the vocabulary correctly.

**Air flow.**   The volume of air passing a given point (in an air duct). Usually expressed in cubic feet per minute (cfm).

**Air velocity.**   The speed of air passing a given point (in an air duct). Usually expressed in feet per minute (ft/min).

**Burnout.**   The condition that results when resistance wire becomes overheated and breaks. Generally caused by insufficient air flow or improper installation of the heater.

**Circuit.**   A *single-phase* circuit refers to one heating element plus the switching device. A *three-phase* circuit refers to three heating elements plus a switching device.

**Contactor.**   A magnetic relay switch used to control a duct heater. Less costly but more noisy than a silent switch.

**Control circuit.**   A circuit that includes the room thermostats, the holding coil of the switching device, and the auto-reset control device.

**C.S.A.**   Canadian Standards Association.

**Current inrush.**   A surge in power demand caused by actuating a device (a duct heater circuit, for example). Most electric utilities have regulations regarding the amount of current inrush allowable at one time.

**Dielectric test.**   A test run, using very high voltage, performed to be certain that equipment will not short out even under extreme conditions.

**Fan relay.**   A relay designed to provide interlocking fan operation with heater operation.

**High-limit switch.**   Also called a *high-limit control* or a *thermal cut-out*. A safety device that automatically breaks the circuit when temperatures reach a given limit. There are two kinds. An *auto reset*, pictured in Figure 10-1, is a safety device that automatically closes the circuit when the temperature drops below another preset point. A *manual reset*, pictured in Figure 10-2, is a safety device that remains open until the plunger is pushed back into the closed position.

**N.E.C.**   National Electrical Code.

**Open-coil elements.**   Heating elements that have the helical coiled resistance wire exposed to the flow of air through the heater. The *rows of coils* refers to the number of helical coils of resistance wire, side by side, in the heater.

**Secondary contactor.**   A contactor that must break all legs of the power supply to the duct heater. Its contacts are made continuously. Also known as a *back-up contactor*.

**Secondary control circuit.**   A circuit that includes the holding coil of the secondary contactor and the manual reset control device.

**Silent switch.**   A switch that operates noiselessly—as opposed to contactors, which

INDEECO

**FIGURE 10-1.** *Automatic reset thermal cut-out*

make snapping noises when operating. Silent switches are available to make in sequence to prevent excessive demand surges.

**Staging.**    Providing circuitry and controls to allow the full output of a heater to be divided into segments. The segments are energized individually, according to the demand for heat. Also called *stepping*.

**Transition.**    Increasing or decreasing the size of the ductwork to accommodate the duct heater.

**U.L.**    Underwriters' Laboratories, Inc.

**FIGURE 10-2.** *Manual reset thermal cut-out*

**Watt density.**    The number of watts of electric heat produced in a given area. Generally expressed in watts per square inch.

**Zero clearance.**    When used with duct heaters, this term means that air space or insulation is not required around the ductwork where the heater is inserted. Combustible materials may butt right up to the duct. Control or terminal panels must be accessible.

## ELECTRIC DUCT HEATER INSTALLATION

The following important points pertain to the installation of electric duct heaters. Some of them are illustrated in Figure 10-3 on the next page:

- Install duct heaters at least 4 ft downstream from heat pumps or central air conditioners, as shown in Figure 10-3A.

- Install duct heaters at least 2 ft downstream from an air handler, as shown in Figure 10-3B.

- Install duct heaters at least 2 ft on either side of an elbow, as shown in Figure 10-3C.

- In vertical ducts, you may install heaters from any of the four sides.

- Install duct heaters at least 18 in. from any canvas duct connector, as shown in Figure 10-3D. If the heater must be closer, replace the canvas connector with a high-temperature connector.

- In horizontal ducts, you may install heaters from either side, but never from the top or bottom. Custom heaters for bottom mount installations are available.

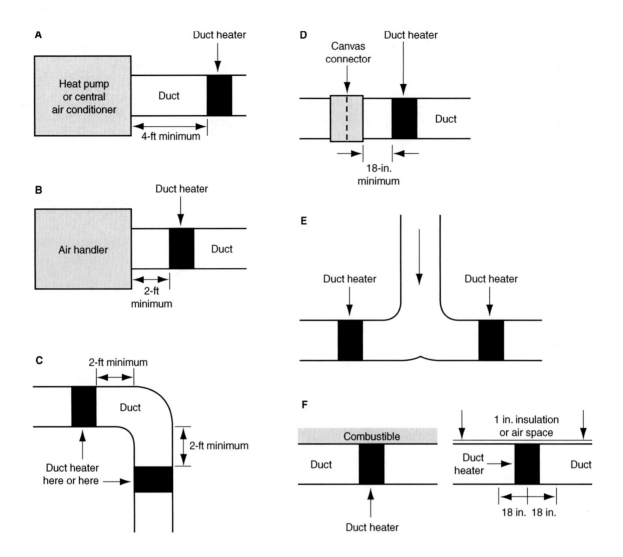

**FIGURE 10-3.** *Duct heater installation guidelines*

- Do not mount heaters side by side. If greater capacity is required, proportion smaller heaters in separate runouts, as shown in Figure 10-3E.

- Nykelkrom® heaters rated at 250 kW or less do not need the spacing normally required from combustible surfaces around the duct. As shown in Figure 10-3F, a 1-in. space—either insulation or air space— is mandatory for units rated in excess of 250 kW. This space is required around the duct for 18 in. on each side of the center of the heater. Such units are to be remote-controlled.

Here are some other important points to remember:

- Heaters and fan motors must be wired so that the heater cannot operate unless the fan is on. This applies unless a fan delay control is prewired into the control system by the manufacturer. When a fan interlock is provided, always connect to the high-voltage side of system.

- The coil of a secondary contactor (general-purpose, continuous duty, rated 6,000 cycles) must be wired in series with a manual reset high-limit control where used.

- Heater control or terminal boxes must be completely accessible. Refer to local codes.

- Pressure drop across a heater depends on air velocity and heater thickness.

- Flange-mounted heaters usually come with a 1-in. minimum flange. Slide-in models normally have a 9/16-in. minimum flange.

Duct heaters are approved for use with heat pumps, air conditioners, and other forced air systems. Duct heaters may be controlled by either contactors or sequential relays. (The switches in each relay make in sequence to reduce current inrush when the heater is energized.) Heaters are available for either single-phase or three-phase operation, for voltages up to 600 V.

### How to install duct heaters

These instructions specifically apply to duct heaters for zero clearance installations. First, cut an opening as required in the side of the duct. (Height will be determined by the model.) Slide the heater in the duct. Use the control box as a template to drill screw holes. Mount the unit to the duct with screws. Wire in high and low voltage. Replace the control box cover. Figure 10-4 shows a slide-in duct heater with its control box open.

Remember, do not *bank* heaters (place them side by side). For greater capacity, proportion smaller heaters in separate runouts. Heaters may be installed in the sides of either horizontal or vertical ducts. Never install a heater in the top or bottom of a horizontal duct. There is only one exception to this rule—it is possible to install a duct heater in the bottom of a horizontal duct if it is custom-built for that purpose.

INDEECO

**FIGURE 10-4.** *Slide-in open-coil duct heater*

Heater control boxes must be completely accessible. They must be located to provide ventilation at all times. Install air ducts in accordance with:

- Standards of the National Fire Protection Association for Installation of Air Conditioning and Ventilating Systems of other than Residence-Type (Pamphlet No. 90A)

- Residence-Type Warm Air Heating and Air Conditioning Systems (Pamphlet No. 90B).

In Canada, Dominion codes and standards must be adhered to.

Electric heaters are supplied for duct installation in two different ways—*flange mounting* and *slide-in mounting*. Larger heaters are often supplied for flange mounting. The heater is placed between two sections of flanged duct, which are bolted in place or fastened with sheet metal screws. For smaller ducts, the slide-in mount is used. It is installed as previously described. With either type of mounting, be certain that the control box is located for easy access.

## AIR VELOCITY DATA

### Minimum air velocities

Sufficient minimum air flow is required for the proper operation of any duct heater. Figure 10-5 shows a performance data chart that graphically indicates minimum air velocity (in ft/min) for any given wattage per square foot. Note that the higher the incoming air temperature, the higher the velocity required.

**Example:** For 10,000 W per square foot, the approximate air velocity would be:

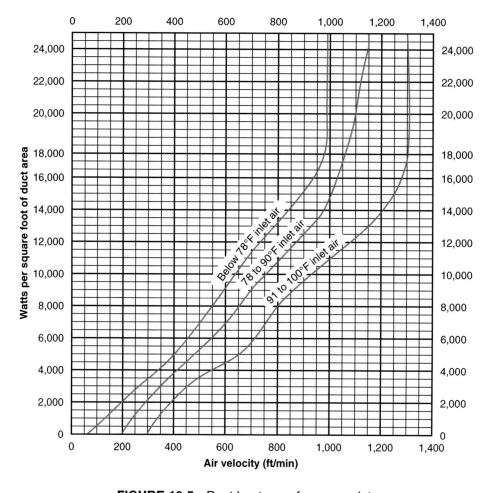

**FIGURE 10-5.** *Duct heater performance data*

- 630 ft/min for inlet air below 78°F

- 730 ft/min for inlet air of 78 to 90°F

- 905 ft/min for inlet air of 91 to 110°F.

The following six equations are useful for computing individual requirements:

1.  total kW required $= \dfrac{\text{Btu heat loss}}{3,413}$

2.  watts per square foot $= \dfrac{\text{kW required} \times 1,000}{\text{duct area in square feet}}$

3.  minimum air flow in cfm $=$ velocity in ft/min $\times$ duct area in square feet

4.  input air velocity in ft/min $= V = \dfrac{PvK}{A(T_2 - T_1)}$

5.  power input in kW $= P = \dfrac{VA(T_2 - T_1)}{K}$

6.  temperature rise $= \Delta T = \dfrac{PvK}{AV}$

where:

$v =$ specific volume of air in ft³/lb (12.5)

$A =$ cross-sectional area of duct in ft²

$K =$ constant (237 for °F)

$T_1 =$ input air temperature

$T_2 =$ output air temperature.

## CONTACTOR POWER CIRCUITRY

### Control contactor types

Control contactors receive the "go" signal from the temperature control system. They then act to provide heat by switching the heating circuits on and off as required. One contactor is generally used for each step, but it is not uncommon for two, three, or four contactors to control a single step in the staging process.

Basically there are two types of control contactors used in electric duct heater systems:

- de-energizing

- disconnecting.

The *de-energizing* type renders only the heating element inoperative. The *disconnecting* type completely isolates the heating element from electric power. The schematic circuitry of both types is shown in Figure 10-6.

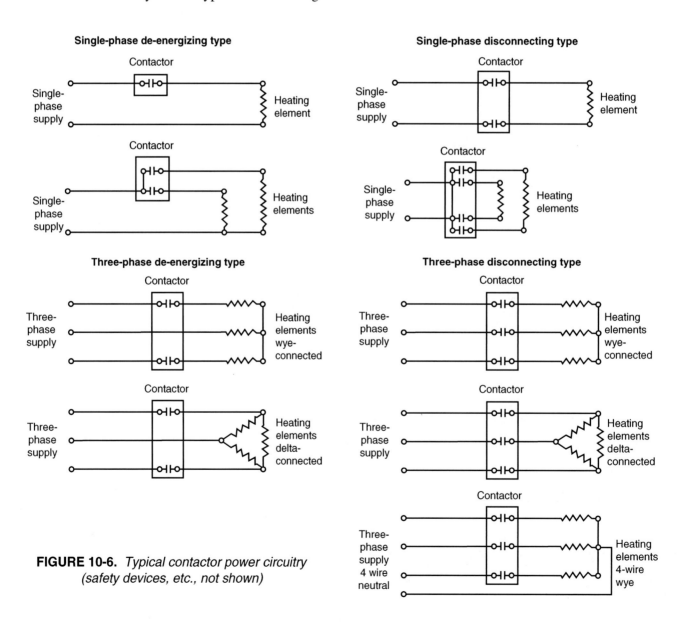

**FIGURE 10-6.** *Typical contactor power circuitry (safety devices, etc., not shown)*

### Backup contactors

*Backup* contactors, when specified, are used in conjunction with pilot-duty, bulb-type, manual reset safety devices. They cut electric power to a heating element to prevent its overheating. Backup contactor holding coil voltage will be the same as the line voltage unless otherwise specified.

### Mercury contactors

Factory built-in *mercury* contactors are most suitable where noise must be held at a low level. Figure 10-7 shows an example of a mercury contactor. Typical installations include locations where duct heater controls are located above a suspended ceiling, in buildings such as schools, offices, hospitals, etc. Because of their durability, mercury contactors are used with certain proportioning-type controllers whose frequent demand for repetitive cycling would not permit the use of magnetic contactors.

Mercury contactors are position-sensitive. They must be installed so that tubes are in an upright position. It is essential to mount duct heater assemblies with mercury contactors in strict accordance with the manufacturer's instructions.

Do not mount a mercury contactor on a heater whose control cabinet is on the bottom of the heater. In this type of application, the contactor must be remotely located. Mercury contactors, like their magnetic counterparts, come in both de-energizing and disconnecting types. Refer to Figure 10-6 for schematic wiring diagrams.

INDEECO

**FIGURE 10-7.** *Mercury contactor*

## GENERAL WIRING DATA

All wiring for electric duct heaters must follow U.S. National or Canadian Electrical codes and any local codes or ordinances. Use Type RH wire or its equivalent, suitable for 75°C, for connections to heater terminals or the control box.

### Typical wiring diagrams

Examples of typical wiring for various applications of electric duct heaters are shown in Figures 10-8, 10-9, and 10-10 on the following pages. Both single-phase and three-phase alternating current sources are shown. Some diagrams

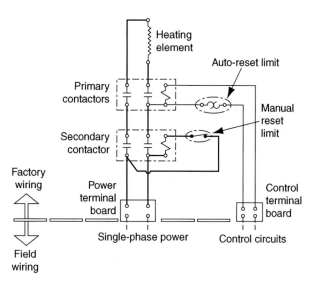

**Single-phase, single-stage heater drawing not more than 48 A total with built-in thermal cut-outs and contactors**

**Single-phase multi-stage heater drawing not more than 48 A total with built-in thermal cut-outs and contactors**

show that the connected heater load draws not more than 48 A total. Others specify that the connected heater load draws more than 48 A total. Note that where connected heater load draws in excess of 48 A, the emphasis is on greater circuit protection. The reason for this is existing electrical codes. They require that the current (amperage) load of electric duct heaters in a single circuit not exceed 48 A. Heaters drawing more than 48 A total load must be subdivided into internal circuits. None may exceed 48 A load. Each internal circuit must be protected by an overcurrent device, or fused at not more than 60 A. This is in addition to the normal branch fusing required.

Prepared charts, tables, graphs, and other reference sources are always valuable teaching aids. The information contained in Table 10-1 at the end of this Lesson is such an aid. It will be helpful to anyone who aspires to be an electric heating system troubleshooter. Study and use Table 10-1 to increase your ability to manipulate electrical values such as kilowatts, watts, voltage, and amperage. Other Lessons in this series deal in greater detail with these factors, and they present other important data. Please refer to them for valuable supplementary information.

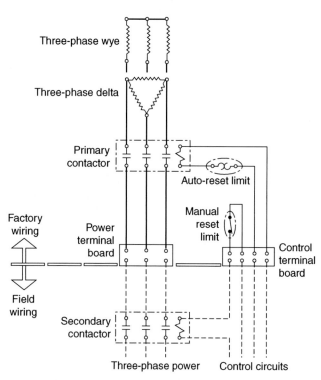

**Three-phase, single-stage heater drawing not more than 48 A total with built-in thermal cut-outs and contactors**

**FIGURE 10-8.** *Typical wiring circuits for electric duct heaters*

## PNEUMATIC AIR FLOW SWITCHES

Air flow switches, as the name implies, detect air flow or its absence in ducts. They are available in two types:

- pneumatic

- positive static pressure.

A *pneumatic* air flow switch responds only to the velocity of air movement. The control port opens on no flow and closes on air flow. Install it in a horizontal duct whenever possible, and where ambient temperatures do not exceed 180°F. You may mount a pneumatic switch on the top, side, or bottom of a duct. Avoid locations near elbows, dampers, fans, duct openings, or other places where excessive turbulence occurs. Mount the control away from such areas at least five times the distance of the smallest duct dimension. For example, in a 3-in. × 8-in. duct, mount it at least 15 in. from the nearest bend.

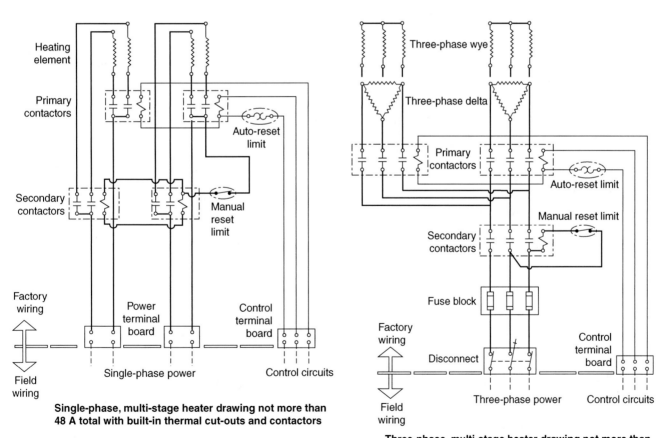

**Single-phase, multi-stage heater drawing not more than 48 A total with built-in thermal cut-outs and contactors**

**Three-phase, multi-stage heater drawing not more than 48 A total with built-in thermal cut-outs, contactors, and disconnect switch**

**FIGURE 10-9.** *Typical wiring circuits for electric duct heaters*

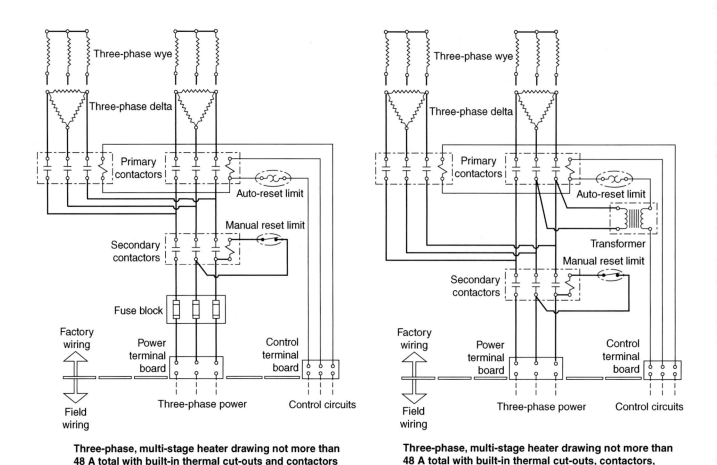

**FIGURE 10-9.** *Typical wiring circuits for electric duct heaters (continued)*

To install, proceed as follows:

1.  Select the proper location.

2.  Use the mounting plate gasket as a convenient template to mark hole positions.

3.  Drill or punch screw holes.

4.  Cut the center hole large enough for the paddle to pass through. The paddle may be trimmed to install in ducts as small as 3 in. × 6 in.

5.  In a horizontal duct, the case must be level. The paddle should be at a right angle to the air flow.

6.  A duct may not be horizontally true. Check with a level and place a shim under the control mounting plate.

If the switch must be in a vertical duct with downward air flow, it must be readjusted. To readjust, turn the range screw, usually in a clockwise direction. Turn it until the switch functions properly with no air flow. Then turn the screw one more turn in the same direction. Figure 10-11 on page 225 shows a typical pneumatic air flow switch installation.

### Operation

The control port on the switch stays closed when there is air flow in the line. When air flow falls below a minimum level, the port opens and bleeds the pressure line. An air flow switch acts as an automatic operating control.

### Adjustment

Pneumatic air flow switches are factory-set for a predetermined minimum flow rate. A specification provided with the switch will show the rate. The graph in Figure 10-12 on page 225 is an example. Do not turn the adjusting screw to get a minimum flow rate setting below the factory setting.

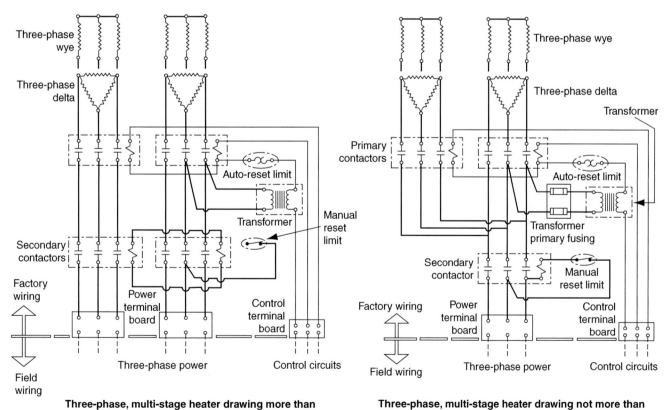

**Three-phase, multi-stage heater drawing more than 48 A total with built-in thermal cutouts, contactors, and transformer with secondary backup contactors**

**Three-phase, multi-stage heater drawing not more than 48 A total with built-in thermal cut-outs, contactors, and transformer with primary fusing**

**FIGURE 10-10.** *Typical wiring circuits for electric duct heaters*

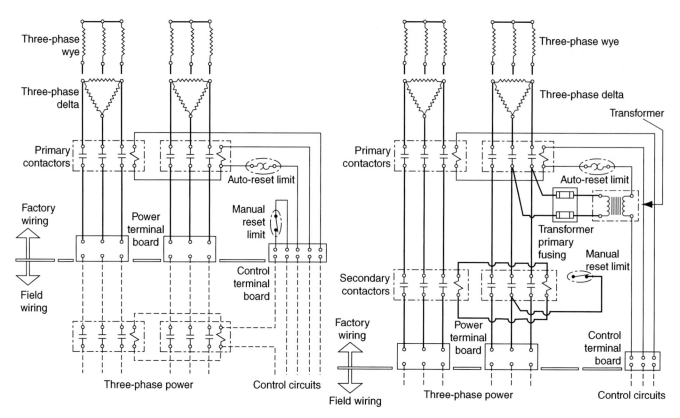

**Three-phase, multi-stage heater drawing more than 48 A total with built-in thermal cut-outs and contactors**

**Three-phase, multi-stage heater drawing not more than 48 A total with built-in thermal cut-outs, contactors, and transformer with primary fusing and secondary backup contactors**

**FIGURE 10-10.** *Typical wiring circuits for electric duct heaters (continued)*

A certain air flow velocity (in feet per minute) is required to actuate the switch. This varies with different duct sizes. Velocities for any given duct size (horizontal or vertical downward flow) are shown in graph curves, like the one in Figure 10-12. (The curves are based on a standard air density of 0.075 pounds per cubic foot.) In a vertical duct with upward air flow, the minimum closing point is about 650 ft/min.

If there is a heat pump coil upstream from the duct heater, the velocity will have to be greater than 650 ft/min, as shown in Figure 10-5. Another guide would be to use the manufacturer's information and adjust the air flow based on the manufacturer's instructions.

## POSITIVE PRESSURE AIR FLOW SWITCHES

A typical model of a *positive pressure* air flow switch is shown in Figure 10-13 on page 226. It responds to positive static pressure in the duct. Install it on the pressure side of the blower or fan, upstream from the heater, in a location with little vibration.

A positive pressure air flow switch has specific installation requirements. Install it in a portion of the duct system where the minimum combined velocity and static pressure will be at least 0.07 in. w.g. (water column) when the blower or fan is running. Air flow may be left or right, up or down, but the air flow switch itself must be mounted on the side of the duct. Other mounting positions require the use of a special control.

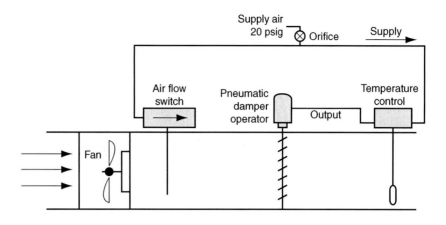

**FIGURE 10-11.** *Typical pneumatic air switch installation*

Positive pressure air flow switches are not designed to operate in locations where the pressure around the switch may be higher than atmospheric pressure. A pressurized ceiling plenum is an example.

### Mounting procedure

1.  Use the dimensional data provided with the air flow switch. Drill or punch a hole 1¼ in. to 2 in. in diameter in the side of the duct where the switch is to be located.

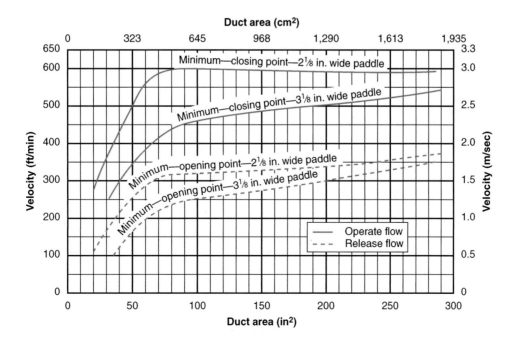

**FIGURE 10-12.** *Typical pneumatic switch minimum and operating velocity settings*

225

INDEECO

2. Attach the switch to the mounting bracket provided. Connect the fitting on the tubing to the threaded fitting on the switch.

3. Mount the assembly as dictated by the duct position. The end of the sensing tube should be turned to face upstream, toward the blower or fan.

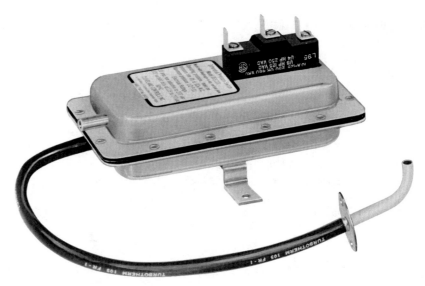

**FIGURE 10-13.** *Typical positive pressure air flow switch*

A number of electric duct heaters incorporate a built-in positive pressure air flow switch, with the switch mechanism accessible in heater control component cabinet. A heater so equipped is usually shipped with the air flow switch sensing tube opening pointing down. Before placing the heater in operation, loosen the brass fitting connecting the tube to the switch. Rotate the tubing until the opening in the curved end faces upstream toward the fan or blower.

### Operation

Positive pressure air flow switches are factory-set to close at a minimum pressure of 0.07 in. w.g., and to operate with a maximum of 10 psi. After the air distribution system has been properly balanced and before power is applied to the heater, a test should be made to determine that sufficient air flow is provided. Make the test as follows:

1. Be sure that power is disconnected from the heater and air flow switch.

2. With the fan on, check continuity between the terminals on the air switch marked *common* and *normally open*. The air flow switch should be closed and indicate zero resistance on an ohmmeter, or a short circuit with a test light.

3. With the fan off, check continuity as in Step 2. The switch should now be open. An ohmmeter should indicate no continuity.

If the switch does not close when the fan is on, or causes the contactors to chatter when in operation, there is most likely insufficient pressure in the duct. Do not alter or jump out the air flow switch. Disconnect the power and find out why there is not enough pressure, or determine if there is a malfunction in the air switch. Unhook the wires to the air switch. Use an ohmmeter to see if the switch is open or closed.

It is imperative that you have either a *slope gauge* or a *magnehelic differential pressure gauge* that can read pressures between 0.05 and 0.25 in. w.g. It should have minor divisions of 0.01 in. w.g.

If the tube on the pressure switch has an elbow, the tube on the slope gauge or magnehelic gauge must be the same. You will need information from the manufacturer on pressure switch settings so that you can measure the pressure and determine if the problem is an air flow problem or a pressure switch problem.

### Service

After the initial test during installation, an air flow switch should not normally require readjustment or service. However, malfunctions may occur. A typical problem and possible solution outline follows. Studying such problems helps a troubleshooter reach a correct diagnosis of the cause of the condition and the solution to the problem more rapidly.

**Problem 1:** The air flow switch will not operate.

Possible solutions:

1. The fan may be off or not delivering enough air.

2. The air flow switch should be on the pressure side (downstream) of the fan. If located on the suction side (upstream), the air flow switch will not operate, and must be relocated.

3. The switch is calibrated for side mounting, and will not work properly if inserted from the top or bottom of a horizontal duct.

4. The sensing tube may be facing the wrong way. Turn the tube so that it faces upstream toward the fan.

5. The air flow switch will not close unless the combined velocity and static pressure in the duct at the air flow switch is at least 0.07 in. w.g. If the switch is located too close to the end of the duct (within 2 ft of the register) or in other locations where the air flow is very low or irregular

(near bends or transitions), it may not close or may chatter. Relocate the switch.

6. Check for continuity in wiring.

7. Check the relief vent on the switch for blockage.

8. The air flow switch will not work if mounted in a plenum or false ceiling where the pressure surrounding the switch body is greater than atmospheric pressure. Relocate the switch.

**Problem 2:** The air flow switch chatters.

Possible solutions:

1. Insufficient static pressure in the duct may cause the air flow switch to chatter. At least 0.07 in. w.g. of combined velocity and static pressure is required to operate the switch. See also item 5 above.

2. The switch is calibrated for side mounting and may chatter if mounted on the top or bottom of a horizontal duct. Relocate the switch.

3. Check for possible intermittent wire connections.

**Problem 3:** The air flow switch stops working after a period of normal operation.

Possible solutions:

1. The sensing tube may have become clogged. Remove it from the duct and unscrew the brass fitting to remove the tubing. Clean the tubing and reinstall.

2. Air flow may have stopped or diminished. Check for dirty filters, closed fire doors or balancing dampers, a loose or broken fan belt, etc.

3. Be sure that the sensing tube is still facing into the airstream. It may have moved due to vibration, etc.

4. Check for continuity in wiring.

5. To be sure that the air flow switch itself is at fault, perform the operational test outlined above under the "Operation" heading.

| Btuh | kW | 120 V 1Φ | 208 V 1Φ | 208 V 3Φ | 220 V 1Φ | 220 V 3Φ | 230 V 1Φ | 230 V 3Φ | 240 V 1Φ | 240 V 3Φ | 277 V 1Φ | 440 V 1Φ | 440 V 3Φ | 460 V 1Φ | 460 V 3Φ | 480 V 1Φ | 480 V 3Φ | 550 V 1Φ | 550 V 3Φ | kW |
|---|---|---|---|---|---|---|---|---|---|---|---|---|---|---|---|---|---|---|---|---|
| 3,413 | 1 | 8.3 | 4.8 | 2.8 | 4.5 | 2.6 | 4.3 | 2.5 | 4.2 | 2.4 | 3.6 | 2.3 | 1.3 | 2.2 | 1.3 | 2.1 | 1.2 | 1.8 | 1.1 | 1 |
| 6,826 | 2 | 16.7 | 9.6 | 5.5 | 9.1 | 5.2 | 8.7 | 5.0 | 8.3 | 4.8 | 7.8 | 4.5 | 2.6 | 4.3 | 2.5 | 4.2 | 2.4 | 3.6 | 2.1 | 2 |
| 10,239 | 3 | 25.0 | 14.4 | 8.3 | 13.6 | 7.9 | 13.0 | 7.5 | 12.5 | 7.2 | 10.8 | 6.8 | 3.9 | 6.5 | 3.8 | 6.2 | 3.6 | 5.4 | 3.2 | 3 |
| 13,652 | 4 | 33.3 | 19.2 | 11.1 | 18.2 | 10.5 | 17.4 | 10.0 | 16.6 | 9.6 | 14.4 | 9.1 | 5.2 | 8.7 | 5.0 | 8.3 | 4.8 | 7.2 | 4.2 | 4 |
| 17,065 | 5 | 41.7 | 24.0 | 13.9 | 22.7 | 13.1 | 21.7 | 12.6 | 20.8 | 12.0 | 18.1 | 11.4 | 6.6 | 10.9 | 6.3 | 10.4 | 6.0 | 9.1 | 5.3 | 5 |
| 20,478 | 6 | 50.0 | 28.9 | 16.6 | 27.2 | 15.7 | 26.0 | 15.1 | 25.0 | 14.4 | 21.7 | 13.6 | 7.9 | 13.0 | 7.5 | 12.5 | 7.2 | 10.9 | 6.3 | 6 |
| 23,891 | 7 | 58.3 | 33.7 | 19.4 | 31.8 | 18.3 | 30.4 | 17.6 | 29.1 | 16.8 | 25.3 | 15.9 | 9.2 | 15.2 | 8.8 | 14.6 | 8.4 | 12.7 | 7.4 | 7 |
| 27,304 | 8 | 66.6 | 38.5 | 22.2 | 36.3 | 21.0 | 34.7 | 20.1 | 33.3 | 19.2 | 28.9 | 18.2 | 10.5 | 17.4 | 10.0 | 16.6 | 9.6 | 14.5 | 8.4 | 8 |
| 30,717 | 9 | 75.0 | 43.3 | 24.9 | 40.9 | 23.6 | 39.1 | 22.6 | 37.4 | 21.6 | 32.5 | 20.4 | 11.8 | 19.5 | 11.3 | 18.7 | 10.8 | 16.3 | 9.5 | 9 |
| 34,130 | 10 | 83.3 | 48.1 | 27.7 | 45.4 | 26.2 | 43.4 | 25.1 | 41.6 | 24.0 | 36.1 | 22.7 | 13.1 | 21.7 | 12.5 | 20.8 | 12.0 | 18.1 | 10.5 | 10 |
| 37,543 | 11 | 91.6 | 52.9 | 30.5 | 49.9 | 28.8 | 47.7 | 27.6 | 45.8 | 26.4 | 39.7 | 25.0 | 14.4 | 23.9 | 13.8 | 22.9 | 13.2 | 19.9 | 11.6 | 11 |
| 40,956 | 12 | 100.0 | 57.7 | 33.2 | 54.5 | 31.4 | 52.1 | 30.1 | 49.9 | 28.8 | 43.3 | 27.2 | 15.7 | 26.0 | 15.0 | 25.0 | 14.4 | 21.7 | 12.6 | 12 |
| 44,369 | 13 | 108.3 | 62.5 | 36.0 | 59.0 | 34.1 | 56.4 | 32.6 | 54.1 | 31.2 | 46.9 | 29.5 | 17.0 | 28.2 | 16.3 | 27.0 | 15.6 | 23.5 | 13.7 | 13 |
| 47,782 | 14 | 116.6 | 67.3 | 38.8 | 63.6 | 36.7 | 60.8 | 35.1 | 58.2 | 33.6 | 50.5 | 31.8 | 18.3 | 30.4 | 17.5 | 29.1 | 16.8 | 25.3 | 14.7 | 14 |
| 51,195 | 15 | 125.0 | 72.1 | 41.6 | 68.1 | 39.3 | 65.1 | 37.7 | 62.4 | 36.0 | 54.2 | 34.1 | 19.7 | 32.6 | 18.6 | 31.2 | 18.0 | 27.2 | 15.8 | 15 |
| 54,608 | 16 | 133.3 | 76.9 | 44.3 | 72.6 | 41.9 | 69.4 | 40.2 | 66.6 | 38.4 | 57.8 | 36.3 | 21.0 | 34.7 | 20.0 | 33.3 | 19.2 | 29.0 | 16.8 | 16 |
| 58,021 | 17 | 141.6 | 81.8 | 47.1 | 77.2 | 44.5 | 73.8 | 42.7 | 70.7 | 40.8 | 61.4 | 38.6 | 22.3 | 36.9 | 21.3 | 35.4 | 20.4 | 30.8 | 17.9 | 17 |
| 61,434 | 18 | 150.0 | 86.5 | 49.9 | 81.7 | 47.2 | 78.1 | 45.2 | 74.9 | 43.2 | 65.0 | 40.9 | 23.6 | 39.1 | 22.5 | 37.4 | 21.6 | 32.6 | 18.9 | 18 |
| 64,847 | 19 | 158.3 | 91.4 | 52.6 | 86.3 | 49.8 | 82.5 | 47.7 | 79.0 | 45.6 | 68.6 | 43.1 | 24.9 | 41.2 | 23.8 | 39.5 | 22.8 | 34.4 | 20.0 | 19 |
| 68,260 | 20 | 166.6 | 96.2 | 55.4 | 90.8 | 52.4 | 86.8 | 50.2 | 83.2 | 48.0 | 72.2 | 45.4 | 26.2 | 43.4 | 25.0 | 41.6 | 24.0 | 36.2 | 21.0 | 20 |
| 71,673 | 21 | 174.9 | 101.0 | 58.2 | 95.3 | 55.0 | 91.1 | 52.7 | 87.4 | 50.4 | 75.8 | 47.7 | 27.5 | 45.6 | 26.3 | 43.7 | 25.2 | 38.0 | 22.1 | 21 |
| 75,086 | 22 | 183.3 | 105.8 | 60.9 | 99.9 | 57.6 | 95.5 | 55.2 | 91.5 | 52.8 | 79.4 | 49.9 | 28.8 | 47.7 | 27.5 | 45.8 | 26.4 | 39.8 | 23.1 | 22 |
| 78,499 | 23 | 191.6 | 110.6 | 63.7 | 104.4 | 60.3 | 99.8 | 57.7 | 95.7 | 55.2 | 83.0 | 52.2 | 30.1 | 49.9 | 28.8 | 47.8 | 27.6 | 41.6 | 24.2 | 23 |
| 81,912 | 24 | 200.0 | 115.4 | 66.5 | 109.0 | 62.9 | 104.2 | 60.2 | 99.8 | 57.6 | 86.6 | 54.5 | 31.4 | 52.1 | 30.0 | 49.9 | 28.8 | 43.4 | 25.2 | 24 |
| 85,325 | 25 | 208.3 | 120.2 | 69.3 | 113.5 | 65.5 | 108.5 | 62.8 | 104.0 | 60.0 | 90.3 | 56.8 | 32.8 | 54.3 | 31.3 | 52.0 | 30.0 | 45.3 | 26.3 | 25 |
| 88,738 | 26 | 216.6 | 125.1 | 72.0 | 118.0 | 68.1 | 112.8 | 65.3 | 108.2 | 62.4 | 93.9 | 59.0 | 34.1 | 56.4 | 32.5 | 54.1 | 31.2 | 47.1 | 27.3 | 26 |
| 92,151 | 27 | 225.0 | 129.9 | 74.8 | 122.6 | 70.7 | 117.2 | 67.8 | 112.3 | 64.8 | 97.5 | 61.3 | 35.4 | 58.6 | 33.8 | 56.2 | 32.4 | 48.9 | 28.4 | 27 |
| 95,564 | 28 | 233.3 | 134.7 | 77.6 | 127.1 | 73.4 | 121.5 | 70.3 | 116.5 | 67.2 | 101.1 | 63.6 | 36.7 | 60.2 | 35.0 | 58.2 | 33.6 | 50.7 | 29.4 | 28 |
| 98,977 | 29 | 241.6 | 139.5 | 80.3 | 131.7 | 76.0 | 125.9 | 72.8 | 120.6 | 69.6 | 104.7 | 65.8 | 38.0 | 63.0 | 36.3 | 60.3 | 34.8 | 52.5 | 30.5 | 29 |
| 102,390 | 30 | 250.0 | 144.3 | 83.1 | 136.2 | 78.6 | 130.2 | 75.3 | 124.8 | 72.0 | 108.3 | 68.1 | 39.3 | 65.1 | 37.5 | 62.4 | 36.0 | 54.3 | 31.5 | 30 |
| 105,803 | 31 | 258.3 | 149.1 | 85.9 | 140.7 | 81.2 | 134.5 | 77.8 | 129.0 | 74.4 | 111.9 | 70.4 | 40.6 | 67.3 | 38.8 | 64.5 | 37.2 | 56.1 | 32.6 | 31 |
| 109,216 | 32 | 266.6 | 153.9 | 88.6 | 145.3 | 83.8 | 138.9 | 80.3 | 133.1 | 76.8 | 115.5 | 72.6 | 41.9 | 69.4 | 40.0 | 66.6 | 38.4 | 57.9 | 33.6 | 32 |
| 112,629 | 33 | 275.0 | 158.7 | 91.4 | 149.8 | 86.5 | 143.2 | 82.8 | 137.3 | 79.2 | 119.1 | 74.9 | 43.2 | 71.6 | 41.3 | 68.6 | 39.6 | 59.7 | 34.7 | 33 |
| 116,042 | 34 | 283.3 | 163.5 | 94.2 | 154.4 | 89.1 | 147.6 | 85.3 | 141.4 | 81.6 | 122.7 | 77.2 | 44.5 | 73.8 | 42.5 | 70.7 | 40.8 | 61.5 | 35.7 | 34 |
| 119,455 | 35 | 291.7 | 168.4 | 97.0 | 159.0 | 91.7 | 151.9 | 87.9 | 145.6 | 84.0 | 126.4 | 79.5 | 45.9 | 76.0 | 43.8 | 72.8 | 42.0 | 63.4 | 36.8 | 35 |
| 122,868 | 36 | 300.0 | 173.2 | 99.7 | 163.4 | 94.3 | 156.2 | 90.4 | 149.8 | 86.4 | 130.0 | 81.7 | 47.2 | 78.1 | 45.0 | 74.9 | 43.2 | 65.2 | 37.8 | 36 |
| 126,281 | 37 | 308.3 | 178.0 | 102.5 | 168.0 | 96.9 | 160.6 | 92.9 | 153.9 | 88.8 | 133.6 | 84.0 | 48.5 | 80.3 | 46.3 | 77.0 | 44.4 | 67.0 | 38.9 | 37 |
| 129,694 | 38 | 316.7 | 182.8 | 105.3 | 172.5 | 99.6 | 164.9 | 95.4 | 158.1 | 91.2 | 137.2 | 86.3 | 49.8 | 82.5 | 47.5 | 79.0 | 45.6 | 68.8 | 39.9 | 38 |
| 133,107 | 39 | 325.0 | 187.6 | 108.0 | 177.1 | 102.2 | 169.3 | 97.9 | 162.2 | 93.6 | 140.8 | 88.5 | 51.1 | 84.6 | 48.8 | 81.1 | 46.8 | 70.6 | 41.0 | 39 |
| 136,520 | 40 | 333.3 | 192.4 | 110.8 | 181.6 | 104.8 | 173.6 | 100.4 | 166.4 | 96.0 | 144.4 | 90.8 | 52.4 | 86.8 | 50.0 | 83.2 | 48.0 | 72.4 | 42.0 | 40 |
| 139,993 | 41 | 341.7 | 197.2 | 113.6 | 186.1 | 107.4 | 177.9 | 102.9 | 170.6 | 98.4 | 148.0 | 93.1 | 53.7 | 89.0 | 51.3 | 85.3 | 49.2 | 74.2 | 43.1 | 41 |
| 143,346 | 42 | 350.0 | 202.0 | 116.3 | 190.7 | 110.0 | 182.3 | 105.4 | 174.7 | 100.8 | 151.6 | 95.3 | 55.0 | 91.1 | 52.5 | 87.4 | 50.4 | 76.0 | 44.1 | 42 |
| 146,759 | 43 | 358.3 | 206.8 | 119.1 | 195.2 | 112.7 | 186.6 | 107.9 | 178.9 | 103.2 | 155.2 | 97.6 | 56.3 | 93.3 | 53.8 | 89.4 | 52.6 | 77.8 | 45.2 | 43 |
| 150,172 | 44 | 366.7 | 211.7 | 121.9 | 199.8 | 115.3 | 191.0 | 110.4 | 183.0 | 105.6 | 158.8 | 100.0 | 57.6 | 95.5 | 55.0 | 91.5 | 52.8 | 79.6 | 46.2 | 44 |
| 153,585 | 45 | 375.0 | 216.5 | 124.7 | 204.3 | 117.9 | 195.3 | 113.0 | 187.2 | 108.0 | 162.5 | 102.2 | 59.0 | 97.7 | 56.3 | 93.6 | 54.0 | 81.5 | 47.3 | 45 |
| 156,998 | 46 | 383.3 | 221.3 | 127.4 | 208.8 | 120.5 | 199.6 | 115.5 | 191.4 | 110.4 | 166.1 | 104.4 | 60.3 | 99.8 | 57.5 | 95.7 | 55.2 | 83.3 | 48.3 | 46 |
| 160,411 | 47 | 391.7 | 226.1 | 130.2 | 213.4 | 123.1 | 204.0 | 118.0 | 195.5 | 112.8 | 169.7 | 106.7 | 61.6 | 102.0 | 58.8 | 97.8 | 56.4 | 85.1 | 49.4 | 47 |
| 163,824 | 48 | 400.0 | 230.9 | 133.0 | 217.9 | 125.8 | 208.3 | 120.5 | 199.7 | 115.2 | 173.3 | 109.0 | 62.9 | 104.2 | 60.0 | 99.8 | 57.6 | 86.9 | 50.4 | 48 |
| 167,237 | 49 | 408.3 | 235.7 | 135.7 | 222.5 | 128.4 | 212.7 | 123.0 | 203.8 | 117.6 | 176.9 | 111.3 | 64.2 | 106.3 | 61.3 | 101.9 | 58.8 | 88.7 | 51.5 | 49 |
| 170,650 | 50 | 416.6 | 240.5 | 138.5 | 227.0 | 131.0 | 217.0 | 125.5 | 208.0 | 120.0 | 180.5 | 113.5 | 65.5 | 108.5 | 62.5 | 104.0 | 60.0 | 90.5 | 52.5 | 50 |

**Formula for calculating line currents:**

Single-phase (1Φ)

$$\text{amperes} = \frac{\text{watts}}{\text{line voltage}}$$

To convert kW to watts, multiply kW by 1,000

Three-phase (3Φ)

$$\text{amperes} = \frac{\text{watts}}{\text{line voltage} \times 1.73}$$

$208 \times 1.73 = 359.8$  
$220 \times 1.73 = 380.6$  
$230 \times 1.73 = 397.9$

$240 \times 1.73 = 415.2$  
$440 \times 1.73 = 761.2$  
$460 \times 1.73 = 795.8$

$480 \times 1.73 = 830.4$  
$550 \times 1.73 = 951.5$  
$600 \times 1.73 = 1,038.0$

**TABLE 10-1.** *Btuh, kilowatts, and amperes, with a formula for calculating line currents*

1. What is a *dielectric* test?

2. What are open-coil elements?

3. What is a secondary control circuit?

4. How far should duct heaters be installed downstream from heat pump and central air conditioner coils?

5. How far must a duct heater be located from a canvas connector?

6. How should duct heaters be installed in horizontal ducts?

7. What determines the pressure drop across the heater?

8. Why do sequencers delay energizing certain heaters?

9. What standards govern proper installation of air ducts?

10. Why type of mounting is generally provided for large duct heaters?

11. What precaution must you take when installing either a flange-mounted or a slide-in duct heater?

12. What must be done to ensure the correct operation of duct heater?

13. If the temperature of the incoming air is raised, the required velocity is _____.

14. What is the recommended velocity for inlet air temperature of 80°F?

15. Using the chart in Figure 10-5, what is the minimum ft/min with 75°F inlet air and 10,000 watts per square foot of duct area?

16. How many phases are disconnected when a three-phase unit is shut off by a de-energizing type control system?

17. How many lines are broken on a single-phase supply using a de-energizing type control?

18. Which wire is never disconnected in a four-wire wye system?

19. What type of contactors should be used in applications where a low level of noise is a requirement?

20. What must be the position of the tubes in a mercury contactor?

21. What is the maximum ampere value allowed on a single circuit for electric duct heaters?

22. What is the maximum fuse size for a single circuit supplying duct heaters?

23. Using Table 10-1, determine the Btu output for a 10-kW heater.

24.     Using Table 10-1, determine the amperes for 10 kW at 277 V.


25.     What do air flow switches detect?


26.     Name two types of air flow switches.


27.     Why should a pneumatic air switch *not* be installed near an elbow?


28.     How far from the nearest bend in a 3-in. × 8-in. duct should a pneumatic air switch be located?


29.     What position should the air flow switch be in when the fan is running?

# Multi-Step Controllers (Part I)

## INTRODUCTION

When staging is required in an electric heating system, the necessary staging (heating steps) may not lend itself to control by a two-stage or three-stage thermostat. It so, a more sophisticated method of staging may be needed. That method is the *multi-step controller*. This device may operate mechanically, or function through solid-state circuitry. Mechanical controllers will be discussed first. They include *cam-operated* and *pneumatic* types.

## CAM-OPERATED STEP CONTROLLERS

Cam-operated step controllers can provide sequencing control of up to ten stages of electric heating. *Switching cams* control various heat stages. The cams are rotated by a drive motor, and activate *snap switches*. The switches each complete or interrupt the power or control circuit to one or more heating elements. (The type of circuit depends on whether the system power source is single-phase or three-phase.) A *balancing relay* controls the drive motor operation and the corresponding cam movement. The balancing relay is actuated by potentiometer-type temperature sensors.

233

Some controllers are equipped with a single potentiometer. Others incorporate an additional potentiometer. These dual-potentiometer models control a damper motor in the air circulation system.

Figure 11-1 is a typical combination schematic and pictorial hookup diagram. It clearly indicates the need for specialized knowledge to service this type of

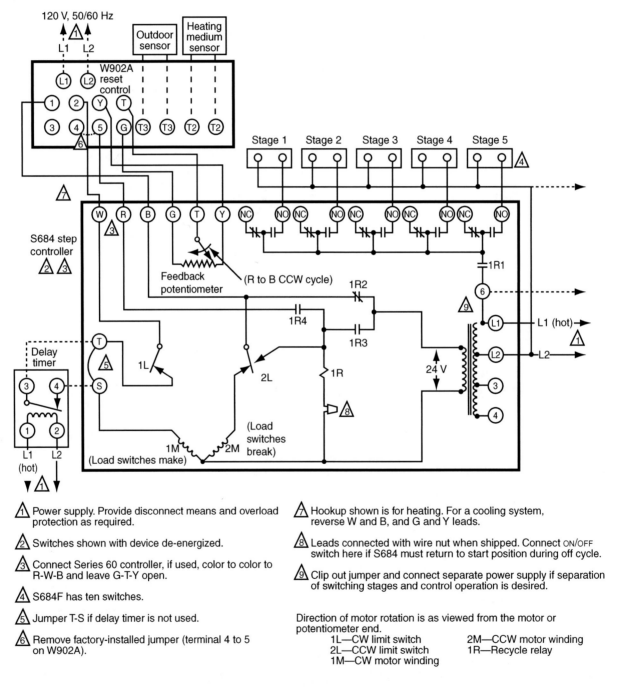

1. Power supply. Provide disconnect means and overload protection as required.

2. Switches shown with device de-energized.

3. Connect Series 60 controller, if used, color to color to R-W-B and leave G-T-Y open.

4. S684F has ten switches.

5. Jumper T-S if delay timer is not used.

6. Remove factory-installed jumper (terminal 4 to 5 on W902A).

7. Hookup shown is for heating. For a cooling system, reverse W and B, and G and Y leads.

8. Leads connected with wire nut when shipped. Connect ON/OFF switch here if S684 must return to start position during off cycle.

9. Clip out jumper and connect separate power supply if separation of switching stages and control operation is desired.

Direction of motor rotation is as viewed from the motor or potentiometer end.
1L—CW limit switch    2M—CCW motor winding
2L—CCW limit switch    1R—Recycle relay
1M—CW motor winding

**FIGURE 11-1.** *Internal schematic and typical hookup for cam-operated step controller with electronic balance relay for proportioning control*

equipment. The installer must, of course, comply with all applicable codes, ordinances, and regulations. The cam-operated step controller may be used with 120-, 208-, 220-, or 240-V ac supply. The terminal block will show the correct terminal for the available power source.

If desired, the system ON/OFF switch can be connected so that power is cut to the recycle relay (1R in Figure 11-1) while leaving the controller powered. With this arrangement, all stages go off when the system is turned off. The step controller returns to its starting point. When the system is turned back on, stages can begin to sequence on immediately.

### Settings and adjustments

Cam-operated step controllers are usually shipped from the factory with make points of load switches equidistant over the 160° of motor rotation. The stage differential is adjusted to 13 to 20°. (The differential on models with 13½-minute motor timing is set at 5°, as shown in Figure 11-2.)

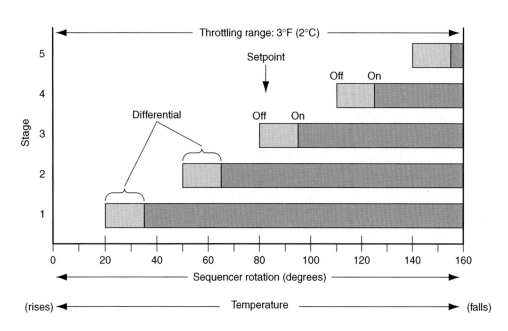

**FIGURE 11-2.** *Typical switch settings for five-stage control of electric duct heaters (factory-shipped with this switch configuration)*

All models are shipped with the motor in full counterclockwise position. This is the position as viewed from the motor or potentiometer end. In this position, all load switches are open.

You can adjust switch cams to operate the switches at any point of motor shaft rotation. You can adjust the switch differential from 5° to nearly 160° maximum. If the step control is mounted with the base upward, make sure that terminal guards cover the switch terminals before adjusting the switch cams.

### Determining switch settings

Proper system operation depends on selecting correct sequencer timing and a controller with the correct throttling range. Adjust switch make and break points to make the best use of full camshaft rotation. Consider motor timing and the amount of temperature rise provided by each stage when selecting switch settings. A delay timer may be added to slow camshaft rotation when energizing stages.

The controller throttling range should be as narrow as possible without causing *hunting*, or rapid cycling, regardless of load conditions. To find the degrees of motor rotation for each degree of change in temperature at the controller, divide the controller throttling range into 160 (full motor rotation, in angular degrees).

**Example 1.**  Controller throttling range: 16°F
Full motor rotation: 160°

$$\frac{160}{16} = 10$$

The motor shaft rotates 10° for every 1°F change at the controller.

**Example 2.**  Controller throttling range: 10°C
Full motor rotation: 160°

$$\frac{160}{10} = 16$$

The motor shaft rotates 16° for every 1°C change at the controller.

General control requirements depend on numerous variables. Consult the controller application data for the type used to obtain the manufacturer's suggested settings. Instability or hunting may occur at the suggested setting. If so, either widen the controller throttling range or use a delay timer to lengthen step control timings.

### Using a delay timer

Use a 30-second or 60-second timer that has an ON period adjustable from 1 to 7 seconds. The ON period should occur once every 30 seconds or once every 60 seconds. The sequencer motor shaft will rotate only when the timer switch contacts are closed. The delay timer is connected to the T and S terminals on the sequencer. If a timer is not used, these terminals must be jumpered.

### Electric duct heating requirements

Electric duct heating systems require narrow stage differentials with switches set equidistant over the range of the step control (refer back to Figure 11-2). A long timing motor (5 or 13½ minutes) should be used for stability. A fast-response Series 90 thermostat with narrow throttling range coupled with the 13½-minute controller is recommended.

### Procedure

The controller switches are preset for a specific function. Switches can be adjusted using the following procedure, if desired:

1.  Make sure that the motor is in the full counterclockwise position. All switches should be in the open, or break, position. (Controls are shipped in this position.)

2.  On all switches, loosen the setscrews in the bushings and the cam adjustment screws. If the setscrews are not easily accessible, operate the motor to rotate the cams and bushings until they are. Short terminals R to B for counterclockwise rotation, and R to W for clockwise rotation.

3.  Short R to B to return the motor to the full counterclockwise position.

4.  Short R to W to run the motor to the desired make point of the first switch. Stop the motor at this point by removing the S-T jumper.

5.  Turn the operational cam for the first switch clockwise until the switch clicks as the roller moves up the cam rise to the high cam level. This is the switch make point. Lock the setscrew in the bushing.

6.  Set make points of each of the switches as described above. Move the motor to each switch make point by jumpering S-T. Remove the jumper when the motor reaches the desired setpoint for the next switch.

7.  To set the switch differentials, short terminals R to B on the motor. Run it to the desired break point of the last switch. Stop the motor at this point by removing power at L1.

8.  Move the differential cam clockwise so that the roller is on the high cam level. Pull back and release the cam roller to make sure that the switch is made.

9.  Turn the differential cam counterclockwise until the roller drops to the low cam level and clicks. This is the switch break point. Lock the hex screw.

10. Repeat steps 7 through 9 for each switch.

**OPERATION**

(*Note*: There are frequent references in this section to clockwise and counterclockwise rotation. This is as viewed from the motor or potentiometer end.)

**Condition:**

The control system is energized and operating through step control.

**Effect:**

■ The load switches energize the load stages according to the requirements of the primary controller or panel.

■ The delay timer (if used) slows down the camshaft rotation on the clockwise cycle, but allows the camshaft to rotate counterclockwise at full motor timing. The slowing action of the delay timer provides smooth system operation. It prevents short cycling of individual load stages.

**Condition:**

The recycle relay is de-energized. The system remains powered. (This occurs only when the optional connection for an ON/OFF switch is used.)

**Effect:**

■ The load contacts in the recycle relay open.

■ All load stages are de-energized.

■ The step control returns to the start position. It is ready for immediate sequencing of load stages when the recycle relay is re-energized.

**Condition:**

The control system is de-energized.

**Effect:**

■ The load contacts open in the recycle relay.

■ All load stages are de-energized.

**Condition:**

The control system is energized after a power interruption.

**Effect:**

- The camshaft rotates counterclockwise until all step switches are open.

- The load contacts close in the recycle relay.

- The camshaft rotates clockwise to the position called for by the primary controller. It closes required step switches and energizes corresponding load stages.

Certain cam-operated step controllers are specifically designed to provide cold deck sequencing and control of an outdoor air damper. Switching sequences and switch differentials are preset to operate as shown in Figure 11-3. Note that the auxiliary potentiometer goes from 0 to 135 Ω in the first 80° of camshaft rotation.

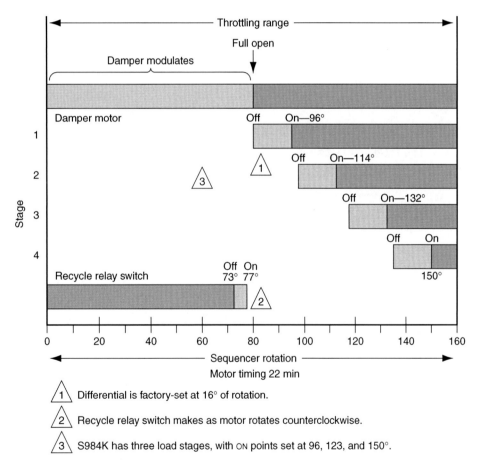

**CHECKOUT**

**Recycle feature**

The step control is designed to drop out an integral load contact (1R1 in Figure 11-1) when panel power is off. On resumption of power, the camshaft rotates to the counterclockwise limit. This opens all load switches. The recycle relay then energizes, pulling in the load contact. Finally, the camshaft rotates clockwise to the position called for by the primary controller. It energizes, in sequence, the required load stages.

⚠ 1 Differential is factory-set at 16° of rotation.

⚠ 2 Recycle relay switch makes as motor rotates counterclockwise.

⚠ 3 S984K has three load stages, with ON points set at 96, 123, and 150°.

**FIGURE 11-3.** *Modulating cooling/sequenced heating control*

239

The function of the recycle feature is nearly the same on controllers that provide cold deck sequencing. The difference is that when power is restored after failure, a fourth snap switch allows the camshaft to return only to its midpoint (80° of rotation). At this point, all stages of refrigeration are off, but the auxiliary potentiometer is at the 135-$\Omega$ position.

### Procedure

After completing installation and adjustment of make and break points, interrupt power to the unit. This allows the recycle feature to run the step control to the start position (midpoint on the cold deck models). Short R to B, and run the controller counterclockwise through the break of each switch. This verifies the switching sequence and ensures proper operation.

**Condition:**

The control system is energized and operating through step control.

**Effect:**

- The camshaft begins its clockwise rotation. During the first 80° of rotation, the auxiliary potentiometer wiper moves from 0 to 135 $\Omega$ and opens the outdoor air damper. The introduction of outdoor air acts as the first cooling stage. No cooling loads are energized during this period.

- If 100% outdoor air doesn't meet cooling demands, the rotation of the camshaft continues. It energizes load stages as required.

**Condition:**

The recycle relay is de-energized. The system remains powered. (This occurs only when the optional connection for an ON/OFF switch is used.)

**Effect:**

- The load contacts in the recycle relay open.

- All load stages are de-energized.

- The step control returns to the original start position. It is ready for immediate sequencing of load stages when the recycle relay is re-energized.

**Condition:**

The control system de-energized.

**Effect:**

- All load stages are de-energized.

- The load contacts in the recycle relay open.

**Condition:**

The control system is energized after a power interruption.

**Effect:**

- When the motor is stopped between 0 and 80°, the motor advances to midpoint, moving the outside air damper to the full open position. At midpoint, the load contacts close in the recycle relay. When the motor is stopped between 80 and 160°, the motor rotates counterclockwise to midpoint (80°). At midpoint, the load contacts close in the recycle relay. The outside air damper remains full open.

- The motor rotates clockwise and energizes cooling stages as required by the primary controller.

## PNEUMATIC STEP CONTROLLERS

The *pneumatic step controller*, like the cam-operated control, is a mechanical device. However, its direct power source is air pressure. In a pneumatic step controller, a pneumatic (air pressure) signal is converted to an electrical signal by means of a PE (pneumatic-electric) switch. Figure 11-4 on the next page shows a typical flow diagram for PE switches. The initial temperature-sensing device (pneumatic thermostat, etc.) sends a signal to the temperature converter. The signal is proportionate to the temperature being sensed. The temperature converter, in turn, sends an air signal to the PE switches. The air signal is proportional to temperature, generally in the 3 to 15-psi range. When the air signal from the temperature converter reaches the setpoint of the PE switches, they will operate. Their operation allows the controlled heaters to be energized through the controller circuits.

PE switches are normally wired to close on a rise in pressure. They are more often used as pilot devices than in direct load switching. That is, they switch

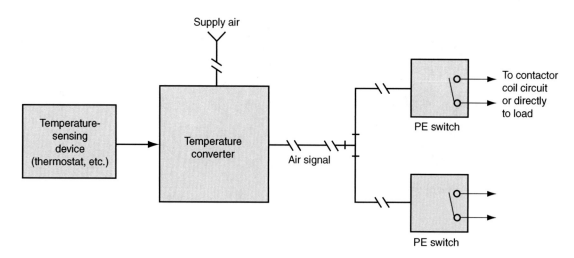

**FIGURE 11-4.** *Typical PE switch flow diagram*

power to the holding coil of a contactor, which in turn carries the heating element load. Three-phase control applications require PE switches to be used in this manner in a pneumatic step controller. Single-phase duct heaters may be controlled directly within the electrical ratings of the controller.

Figure 11-5 shows how to interwire a single-phase duct heater with a pneumatic step controller. The control transformer is required in this case, since it is a 480-V single-phase application and the automatic reset limit control rating is 277 V. For this reason, the safety contactor is also required. When the voltage supply is 277 V or less, the automatic reset limit control may be wired in place of the contactor contact if the connected load does not exceed 30 A. Under these conditions, the transformer and safety contactor may also be eliminated, if desired.

## SOLID-STATE MULTI-STEP CONTROLLERS

Fully *modulating* or *proportional* control is the ultimate control method for space heating. Proportional control gives an exact match between the heat being added to a space and the heat being lost under varying conditions. Until recently, however, truly proportional control of electric heat required the use of expensive, bulky, and heavy equipment. As such, it was not widely used.

These deterrents were eliminated with the introduction of high-power *silicon-controlled rectifiers* (SCR) and *triacs*. Solid-state proportional power controllers are economically practical. In addition, they are compact and lightweight. They may be conveniently incorporated in electric heater control packages. Solid-state controllers offer more than excellent temperature control. They are completely silent in operation, and show a durability potential unknown with mechanical step control devices.

### Theory of operation

A typical solid-state step controller is composed of three basic assemblies:

- a triac or silicon-controlled rectifier in newer equipment

- logic and control circuits

- a low-voltage power supply.

The triac or SCR is a semiconductor power-switching device. It energizes the heater in response to signals from the logic and control circuits. Rating the triac or SCR conservatively and mounting it in a large finned heat sink provides insurance against triac failure. The heat sink is in close thermal contact with the triac or SCR, but is electrically isolated from line voltages. Figure 11-6 on the next page shows the triac assembly and its functional role.

The logic and control circuits obtain proportional control by establishing a base time interval. They energize the heater for a number of ac cycles during each interval, depending on the amount of heat required. The length of this interval is critical. If it is too short, there will be too few ac cycles for precise control. If it is too long, the heating elements will heat up and cool down in each interval. The resulting thermal stresses could reduce the life expectancy of the element and cause wide swings in the discharge air temperature.

In some controllers, a 4-second interval is used. At the beginning of each interval, the logic circuit analyzes the signal from the thermostat. It determines how many ac cycles are required to supply the correct amount of heat. It uses a zero

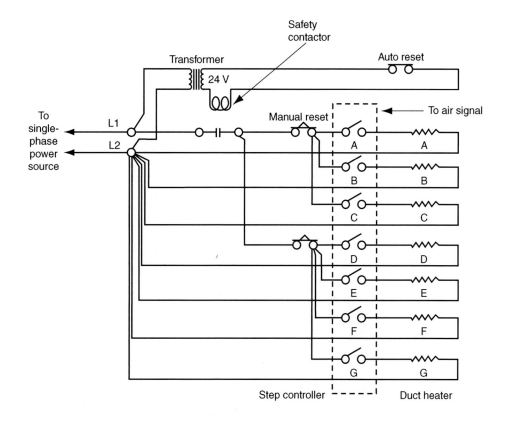

**FIGURE 11-5.** *Single-phase wiring diagram (under 48 A)*

voltage switching system to minimize radio frequency interference. The control circuit turns the triac on for the appropriate number of cycles. At the end of each interval, the circuitry is retriggered to repeat this chain of events continuously.

An internal power supply provides the low-voltage, current-limited power required by the logic and control circuit. This low voltage (less than 10 V) is used on all thermostat and interlock controls. This means that field wiring to these controls need only conform to N.E.C. Class 2 wiring requirements.

The logic and control circuits and power supply are assembled on the triac heat sink assembly so that the control may be installed through the wall of the heater terminal box. The heat sink remains outside the terminal box. This allows convection cooling for the triac and heat sink assembly, yet gives full protection for electronic circuits.

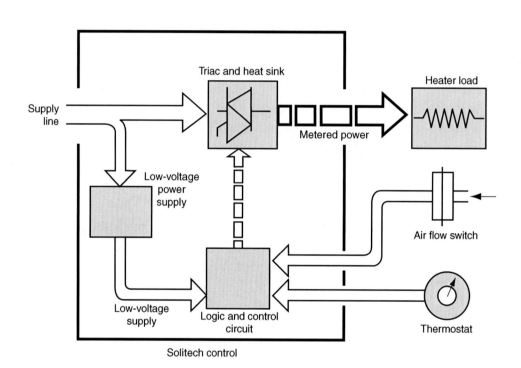

**FIGURE 11-6.** *Solid-state functional diagram*

**Selection and listings**

Take care in specifying and selecting heaters for use with solid-state controllers to achieve maximum economy. Where possible, single-phase heaters should be specified. Keeping the single-phase rating less than the capacity of the automatic reset thermal cut-out eliminates the need for a safety contactor. Typical single-phase solid-state components are represented in Figure 11-7.

Review the kW ratings of controllers being considered when heater ratings are established. Often, a relatively small decrease in heater kW will result in a substantial reduction in the cost of the solid-state controller. These controls supply only the exact amount of heat required to satisfy the input signal. Therefore, it is feasible to standardize heater kW ratings to take advantage of price considerations.

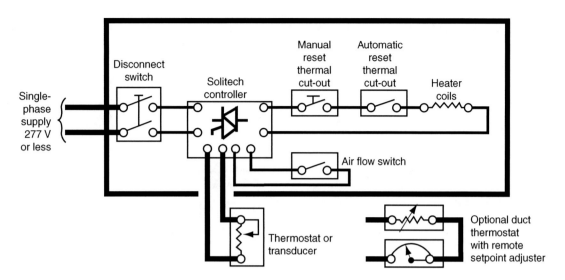

**FIGURE 11-7.** *Typical single-phase low-kW duct heater with built-in disconnect, solid-state controller, air flow switch, and load-carrying automatic and manual reset thermal cut-outs*

For control of a 480-V, three-phase heater with a solid-state controller, a four-wire line must be used. The neutral line must be connected to the heater. Because of this requirement, safety contactors and manual reset thermal cut-outs used on 480-V heaters must break all ungrounded lines. When voltage (three-phase) is 240 V or less, the conventional three-wire network will meet electrical requirements. A typical three-phase 240-V system hookup is shown in Figure 11-8.

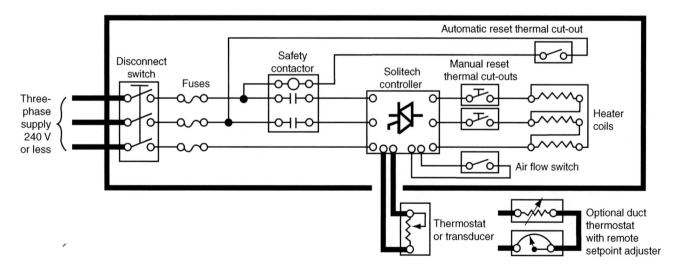

**FIGURE 11-8.** *Typical three-phase duct heater with built-in disconnect, solid-state controller, air flow switch, load-carrying manual reset thermal cut-outs, and pilot-duty automatic reset thermal cut-out with safety contactor*

245

1.  The switches of a mechanical step controller are operated by
    _____.

2.  Can a mechanical step controller control three-phase loads?

3.  What controls the drive motor operation in a mechanical step controller?

4.  What is the function of the second potentiometer in a dual-potentiometer
    step controller?

5.  In Figure 11-1, is the power supply single-phase or three-phase?

6.  What does 2L represent in Figure 11-1?

7.  What happens if the controller throttling range is too narrow?

8.  How many degrees of motor rotation can be obtained on a cam-
    operated step controller?

9.  What should be done if instability or hunting occurs at the suggested
    setting?

10. When will the sequencer motor shaft rotate?

11. Electric duct heater applications require a(n) _____ stage
    differential.

12. Which two terminals in Figure 11-1, if shorted, would cause
    counterclockwise rotation?

13. What does a delay timer do to camshaft rotation?

14. In modulating cooling/sequenced heating control, what happens to the camshaft when power is restored after a failure?

15. What is the direct power source for a pneumatic step controller?

16. How is pneumatic power converted to electric power?

17. What pressure is generally used as a signal by the temperature-sensing device?

18. PE switches are generally used as _____.

19. Proportional control establishes an exact match between _____ to a space and _____.

20. What voltage is required by the logic and control circuit in a solid-state step controller?

# 12

LESSON

# Multi-Step Controllers (Part 2)

## A "BUILDING BLOCK" APPROACH

Several different types of systems are available for controlling electric heating systems. Always follow national and local electrical codes and the manufacturer's installation instructions. One system takes a "building block" approach to controlling electric heat. It is made by Johnson Controls. This system consists of a several controls that can be connected together.

### Control of contactors or sequencers

The first control is an electronic temperature control that has a SPDT (single-pole, double-throw) relay. It can control the contactors or sequencers for the electric heat coils. This temperature control has a wide temperature range, with a differential that ranges from 1 to 30°F. If a cooling thermostat is also included, the thermostats must be set so that heating and cooling do not run at the same time. There should be at least 2°F difference between the heating setting and the cooling setting. Figure 12-1 on the next page shows an electronic temperature control.

**FIGURE 12-1.** *Electronic temperature control*

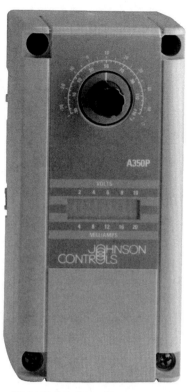

**FIGURE 12-2.** *Electronic PI temperature control*

**FIGURE 12-3.** *Temperature stage module*

### Control of SCR power controllers

The second control is an electronic temperature control with a 0 to 10-V dc output or a 0 to 20-mA output. It can be used to control electronic SCR power controllers. The thermostat has a 10-segment LED that indicates the percentage of output. Figure 12-2 shows this electronic proportional plus integral temperature control. The proportional plus integral (PI) control option holds setpoint regardless of load shifts on the system.

### Adding stages of control

The third control is a *temperature stage module*. It can add up to nine additional stages of control for either the first or second electronic control above. The differential ranges from 1 to 30°F. Figure 12-3 shows a temperature stage module that can be used for multiple staging of boilers or chillers, for staging of refrigeration compressors, or for multiple fan staging for cooling towers.

Outside thermostats can be used with the temperature stage module. This could provide even more stages of heat, or the same number of stages with less temperature differential. This system would also reduce the demand rate if a night setback thermostat were used. With night setback, the demand rate would be less because the space temperature would cool off at night. All of the stages of electric heat would be on until the space temperature reached the setpoint of the space thermostats. With outside thermostats, the outside temperature would control the number of heaters that would come on in the morning. There is a disadvantage, however. It would take longer to recover the space temperature in the morning after a night setback of 5°F or more.

### Controlling discharge air temperature

The fourth control is an electronic *temperature reset control*, shown in Figure 12-4. This module controls the discharge temperature of the electric heat coils. It helps heat the building evenly. The discharge air temperature setting would depend on the air flow, and the heating load of the building. The electronic temperature reset control will adjust the discharge air temperature depending on outside temperature. In other words, the colder the outside temperature, the warmer the discharge air. Using a night setback thermostat reduces the demand rate on all but the coldest days. This is because the space temperature is well below the setpoint of the multi-stage thermostats that are located in the space. All heaters would be on until the space temperature approached the setpoints of the thermostats.

### Temperature display module

The fifth control is a *temperature display module*, shown in Figure 12-5. It displays the actual temperature of the space. The setpoint can also be displayed. All of these controls can be surface-mounted to the wall, or can use DIN rail mounting.

### Other controls

Other modules for sensing pressure and humidity are available. A large SCR power controller, for example, can be controlled by 0 to 5 V dc, 4 to 20 mA, or a 1,000-Ω potentiometer. Some power controller models can handle over 200 A for three-phase heaters. Other models can handle over 550 A for three-phase heaters.

Another type of control system is made by Honeywell. It consists of a thermostat control with either an internal or a remote sensor. The remote sensor can be placed in a secure place to eliminate tampering. There is also a module that is placed in the heating or cooling unit. It has pilot relays that control the heating and cooling functions of the unit. There is

**FIGURE 12-4.** *Electronic temperature reset control*

**FIGURE 12-5.** *Temperature display module*

also an output that is used to control the return air and fresh air damper motor for the economizer function.

This system is available for up to four stages of heat with two stages of cooling. It is also available with three stages of heating and cooling. There is another advantage to this system. Only four thermostat wires need to be run between the thermostat control and the module in the heating or cooling unit. This feature makes retrofit to old units easy. This control system keeps the demand rate low by recovering from night setback by using longer recovery times, if necessary. The economizer keeps air conditioner electricity usage at a minimum.

1. How can you make sure that the heating and cooling do not run at the same time on separate modular thermostats?

2. How does the first modular thermostat, shown in Figure 12-1, control the electric heat coils?

3. How does the second modular thermostat, shown in Figure 12-2, control the electric heat coils?

4. If temperature stage modules are added to either of the above thermostats, how many stages of heat can be controlled?

5. What is the temperature differential range of a temperature stage module?

6. Using outside thermostats with a temperature stage module can provide _____ stages of heat, or the same number of stages with _____ temperature differential.

7. When do outside thermostats reduce the electric demand rate?

8. What are two benefits of an electronic temperature reset control?

9. How much current can a large three-phase SCR power controller carry?

10. Why is a remote sensor for the thermostat desirable?

# Electronic Sequencing Control

## INTRODUCTION

There are numerous control components and assembled units of different manufacture found in the field. You will find both OEM (original equipment manufacturer) equipment and replacements for the original product. Because of this diversity, instructional material must be specific. It is difficult to describe any one component as "typical." This is especially true when electronic and solid-state circuits are involved. Accordingly, this Lesson will concentrate specifically on the Honeywell Models W973 and W7080 electronic sequencing controls. In working with such controls, always follow national and local electrical codes, and the manufacturer's installation instructions.

## W973 ELECTRONIC SINGLE-ZONE SYSTEM

### Design characteristics

Figure 13-1 on the next page is a schematic showing the various components that make up the W973 electronic single-zone system. The component pictured in

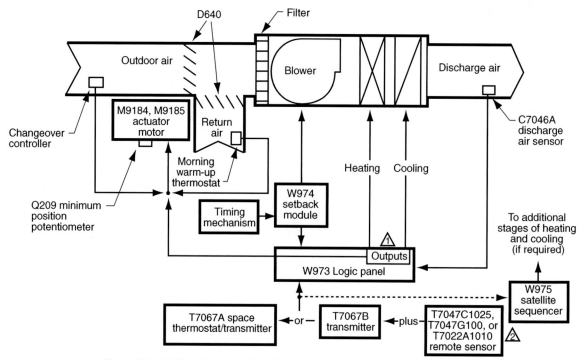

For additional information and wiring diagrams, refer to W973 specification sheet, 60-2428.

⚠ 1  Use switching or modulating outputs as required.

⚠ 2  Use T7047C or T7022 if T7067B is used.

**FIGURE 13-1.** *Typical W973 single-zone system schematic*

Figure 13-2 is the T7067A thermostat and transmitter. It controls the W973 logic panel. It has a temperature adjustment range of 55 to 85°F. The adjustable *deadband* is from 3 to 30°F. Recall that the *deadband* is the area in degrees in which neither cooling nor heating will be called for. If cooling is set for 72°F and heating for 75°F, for example, there is a deadband of 3°F. The thermostat can be ordered with an *integral* temperature sensor or a *remote* temperature sensor. With the remote sensor, the controller can be in a manager's office or a control room and the sensor in the controlled space. This feature helps prevent tampering and vandalism.

The thermostat fits on the *subbase*. It has switches for cooling and heating selections, as well as for fan selections. A *status panel* with six indicator lights for monitoring heating, cooling, and fan functions allows the operator to see what is happening with the mechanical equipment.

The W973 *logic panel* is shown in Figure 13-3. It is designed for surface mounting, and can be mounted in any position. Since there are exposed terminals, the W973 and W975 modules must be mounted

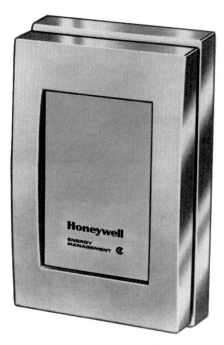

**FIGURE 13-2.** *T7067 thermostat and transmitter*

**FIGURE 13-3.** *W973 logic panel*

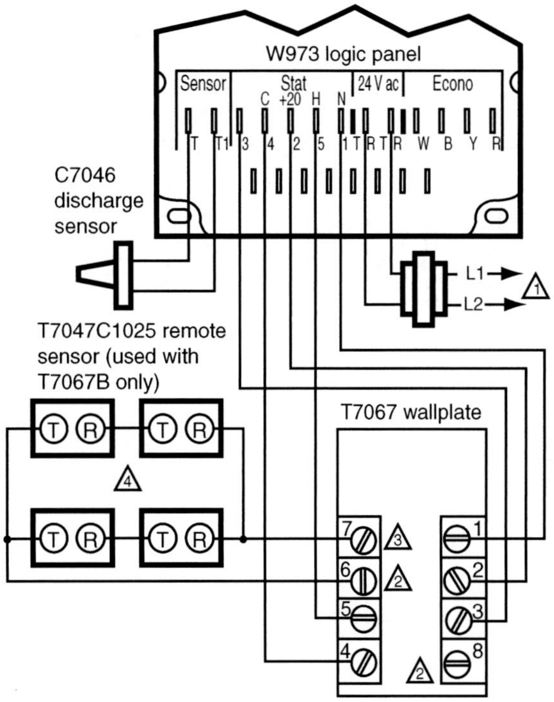

in a panel. The modules are designed for a temperature range of –40 to +150°F. Up to six W973 modules can be controlled from one thermostat. W975 electronic *satellite sequencers* are also available. They increase the number of heating or cooling stages, up to a maximum of ten.

The W974 *setback module* closes the fresh air damper and changes the fan from constant to intermittent during the night setback period. The heating setback is switch-selectable for 5, 10, or 15°F. Depending on the module, the air conditioning can be shut down for the night, or a setback of 5, 8, or 12°F can be selected.

Figure 13-4 on the next page is a diagram for a W973 logic panel with two W975A satellite sequencers. The sequencer on the left can handle up to ten stages of electric heat. The diagram in Figure 13-5 above shows the connection of four remote sensors. They provide an average zone temperature signal. This is useful in a large zone, or if there are windows on one side of the zone. The four sensors will sample temperatures from up to four areas. The average of the four temperatures is sent through the thermostat/transmitter to the logic panel.

The thermostat and transmitter is equipped with heating and cooling LEDs. These lights come on if there is a call for heating or cooling. The lockscrews are tightened so that the heating and cooling levers do not move.

⚠ Power supply. Provide disconnect means and overload protection as necessary.

⚠ Terminal 8 is used with the W774A,B only. Terminal 6 is used with the W974A,B and/or remote sensing element.

⚠ Terminals 6 and 7 are used to connect the remote sensing element to the T7067B only. No screw is provided for terminal 7 with the T7067A.

⚠ Four remote sensors connected as illustrated are required to obtain proper system operation.

**FIGURE 13-5.** *Using four remote sensors to provide an average zone temperature signal*

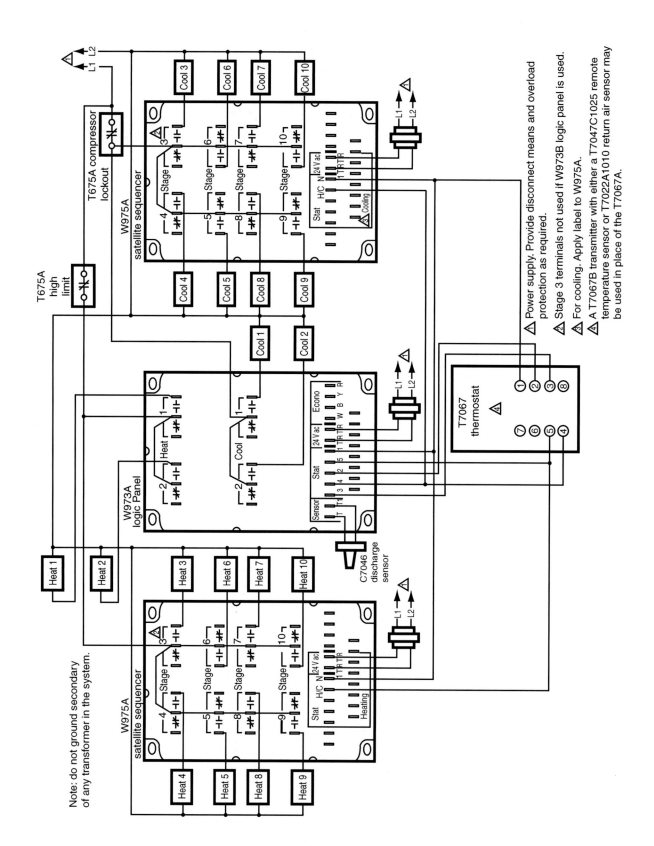

**FIGURE 13-4.** *Using two W975A satellite sequencers to control up to eight additional heating and cooling stages*

## W7080 DUAL-SETPOINT MULTIZONE CONTROL SYSTEM

### Design characteristics

Figure 13-6 shows the various components of the W7080 system. The W7080A *load analyzer* responds to the highest heating and cooling demand signal from the zone thermostats, and controls heating and cooling. This control allows up to three stages of electric heat. Night setback for heat and night cooling shutdown is done by adding a time clock. This unit can be mounted in any position. It works in temperature ranges from –40 to +150°F.

The T7080A thermostat and transmitter controls the W7080A load analyzer. It has a temperature adjustment range of 55 to 85°F. The adjustable deadband is from 3 to 30°F. The thermostat comes with either an integral or remote temperature sensor. With the remote sensor, you can place the temperature controller and transmitter in a control room and the sensor in the controlled

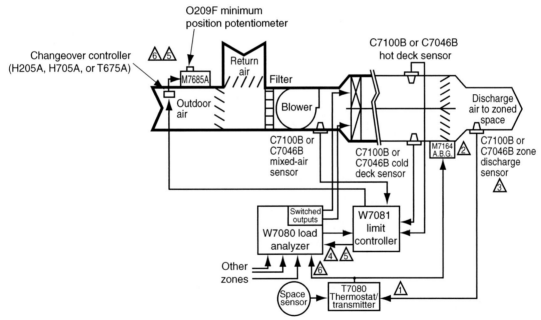

1. Space sensor is integral with T7080A. If remote temperature sensing is desired, use T7080B with T7047C1082 for remote space temperature sensing; use C7100B1013 or C7046B1010 for remote return air temperature sensing.

2. One M7164A, B, G and mixing dampers required for each zone.

3. One C7100B1013 or C7046B1010 required in each zone discharge air stream.

4. Modulated heating and cooling drive signals are available at the HT (heat) and C (cool) terminals of the W7080A load analyzer.

5. Up to six total motors (economizer and modulated valve) can be driven from the V7080 load analyzer. For unison operation. Parallel wire motor drive signal terminals R and C. (Motor O.S. number, signal source, and reference voltage determine actual operation characteristics).

6. The W7080A load analyzer motors require separate transformers. Do not ground any transformer secondary in the system.

**FIGURE 13-6.** *Typical W7080 multizone system schematic*

space. Up to four sensors can be used for one or more areas of a zone to develop an average signal.

The W7081A *limit controller* provides a low limit for the cold deck and a high limit for the hot deck. It also provides economizer and mixed-air low-limit control for the system. The W7083A electronic *heat sequencer* shown in Figure 13-7 is used with the W7080A load analyzer to provide up to five ON/OFF stages of electric heat. The W7084A *zone adder* is used with the W7080A load analyzer to expand the number of zones that can be handled by the load analyzer. Each zone adder handles up to 12 more zones.

The W7001A *discharge air temperature controller* controls either heating or cooling discharge air temperature. With electric heating, this will reduce the kilowatt demand rate. This control is available in heat only, cool only, heat/sequenced, or modulating heat/cool control.

### BUILDING MANAGEMENT SYSTEMS

Building management systems are standard in larger buildings today. A number of different companies manufacture such systems, including such well-known names as Honeywell, Andover, Trane, Johnson Controls, Landis & Gyr, and Robertshaw.

A *building management system* is a DDC (direct digital control) application for controlling lighting, air conditioning, heating, and other equipment such as trash compactors. In many cases, air conditioning or electric heat coils will be turned off for a few minutes if a trash compactor is operating. The system is designed to save energy and keep the demand rate as low as possible.

It is possible from the computer terminal to check the temperature at various points in the ductwork, as well as space temperature. Information such as amperes for blowers, compressors, heating coils, and other equipment is also available. Some systems also can access information for lighting, fire, and other safety information for the building. It is possible to access almost all the parameters of the mechanical system in the building, providing the sensors are installed.

**FIGURE 13-7.** *W7083A electronic heat sequencer*

1.    What is the temperature range of the T7067A thermostat that is used with the Honeywell W973 control system?

2.    What is the temperature range of the adjustable deadband for the T7067A thermostat that is used with the Honeywell W973 control system?

3.    What is a *deadband* for a thermostat?

4.    What is the advantage of the optional remote sensor?

5.    What is the purpose of the optional status panel?

6.    In what position must the W973 logic panel be mounted?

7.    The logic panel can operate in a temperature range of _____ to _____.

8.    How many logic panels can one thermostat control?

9.    What is the purpose of the W975 satellite sequencer?

10.    What is the purpose of the setback module?

11.    What is the advantage of using up to four sensors for the thermostat/transmitter?

12.    What is the purpose of the Honeywell W7078 load analyzer?

13.     In what position must the load analyzer be mounted?

14.     The load analyzer can operate in temperature ranges from _____
        to _____.

15.     What is the temperature adjustment range of the T7080A
        thermostat/transmitter?

16.     What is the deadband range of the T7080A thermostat/transmitter?

17.     How many remote sensors can be used with the T7080A thermostat?

18.     What is the purpose of the W7081A limit controller?

19.     What is the purpose of the W7083A electronic heat sequencer?

20.     What is the purpose of the W7084A zone adder?

21.     What is the purpose of the W7001A discharge air temperature
        controller?

22.     What is the purpose of a building automation or management system?

# 14

LESSON

# Decentralized Electric Heating Systems

## WHAT IS DECENTRALIZED ELECTRIC HEATING?

The term *decentralized* applies to units that do not use a centrally distributed medium to heat a space. Nevertheless, they produce heat in the space. For example, self-contained electric baseboard heaters are decentralized, or non-central, units. Baseboard hot water radiators, however, receive heat from a central boiler. They are considered part of a central heating system.

## TYPES OF DECENTRALIZED HEATING EQUIPMENT

There is a wide variety of types and configurations of decentralized heating equipment. They perform a number of different functions. One type may serve as a *primary source* of heat for an entire building. Another may be intended for *supplemental* use. Supplemental units are typically wall-mounted or portable heaters. They are particularly useful in heating newly added or redecorated space.

263

The most popular types of decentralized units include the following:

- baseboard (either convective or radiant)

- ceiling cable

- radiant ceiling panels

- unit heaters.

Baseboard heaters are a common primary heat source in many homes and buildings. Ceiling cable was used as a source of primary heat in homes a number of years ago. Today it is used rarely, if at all. Unit heaters have been widely used as bathroom and supplementary heaters. Small, fan-equipped unit heater models are now available for whole-house heating.

## HEATING ELEMENTS

Each type of non-central heating unit uses a different type of heating element. *Radiant* or *convective* heaters, which operate at a relatively high temperatures, use open elements. These elements reach operating temperature rapidly when energized. The exact operating temperature varies. It depends on the type of material used for the element, and on the type of heat desired. For example, a radiant heater would probably operate at higher temperatures than a wall-mounted convective heater.

Another element used in non-central heating is the *encapsulated* or completely encased element. The simplest form of encapsulated element is ceiling cable. It has a layer of plastic insulation over it that can withstand the heat. Ceiling cable is designed to operate at very low temperatures. It is used rarely, if at all, today.

Baseboard convectors use a more complicated kind of enclosed element. It has an outer *sheath* of ceramic or metal. The sheath protects the resistance wire from physical damage, corrosion, and deterioration. Electrical insulation between the resistance wire and its outer sheath isolates the element from the enclosure. Heat-dissipating fins add surface area to the element. This increases the rate of heat transfer to the surrounding medium—either air or water.

## BASEBOARD HEATERS

Figure 14-1 shows a typical baseboard heater. It is one of the most popular types of individual room units. Such units are used for general comfort heating in both residential and commercial buildings. They may be used as a total heating plant, or for supplementary heat.

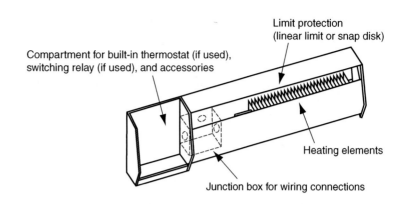

**FIGURE 14-1.** *Typical baseboard heater*

Baseboard units come in a wide range of sizes (heat output ratings). They may use radiant or convective heating methods. Baseboard units have the advantage of taking up little space. They can be placed under windows and along outside walls. This is where the most heat is required to offset heat losses and "cold wall effect." Convective models require only free air circulation across the heating elements. Radiant units, however, require a good "view" of the room. Their use may affect furniture placement.

Nearly all baseboard heaters have built-in limit protection, usually in the form of a *linear limit*. The linear limit has a sensing element that runs the entire length of the baseboard heater. It protects against hot spots caused by blocked circulation. Some baseboard heaters may use *spot-type limits* (snap disks) instead of linear limits.

There are two common methods used to control baseboard heaters. One is a built-in or wall-mounted line-voltage thermostat. The other is a wall-mounted low-voltage thermostat and a switching relay. The control method used will depend on comfort, cost, and installation requirements.

### Baseboard heater with built-in thermostat

The hookup shown in Figure 14-2 shows a typical baseboard heater with a built-in line-voltage thermostat. It is wired to break one side of the power circuit to the heating elements. A built-in limit is wired in series with the thermostat and heating elements. It will break the power circuit if a dangerous over-temperature condition occurs anywhere along the heater length. Baseboards usually use a linear limit. However, they might use one or more snap disks or cartridge limits in series with the heating load.

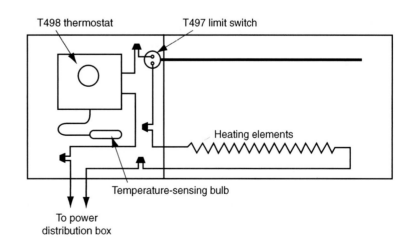

**FIGURE 14-2.** *Baseboard heater with built-in thermostat*

Baseboard units are internally pre-wired. They need only a power connection to put them in operation. The built-in thermostat is very close to the heating elements. It could be affected by heat output of the unit, causing a setpoint *droop*. Avoid this by insulating the wiring compartment from the heating section. There are two other minor points:

- The thermostat is in a less convenient location for reading and setting than it would be on the wall.

- It senses room temperatures near the floor rather than at an average height.

**Baseboard heater with line-voltage wall thermostat**

A line-voltage or low-voltage wall thermostat can control many baseboard heaters. Figure 14-3 shows a single baseboard heater with a line-voltage thermostat.

The thermostat used in this system must be sized to switch the heating load directly. Some local codes require that the thermostat provide a *positive OFF* position. It must break both sides of the power circuit if it is a 108/230, 277, or 480-V circuit. This modification requires running two wires, from the power distribution center to the thermostat and from the thermostat to the heater.

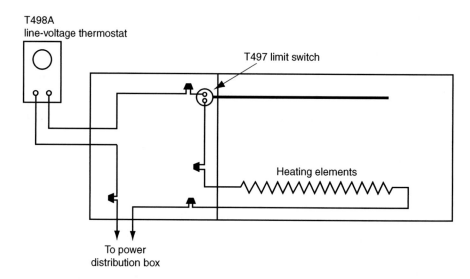

**FIGURE 14-3.** *Baseboard heater with line-voltage wall thermostat*

Installation of this system is not as simple as with built-in thermostat models. It requires line-voltage wiring from the power distribution box to the thermostat and to the baseboard unit. Also, a line-voltage thermostat does not provide the control accuracy of a low-voltage control system.

**Baseboard heater with low-voltage wall thermostat**

Use of a low-voltage wall thermostat requires a *switching relay* in the control system to switch the heating load. The thermostat handles only the power required to energize the low-voltage relay coil. The main advantage of the low-voltage control system is increased control accuracy. Because of its lighter construction, it can use a more sensitive bimetal sensing element. Also, the low-current loads allow the use of adjustable *heat anticipators*. They can be matched exactly to the current draw of the controlled equipment. Internal heat production and droop are not the serious problems they are with the line-voltage thermostat.

Figure 14-4 shows a switching relay controlled by a low-voltage thermostat. The relay is a *direct-following thermal delay relay*. Used with a low-voltage thermostat, it provides four to six cycles per hour. Closing the thermostat contacts energizes a resistance heater in the thermal delay relay. This heat, in turn, actuates a bimetal-operated snap switch. The time delay factor is nominally 75 seconds. High-limit protection is provided by a linear limit control, as in previous hookups.

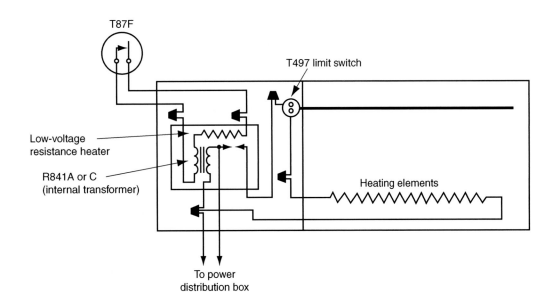

FIGURE 14-4. *Baseboard heater with low-voltage thermostat/switching relay*

The switching relay is usually in the wiring compartment of the baseboard heater. It may, however, be located away from the heater. It can be on a wireway in the basement, in the attic, or almost any location that is convenient.

### Cross control

Switching relays can switch more than one heating load. This makes the low-voltage control system useful in solving special control problems. An example is *cross control*. Cross control can occur when two adjacent spaces have separate heaters under control of separate line-voltage thermostats. It is caused by movement of air from one space to the other. As a result, one thermostat takes control away from the other. This may cause wide temperature swings in one of the spaces.

Attention to thermostat location and setting, and load sizing (Btu output), can minimize cross control. But other variables, such as solar heat and occupancy factors, can still cause problems. The best solution is to control both heaters with a single low-voltage thermostat, with separate relays to switch each heating load. This will cycle all heaters at the same time and give more even heat in the space. Locate the single thermostat where it can sense a representative temperature. Avoid hot or cold locations.

## CEILING CABLE AND PANELS

*Ceiling cable* is another method of non-centralized electric heating. It is used very little, if at all, today. If used, it is usually installed in new homes and apartments during building construction. The cable is embedded directly in the ceiling material. Extra insulation is usually added in the ceiling above the cable.

Common ceiling cable is a continuous length of insulated resistance wire. It has a constant heat output (wattage) for each foot. There are also *radiant ceiling panels* similar in function to ceiling cable. These panels have resistance wire embedded in them, and the entire panel is rated for total heat output.

An advantage of ceiling cable installations is that they are completely out of the usable room space. There is no interference with furniture or drapery location. The warm mass of the total ceiling gives uniform heat delivery. However, because of its large mass, the system cannot respond quickly to changes in demand. Ceiling cable gives room-wide heat distribution. But its radiant warmth does not reach under furniture or other obstructions. Installation limitations may prevent concentration of heat along windows and cold outer walls.

As noted, ceiling cable is a high-mass system. It responds slowly to changes in heat demand. For this reason, it is usually controlled by a line-voltage thermostat, as shown in Figure 14-5. These systems have moderate operating temperatures (100 to 130°F). Thus, no over-temperature limit protection is required.

The first step in using ceiling cable is to calculate the exact amount of heat required for the room. Convert this requirement to the number of feet of ceiling cable that must be used. Then compute the spacing of the cable to provide even room coverage. Mark off the pattern on the ceiling, and staple the cable directly to the under-surface before the finished ceiling is applied. The installer must be aware of code requirements, which may limit the distance that must be left between loops of cable.

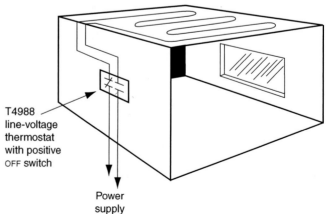

T4988 line-voltage thermostat with positive OFF switch

Power supply

**FIGURE 14-5.** *Ceiling cable with line-voltage thermostat*

Note that cable is often laid out to start and finish in the same spot. Thus, the cable ends can be brought down together to the thermostat and power distribution center. With a double line break (positive OFF) thermostat, shown in Figure 14-5, both ends must be brought to the thermostat. A low-voltage thermostat and relay combination gives closer control. It can also be used to control more than one load from a single thermostat.

In this type of application, the relay and transformer would generally be outside the room, as shown in Figure 14-6. They would usually be on a wireway or J-box near the power distribution center. They could be in the attic (above the ceiling) or some other location closer to each room.

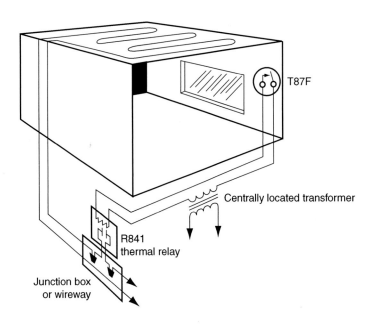

Radiant ceiling panels work on the same principle as embedded ceiling cable. They often respond faster than ceiling cable. The resistance element may be sealed in a medium selected for faster heating characteristics. Glass is an example. The heating element itself is usually in the form of a grid or sheet. It is laminated between layers of the nonconductive material.

Radiant ceiling panels use the same control system as embedded cable. The most common method is a separate line-voltage thermostat for each room.

**FIGURE 14-6.** *Ceiling cable with low-voltage thermostat*

## OTHER DECENTRALIZED HEATING SYSTEMS

Up to this point, this Lesson has covered two types of room-size heating units for residential use—baseboard units and ceiling cable. There are many other types that may be called "room" heaters:

- wall, ceiling, or floor-mounted room heaters

- free-standing room heaters, including decorative fireplace heaters

- portable electric heaters.

Portable electric heaters are usually radiant heating units. Free-standing and wall-mounted types are either radiant or convective heaters.

Radiant heaters are very useful in bathrooms, entry halls, or other areas where quick warmth is desired. Locate them so that heating rays will not be blocked from the desired area. Radiant heaters transfer very little heat to the surrounding air. They effectively heat only objects that are in the direct line of sight of their rays.

Warm air convectors depend on the free circulation of air across the heating elements. They distribute warmth throughout the heated space. Air may circulate through the heater by natural convection, but is often forced through by an internal fan. The fan produces positive circulation and rapid heat distribution. Be careful not to block air circulation. Otherwise, the unit will overheat.

The most common unit in residential applications is the free-standing or wall-mounted heater. It is used for supplementary heat in a bathroom, amusement room, etc. These might be controlled in several ways:

- ON/OFF switch

- built-in thermostat

- line-voltage wall thermostat

- variable switch to select a certain level of constant heat output.

With a built-in or wall thermostat, the control system is the same as that of baseboard heaters. Figure 14-7 shows a typical hookup controlled by a line-voltage thermostat.

## INDUSTRIAL-TYPE UNIT HEATERS

Unit heater design is not limited to the non-central heating equipment used in residential applications. There are a number of different unit-type heaters used in industrial or commercial locations. These are areas that need rugged, heavy-duty heating equipment. The units are usually controlled by a line-voltage thermostat or start/stop switch. Figure 14-8 shows a typical industrial unit heater.

### Operational data by unit size

**Size 0 unit heaters.** These are available in 3, 4, or 5-kW, 208, 240, and 277-V single-phase only. They operate as follows.

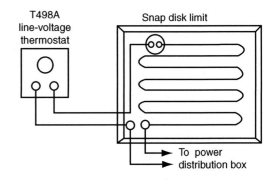

**FIGURE 14-7.** *Unit heater with line-voltage wall thermostat*

The built-in thermostat calls for heat (may not be connected to an external thermostat). This immediately energizes the heating element and fan timer. After a delay of about 20 seconds, the timer contacts close. This allows the fan motor to run. It blows warm air into the space to be heated. When the thermostat is satisfied, the heating element and timer are de-energized. After about 20 seconds, through the action of resetting timer contacts, the fan will shut off. An automatic safety limit control will de-energize the heater upon abnormal temperatures.

**FIGURE 14-8.** *Electric unit heater*

**Size 1 unit heaters.** The unit heater control circuit receives a call for heat. It comes through closing contact action of either a remote low-voltage thermostat connected to the terminals marked "T & T," or a built-in thermostat (optional). This closing thermostat contact action allows contactors R1, R2, and timer to energize. This, in turn, applies power to heating elements. After about 20 seconds, timer contacts will close. This allows the fan to run and blow heated air into the space to be heated. The opposite actions occur when the thermostat is satisfied and its contacts open. Contactors R1, R2, and timer become de-energized. This removes power from heating elements. Through resetting action of the timer, the fan will be de-energized about 20 seconds later. This delay allows stored heat to be removed from the heating elements. There are automatic resetting safety limits in each heating circuit which, upon abnormal temperature, remove element power. They will cycle the elements until the trouble is corrected.

**Field wiring.** Power and low-voltage wiring must be brought in through separate entrances provided. Conduit connections are provided for wiring. The wiring diagram with each heater, inside the control box cover, shows the proper connections.

## FAN COIL UNITS

Another type of de-centralized heating unit for commercial applications is the *fan coil unit* or *unit ventilator*. They are common in motels, schools, and other commercial buildings. Fan coil units are primarily air conditioning units. They may have compressors or receive chilled water from a central source. A heating function may be added by using centrally heated water, or electric coil strip heaters. Classrooms and some other spaces require ventilation as well as heating. Various types of unit ventilators are available. They provide proportional intake of outside air. The air is mixed with the room air, filtered and heated, and then discharged into the occupied space. These units may also include air conditioning.

## MINERAL-INSULATED CABLE

Another variety of de-centralized electric heaters is *mineral-insulated (MI) electric cable*. It is used extensively for pipeline tracing and highway, driveway, and walkway snow removal. It is also effective in heating enclosed areas.

MI cable is available in a wide variety of diameters, voltages, and watts per foot ratings. Watts per foot ratings are nominally 10, 15, 20, 25, 30, 35, 40, 45, and 50 W per linear foot. Cable is produced for use with 120, 208, 240, 277, 440, and 480 supply voltages.

Table 14-1 shows a typical example of MI cable specifications. It gives data for cable with a 10 W per linear foot rating through all of the voltage levels listed above.

### Construction features of MI cable

Cable comes in completely assembled units in lengths ranging from 20 to 2,750 ft. Waterproof end seals are included. This eliminates on-the-job cutting and splicing, and the possibility of moisture infiltration. It also speeds field assembly, and offers an almost foolproof method of installation.

|  | Heated length (ft) | Watts | Amps | Heater diameter |
|---|---|---|---|---|
| **120 V** | 42 | 424 | 3.5 | 0.155 |
|  | 54 | 537 | 4.5 | 0.195 |
|  | 108 | 1078 | 9.0 | 0.246 |
|  | 143 | 1434 | 11.9 | 0.340 |
|  | 181 | 1809 | 15.1 | 0.371 |
|  | 227 | 2268 | 18.9 | 0.402 |
| **208 V** | 74 | 735 | 3.5 | 0.155 |
|  | 93 | 930 | 4.5 | 0.195 |
|  | 187 | 1868 | 9.0 | 0.246 |
|  | 249 | 2486 | 11.9 | 0.340 |
|  | 314 | 3136 | 15.1 | 0.371 |
|  | 393 | 3931 | 18.9 | 0.402 |
| **240 V** | 85 | 848 | 3.5 | 0.155 |
|  | 107 | 1073 | 4.5 | 0.195 |
|  | 216 | 2155 | 9.0 | 0.246 |
|  | 287 | 2868 | 11.9 | 0.340 |
|  | 362 | 3618 | 15.1 | 0.371 |
|  | 454 | 4535 | 18.9 | 0.402 |
| **277 V** | 98 | 979 | 3.5 | 0.155 |
|  | 124 | 1239 | 4.5 | 0.195 |
|  | 249 | 2487 | 9.0 | 0.246 |
|  | 331 | 3311 | 11.9 | 0.340 |
|  | 418 | 4176 | 15.1 | 0.371 |
|  | 523 | 5234 | 18.9 | 0.402 |
| **440 V** | 526 | 5259 | 11.9 | 0.340 |
|  | 663 | 6633 | 15.1 | 0.371 |
|  | 832 | 8315 | 18.9 | 0.402 |
| **480 V** | 574 | 5737 | 11.9 | 0.340 |
|  | 724 | 7236 | 15.1 | 0.371 |
|  | 907 | 9071 | 18.9 | 0.402 |

**TABLE 14-1.** *MI cable specifications for dual-conductor cable at 10 W per foot*

The inorganic materials in MI cable are copper and magnesium oxide. They make it fireproof, non-fire causing, and almost indestructible. Its operational life is affected only by oxidation of the copper sheath that houses the insulation and resistance wire, or in extreme conditions by the melting point of copper (1,083°C). The insulation itself is heat-stable up to 2,800°C. MI cable's solid construction and gas-tight, liquid-tight, seamless copper sheathing make it impervious to dirt, water, and even condensation accumulation.

## INFRARED HEATERS AND ELEMENT TYPES

Spot-type heating may be called for to handle hard-to-heat areas, especially those whose heat losses are excessive and continuous. The answer is usually found in *infrared* heaters. They provide efficient heating for areas such as bus terminals, loading platforms, warehouses, factories, garages, curb markets, etc.

| Type of area | Watt density per square foot of floor area |
|---|---|
| Open areas—marquees, etc. | 30 to 40 |
| Partly sheltered | 20 to 25 |
| Poorly insulated or drafty | 12 to 15 |
| Well-insulated | 6 to 10 |

**TABLE 14-2.** *General rules for selecting watt densities*

The amount of infrared heating required varies widely with design conditions. In calculating heat loss and total watts required, consider that only about half of the energy from this class of heater is transferred to the target area as radiant heat. The other half is dissipated by convection. Data such as those in Table 14-2 will help to develop general rule-of-thumb watt densities, based on total energy per square foot of floor area. The choice between *quartz tube* or *metal-clad element* heaters is a minor matter. Both produce about the same radiation efficiency.

## Application data

A typical intensity pattern of a 60° reflector is shown in Figure 14-9. Actual intensity will vary. It will be about the square of the distance from the heat source to the target area.

Look at the large areas shown in plans A and B in Figure 14-10 on the next page. Tables 14-3 and 14-4 on page 275 give the watt densities and spacing for fixtures in such areas. These factors will provide near-uniform heat distribution.

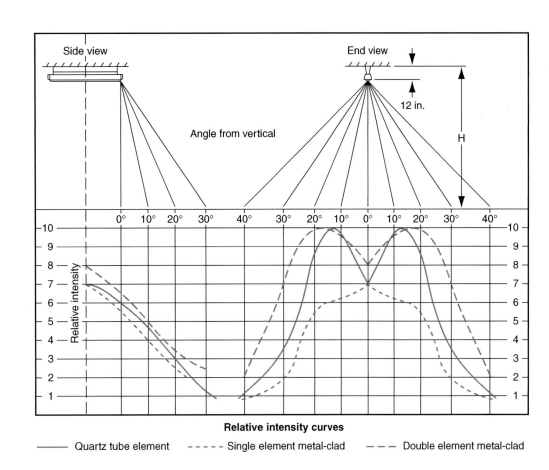

**FIGURE 14-9.** *Intensity pattern for 60° reflector*

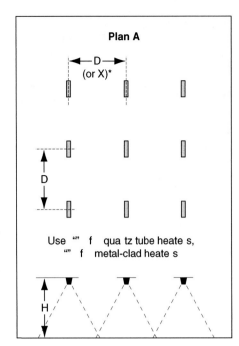
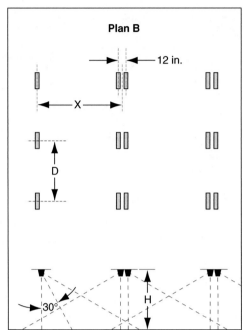

**FIGURE 14-10.** *Spacing arrangements*

Electric infrared heaters are designed to put productive energy exactly where it is wanted. This is done by controlling the angle of radiation with *reflectors*. Reflectors are classed as follows:

- 90° broad beam

- 60° medium beam

- 45° controlled beam

- marquee type.

### Quartz tube elements

The *quartz tube* is a coiled nichrome element within a fused quartz tube. The space inside the tube is air-filled. The element is supported by the tube itself. The tube is capped (not sealed) by porcelain or metal terminal blocks. It stands up well against splashing. It has medium resistance to vibration and low resistance to impact.

The quartz tube has a quicker response time than the metal sheath heater, but with similar low luminosity. It can be controlled by a simple *percentage input timer* with the pulses particularly noticeable visually only on low-percentage settings. It has higher radiating efficiency under percentage timer control than the metal sheath heater.

### Metal sheath elements

The *metal sheath* heater is a nichrome resistor embedded in an electrical insulating refractory within a metal tube. It is the most rugged of the three sources. It stands up well against impact, vibration, and splashing.

| Height "H" (from floor) | Spacing "D" | Approximate square feet | Average watts per square foot for fixtures below | | | | |
|---|---|---|---|---|---|---|---|
| | | | 1,000 W | 1,500 W | 2,000 W | 3,000 W | 4,000 W |
| 8 | 8 | 64 | 15.6 | 23.4 | 31.2 | | |
| 9 | 9 | 81 | 12.3 | 18.5 | 24.6 | 37.0 | |
| 10 | 10 | 100 | 10.0 | 15.0 | 20.0 | 30.0 | 40.0 |
| 11 | 11 | 121 | 8.3 | 12.4 | 16.6 | 24.8 | 33.0 |
| 12 | 12 | 144 | 7.0 | 10.4 | 13.9 | 20.8 | 27.8 |
| 13 | 13 | 169 | 5.9 | 8.9 | 11.8 | 17.8 | 23.6 |
| 14 | 14 | 196 | 5.1 | 7.6 | 10.2 | 15.3 | 17.8 |
| 15 | 15 | 225 | 4.5 | 6.7 | 8.9 | 13.3 | 17.8 |
| 16 | 16 | 256 | | 5.8 | 7.8 | 11.7 | 15.6 |
| 17 | 17 | 289 | | 5.2 | 6.9 | 10.4 | 13.8 |
| 18 | 18 | 324 | | 4.7 | 6.2 | 9.3 | 12.3 |

**TABLE 14-3.** *Approximate coverage and recommended spacing for various mounting heights (H) with vertical radiation (see Figure 14-10, Plan A)*

| Height "H" Spacing "D" | Spacing "X" (ft) | Approximate square feet | Average watts per square foot for fixtures below | | | | |
|---|---|---|---|---|---|---|---|
| | | | 1,000 W | 1,500 W | 2,000 W | 3,000 W | 4,000 W |
| 8 | 12.0 | 48 | 20.8 | 31.2 | | | |
| 9 | 13.5 | 61 | 16.4 | 24.6 | 32.8 | | |
| 10 | 15.0 | 75 | 13.3 | 20.0 | 26.7 | 40.0 | |
| 11 | 16.5 | 91 | 11.0 | 16.5 | 22.0 | 33.0 | |
| 12 | 18.0 | 108 | 9.3 | 13.9 | 18.6 | 27.8 | 37.2 |
| 13 | 19.5 | 127 | 7.9 | 11.8 | 15.7 | 23.6 | 31.5 |
| 14 | 21.0 | 147 | 7.1 | 10.7 | 14.3 | 21.4 | 28.6 |
| 15 | 22.5 | 169 | 6.0 | 8.9 | 11.9 | 17.8 | 23.8 |
| 16 | 24.0 | 192 | 5.2 | 7.8 | 10.4 | 15.6 | 20.8 |
| 17 | 25.5 | 218 | 4.6 | 6.9 | 9.2 | 13.8 | 18.4 |
| 18 | 27.0 | 243 | 4.1 | 6.2 | 8.2 | 12.3 | 16.5 |

**TABLE 14-4.** *Approximate coverage and recommended spacing for radiation at 45° angle, for relatively high-density and low ceiling installations (see Figure 14-10, Plan B)*

The response time of the metal sheath heater is about two to five minutes. This permits the use of a simple percentage input timer control to maintain any temperature from full ON to full OFF fairly consistently because of the thermal mass storage of the element during the OFF period. At full operation, the heaters emit a dull red glow, with no glare even at maximum wattage. Reduced-voltage operation is not recommended because of the drastic reduction of radiating efficiency.

Metal sheath radiant heaters are designed for about 47 W per inch of ⅜-in. diameter tube. They normally operate at 1,200 to 1,500°F. They may be installed in any position. For top efficiency, shield the metal sheath element against wind.

### Quartz lamps

*Quartz tubes* are designed for about 34 W per inch of ⅜-in. diameter tube. They normally operate at 1,200 to 1,500°F. The quartz tube must be horizontal during operation or the element may sag. This will result in element failure. Drafts or wind have little effect on the infrared radiating efficiency of the quartz tube.

The *quartz lamp* consists of a coiled tungsten filament. It is positioned in a straight line and away from the quartz tube by tantalum spacers. The filament is sealed into the ends of the ⅜-in. diameter quartz tube, which is exhausted and filled with inert gas.

Quartz lamps are normally designed for 100 W per inch of ⅜-in. diameter (T-3) lamp. The filament operates at approximately 4,000°F. They have an extremely rapid warm-up time, just a few seconds. They emit a substantial amount of visible light—about 750 lumens per inch of lamp length, compared to the typical fluorescent tube output of about 67 lumens per inch of length.

Drafts or wind have a negligible effect on the infrared radiating efficiency of the quartz lamp. Typical examples of the precise angles of radiation produced by infrared heating are shown in Figure 14-11.

### TYPICAL SPECIFICATIONS

### Broad or medium beam infrared heaters
### (90° or 60° included radiation angle)

The Chromalox RD infrared heater is a typical double-element fixture. It is installed much like an ordinary light fixture. Metal sheath, quartz tube, or quartz lamp elements may be used interchangeably, depending on installation changes and demands. Reflectors can also be interchanged between fixtures of the same size if a change in beam pattern is needed. Fixtures are available in four basic lengths. The element types used are located at the focus of two optically correct reflectors. These fixtures are designed specifically for indoor applications.

All wiring is single-ended, insulated, nickel-plated stranded copper, with 6 in. of wire available for junction box connections. The junction box may be mounted at either end or on top.

Bracket-type fixtures may be fastened directly to the ceiling or wall. They have a standard adjustable mounting bracket that can be positioned at 15, 30, or 45° in either direction. Studs may be used. The fixtures are easily adjusted for either one stud in the center or two studs, one on either end. Another mounting option is the use of one or two 16-gauge steel chains on each end. This is a method for which this fixture is easily adapted.

All lamp reflectors have a polished aluminum finish, either 60° symmetrical, 60° asymmetrical, or 90° symmetrical. Complete control information is provided with every unit.

The Chromalox SKR is another typical infrared heater in the medium beam category. It has a metal sheath element. The heating element is a totally enclosed, refractory-insulated tubular element. It is alloy-sheathed, located at the focus of a parabolic reflector, and mounted on secondary insulation to withstand high voltage.

The reflector is polished aluminum. It is accessible from the face side. Fixture stems provide a minimum 12-in. spacing from combustible ceilings. Each stem has an attractive canopy. Stems may be bent with a conduit-bending tool to direct the radiation pattern where desired.

Wiring is the same kind, and the method of installation is the same, as in type RD. A protective grille to prevent accidental contact with the element is standard equipment. To comply with UL requirements, type SKR heaters must be installed with the following minimum spacings:

- 12 in. from the ceiling, as provided with fixture stems

- 6 ft from the floor

- 24 in. from walls.

90° broad beam

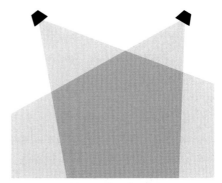
60° medium beam

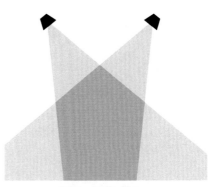
45° controlled beam

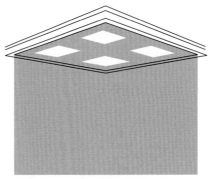
Marquee heater

**FIGURE 14-11.** *Infrared heating patterns*

*Note*: 275-V heaters should *not* be connected in series for 550-V operation.

Chromalox KR heaters have a flexible metallic conduit with a standard polarized male plug instead of fixture stems. They have sliding mounting clamps for attachment to supports. This type of heater is good for portable comfort heating applications since it can be easily mounted by chains, straps, or other common means. It can be mounted at various angles to accommodate a wide range of conditions.

*Marquee* infrared heaters are designed for recess mounting. Infrared marquee heating should be installed with an average intensity of 150 to 200 W per square foot of sidewalk area under the marquee. Multiply the sidewalk area in square feet by 150 and by 200 to find the total minimum and maximum wattage to install. Either quartz tube, quartz lamp, or metal sheath elements may be used for the voltage range available. Metal sheath and quartz tube heating elements rated at 240 V perform at 75% of rated wattage when operated at 208 V. Reflectors are available in 30° symmetrical, 30° asymmetrical, and 60 or 90° symmetrical. Because of vagrant heat, marquee heaters should be installed only in non-combustible marquee construction.

A *controlled beam* infrared heater is designed to contain and control all radiation in a definite, tight pattern. As a result, more positive comfort may be planned and obtained. Radiation is more uniform because heat can be directed effectively. Radiation can be leveled out so that workers in the heat pattern move about with no extremes of radiant energy to produce discomfort.

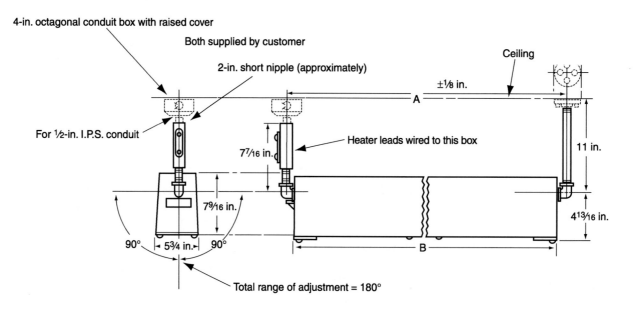

**FIGURE 14-12.** *Suggested method of mounting and wiring fixture*

The heating source in a controlled beam fixture can be a quartz tube, quartz lamp, or metal sheath element. This type of fixture may be installed indoors or outdoors. Accordingly, the construction is weatherproof. Fixture stems provide a minimum 8½-in. spacing below the mounting surface. Wiring is single-end with 6 in. available for connection. Figure 14-12 shows a convenient way of connecting heater wires to the power supply. It also shows a typical mounting method. Since it is designed for high mounting, cranes and tall equipment are no obstacle to the effective use of this system. The controlled beam fixture focuses radiation within the desired area. It gets maximum radiation efficiency from the electrical input by redirecting spill and scatter radiation into the useful controlled pattern.

### Guides to efficient spot heating

Figure 14-13 shows a typical infrared *spot* heater. Follow these principles to design the most efficient infrared comfort installation for spot heating:

1. Irradiate personnel from at least two directions, preferably at about a 45° angle, so more of the area of the person is covered.

2. Tilt so that the upper limit of the beam is about 6 ft above the center of the work station.

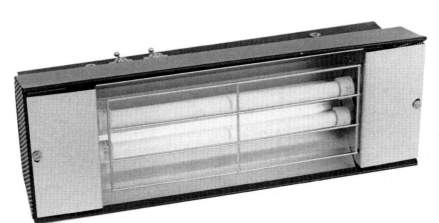

FOSTORIA INDUSTRIES, INC.

3. Keep the total level of radiation as constant as possible throughout the irradiated area.

4. Keep fixtures out of the way of materials being moved.

**FIGURE 14-13.** *Infrared spot heater*

5. Do not irradiate any outside walls.

6. Do not irradiate any surfaces over 6 ft above the floor.

7. Provide means of "stepping" the level of radiation furnished.

8. For outdoor applications, provide wind shields for personnel and twice the level of radiation.

9. Treat the heating of areas over 50 ft minimum dimension as complete areas.

## DETERMINING FIXTURE REQUIREMENTS

Refer to the information contained in Table 14-5 for data drawn from the Chromalox pocket guide for infrared comfort heating.

### Point-by-point analysis method

1. Refer to Tables 14-6, 14-7, and 14-8 on the following pages to find the width of the radiation pattern. The length of the radiation pattern is width plus fixture length.

2. Select tentative mounting locations, and the type of fixture and element to be used. Base your selection on the tabulated width of the pattern, and on details of characteristics of the application.

3. For tentative mounting locations, determine the total watts received at each point in the heated area from all fixtures radiating it. Total watts is based on tabulated 1 ft heated length of the type of element selected. Keep within 20% of average at all important points.

4. Divide the determined average density into design watts input density for this application. This quotient gives the feet of heated length required for each fixture.

5. Different length fixtures or fixtures mounted at different distances from the target may be desired. If so, determine watts input density from each fixture. Adjust the element lengths and distances respectively.

1. 50 W per square foot total from at least two directions (not overhead) focused just below the waist.

2. Install 1 W for each degree of operational temperature desired above the minimum ambient ever reached. (Minimum installed density 12 W per square foot.)

3. For 90° and 60° beam fixtures, add 5% additional capacity for each foot greater than 10 ft between worker and fixture. (SKM, SKL, and SKQ fixtures do not require this adjustment.)

4. For outdoor applications, provide adequate wind shields and 2 W per foot for each degree of operational temperature increase desired.

5. For complete area applications, install 0.5 watt per square foot for each degree of operational temperature desired.

**TABLE 14-5.** *Chromalox pocket guide for infrared comfort heating*

| Distance from fixture (ft) | Width of radiation (ft) | Input density (W/ft²) | | |
| | | Quartz tube 34 W per inch SKL | Metal sheath 47 W per inch SKM | Quartz lamp 100 W per inch SKQ |
|---|---|---|---|---|
| 6 | 5.0 | 13.6 | 18.8 | 40.0 |
| 7 | 5.8 | 10.4 | 14.3 | 30.5 |
| 8 | 6.6 | 8.1 | 11.2 | 23.9 |
| 9 | 7.5 | 6.5 | 8.9 | 18.9 |
| 10 | 8.3 | 5.3 | 7.3 | 15.6 |
| 11 | 9.1 | 4.4 | 6.1 | 13.0 |
| 12 | 9.9 | 3.7 | 5.1 | 10.9 |
| 15 | 12.4 | 2.5 | 3.4 | 7.2 |
| 20 | 16.6 | 1.4 | 1.9 | 4.1 |
| 25 | 20.7 | 0.91 | 1.3 | 2.7 |
| 30 | 24.8 | 0.64 | 0.88 | 1.9 |
| 35 | 29.0 | 0.47 | 0.65 | 1.4 |
| 40 | 33.1 | 0.36 | 0.50 | 1.1 |
| 45 | 37.3 | 0.29 | 0.39 | 0.84 |
| 50 | 41.4 | 0.23 | 0.32 | 0.69 |

**TABLE 14-6.** *45° beam fixture for 1 ft heated length*

### Simplified method

1.  Find the dimensions of the area to be heated.

2.  Choose a tentative location for the fixtures (or set of fixtures).

3.  Select the beam characteristics, and the fixtures and elements to be used.

4.  Based on the results of Steps 2 and 3, determine if the design pattern fits the work station area.

5.  If the pattern doesn't fit the work station well, see if other beam characteristics will fit better.

6.  Determine the watts input density required for the lowest temperature the system is expected to combat.

7.  Multiply the watts input density from Step 6 by the area in square feet of design pattern. The answer is installed watts required.

8.  Select fixtures with the total wattage determined in Step 7. Indicate placement at the tentative locations selected in Step 2.

| Distance from fixture (ft) | Width of radiation (ft) | Input density (W/ft$^2$) | | |
|---|---|---|---|---|
| | | Quartz tube 34 W per inch RDS, RDA | Metal sheath 47 W per inch RDS, RDA, SKR, KR | Quartz lamp 100 W per inch RDS, RDA |
| 6 | 6.9 | 7.6 | 10.5 | 22.4 |
| 7 | 8.1 | 5.5 | 7.7 | 16.3 |
| 8 | 9.2 | 4.4 | 6.0 | 12.8 |
| 9 | 10.4 | 3.4 | 4.8 | 10.1 |
| 10 | 11.5 | 2.8 | 3.9 | 8.3 |
| 11 | 12.7 | 2.3 | 3.2 | 6.9 |
| 12 | 13.9 | 2.0 | 2.7 | 5.8 |
| 15 | 17.3 | 1.3 | 1.8 | 3.8 |
| 20 | 23.1 | 0.73 | 1.0 | 2.2 |
| 25 | 28.9 | 0.47 | 0.65 | 1.4 |
| 30 | 34.6 | 0.33 | 0.46 | 0.98 |
| 35 | 40.4 | 0.24 | 0.34 | 0.72 |
| 40 | 46.2 | 0.19 | 0.26 | 0.55 |
| 45 | 52.0 | 0.15 | 0.21 | 0.44 |
| 50 | 57.7 | 0.12 | 0.17 | 0.35 |

**TABLE 14-7.** *60° beam fixture for 1 ft heated length*

### CONTROLLING INFRARED HEATERS

For controlling quartz lamp installations, provide three or more circuits of about equal capacity. Each should radiate a relatively uniform pattern over the entire area when operated alone. They should overlap for full operation. For reduced capacity in mild weather, operate only the circuits required for comfort.

Control of quartz tube or metal sheath heaters is similar. Provide three or more circuits in the same manner. However, one of the circuits should have an input controller and contactors. In this way, manual switching of circuits plus the one pulsed circuit gives an indefinite number of effective capacities as well as economical operation.

Provide limit thermostats, one for freeze protection and one for limiting ambient buildup. These should be on at least one of the circuits of any system of control suggested above.

### Input controllers

For selective control of one or more heaters, cycling devices on which the desired heat can be dialed are the answer. Operating on a 30-second cycle, the dial is calibrated in percentage of ON time for each cycle. By dialing, wattage is reduced until the desired comfort level is reached on milder days. Both flush and surface-mounted types are available.

A packaged pre-wired combination of input controller, pilot lights, fuse block, and line switch is in reality an input controller panel. To connect to infrared heaters, simply bring two leads from the supply and run two leads to the contactor. Timer motors in these units are available for both 115 and 230-V supply. Contact capacity ranges from 20 to 25 A. In most cases, a 230-V rated motor may be operated on 208 V without any complications. Check with the equipment manufacturer to be sure.

### Line-voltage thermostat control

| Distance from fixture (ft) | Width of radiation (ft) | Input density (W/ft$^2$) | | |
|---|---|---|---|---|
| | | Quartz tube 34 W per inch RDB | Metal sheath 47 W per inch RDB | Quartz lamp 100 W per inch RDB |
| 6 | 12.0 | 2.6 | 3.6 | 7.7 |
| 7 | 14.0 | 1.9 | 2.7 | 5.7 |
| 8 | 16.0 | 1.5 | 2.1 | 4.4 |
| 9 | 18.0 | 1.2 | 1.7 | 3.5 |
| 10 | 20.0 | 0.97 | 1.3 | 2.9 |
| 11 | 22.0 | 0.81 | 1.1 | 2.4 |
| 12 | 24.0 | 0.68 | 0.94 | 2.0 |
| 15 | 30.0 | 0.44 | 0.61 | 1.3 |
| 20 | 40.0 | 0.25 | 0.34 | 0.73 |
| 25 | 50.0 | 0.16 | 0.22 | 0.47 |
| 30 | 60.0 | 0.11 | 0.15 | 0.33 |
| 35 | 70.0 | 0.08 | 0.11 | 0.24 |
| 40 | 80.0 | 0.06 | 0.09 | 0.19 |
| 45 | 90.0 | 0.05 | 0.07 | 0.15 |
| 50 | 100.0 | 0.04 | 0.06 | 0.12 |

**TABLE 14-8.** *90° beam fixture for 1 ft heated length*

Thermostats automatically limit room temperatures. They cut off heaters as needed to maintain a preset maximum temperature, or turn them on for freeze protection. Each thermostat is used with one or more heaters within its electrical rating. Higher ratings require a magnetic contactor. A thermostat must be the snap-action type for use with a contactor.

A typical heavy-duty, single-stage, line-voltage thermostat offers positive accuracy and long, reliable service. It has a patented hydraulic action for rapid response, a rugged snap-action switch with silvered contacts, fully protected against dust, and a tough metallic gray finish. Capacities are as follows: 5,000 W at 277 V, 5,280 W at 240 V, 3,000 W at 120 V ac, SPST, 40 to 80°F range, with a 3°F differential.

### To operate thermostats and VC controllers on higher ratings

Magnetic contactors for ac control are used to energize heating loads that exceed the power-handling capacity of line-voltage thermostats or manual switches. Heavy-duty contacts carry heavier currents at line voltages up to 550 V. Standard holding coil voltages are 120, 208, 240, and 277 V, 60 Hz, UL-listed for line voltages up to 550 V. For a single-phase or two-wire power supply to a heater circuit, a two-pole contactor is used.

### Single-phase operation

All heaters are connected in parallel for single-phase operation. Total single-phase current in amperes is total wattage divided by circuit voltage. If this current does not exceed the input controller or thermostat capacity, then the input controller may be used as shown in Figure 14-14A. It directly controls selected heaters through the limiting thermostat. If the heater load current or voltage rating is greater than the input controller or thermostat capacity, the contactor wired as shown in Figure 14-14B must be used.

### Three-phase operation

Heaters should be selected in multiples of three for the most economical three-phase operation. Total the wattage of each group of three (or six, nine, etc.)

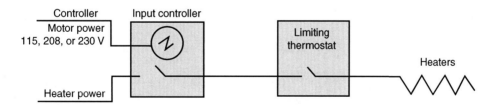

**A. Single phase when heater load is within capacity of input controller and thermostat**

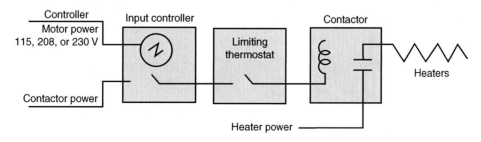

**B. Polyphase or single phase when heater load is greater than capacity of input controller and thermostat**

**FIGURE 14-14.** *Wiring diagrams (ac only)*

identical heaters. Divide by the three-phase voltage and by 1.73. The result is the three-phase current to handle, for which the next larger capacity three-pole contactor is required.

Select an input controller of the same voltage rating as the contactor holding coil. When this is done, the controller motor power supply may be the same as the contactor power supply. Make connections as shown in Figure 14-14B.

### Low-voltage thermostat control

Most heating experts agree that a low-voltage thermostat gives more efficient electric heat control than a line-voltage type. With the low-voltage type of control, a contactor or relay must be installed. This component has a low-voltage holding coil or warp switch heater. It is energized by the low-voltage thermostat circuit (24 V ac) and closes the relay's main contacts to energize heaters.

An application of a low-voltage thermostat to a one-heater system is shown in Figure 14-15. An application in which thermostat is used to control two electric heaters is shown in Figure 14-16.

A line-voltage thermostat on a heater fixture with temperature control problems can be converted to a low-voltage thermostat for better control. If cross control is the problem, a wall-mounted low-voltage thermostat is a sure way of solving the problem and avoiding repeat complaints. The change replaces the line-voltage thermostat with two new components, the T87F low-voltage thermostat and the R841 heating relay.

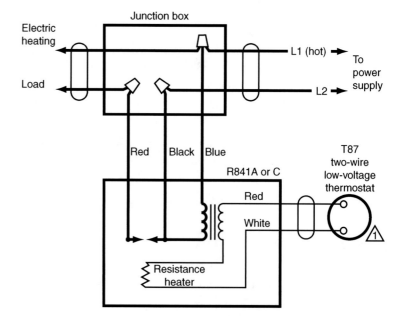

⚠ Set adjustable heat anticipation heater at 0.2 amps.

**FIGURE 14-15.** *Low-voltage thermostat conversion (one heater with one thermostat)*

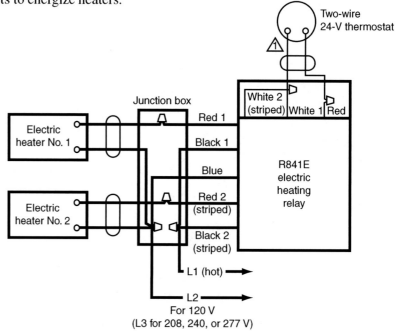

⚠ Set adjustable heat anticipation heaters at 0.4 amps.

**FIGURE 14-16.** *Low-voltage thermostat conversion (two heaters and one R841E relay with one thermostat)*

The first step in electric heating service or repair is to make the equipment safe to work on. First, disconnect all electric power to the heating units to be serviced. Then disconnect and remove the line-voltage thermostat. If it is built-in, open the heater access door, cover, or plate and unfasten the thermostat. Disconnect the wires at the line-voltage thermostat and at the heater, and remove the old thermostat. Install the low-voltage thermostat and relay in the heater control compartment. Connect it as shown in either Figure 14-15 or 14-16, as required. If the low-voltage thermostat is to be wall-mounted, run two thermostat wires to the location chosen. Connect these wires to the thermostat terminals on the relay installed in the electric heater control compartment. Mount and wire the thermostat according to the instructions furnished.

1.  Do baseboard hot water radiators constitute decentralized heat?

2.  Name two general functions of decentralized heating equipment.

3.  Name the most popular types of decentralized electric heating units.

4.  Where are open elements used?

5.  Which would operate at a higher temperature, a radiant heater or a wall-mounted convector?

6.  What type of insulation does ceiling cable have?

7.  What is the outer sheath that protects the heating element of a baseboard heater made of?

8.  What is done to increase the rate of heat transfer from the heating element of a baseboard heater?

9.  Where are baseboard heaters usually located?

10. How does a linear heat limit operate?

11. What type of thermostat generally controls the room temperature of a baseboard heater?

12. Why should the wiring compartment of a baseboard heater be effectively insulated?

13. What must be done to meet electrical code requirements for a positive OFF position?

14. Why are baseboard heaters with built-in thermostats more desirable than wall thermostats?

15. Which is more accurate, a line-voltage system or a low-voltage system?

16. What items required for a low-voltage control circuit are not necessary for a line-voltage installation?

17. Are heat anticipators used with low-voltage or line-voltage controls?

18. Where may the switching relay be located for a baseboard heater?

19. What precautions should be taken when you locate a wall thermostat?

20. When is ceiling cable usually installed?

21. What is the most common ceiling cable?

22. Name two types of ceiling applications.

23. What are the advantages of ceiling cable?

24. Why does a ceiling cable system respond slowly to changes in heat demand?

25. What type of thermostat controls a ceiling cable installation?

26. Do radiant ceiling panels respond slower or faster than embedded ceiling cable?

27. Name some applications for radiant electric heaters.

28. What is MI cable?

29. Where is infrared heating most useful?

30. What are the two types of infrared heaters?

# 15

**LESSON**

# Electric Boilers

## ELECTRIC-HYDRONIC SYSTEMS

Cast iron and steel boilers have been in use for many years. They have utilized solid, liquid, and gaseous fuels. These fuels have been used for residential, commercial, and industrial heating applications. Today there is a fourth "fuel"—electricity.

Electric energy is converted into heat for *hydronic* systems in several ways. One of these is the *electric boiler*. Residential types are compact. They generally have a water capacity of only two or three gallons. They are small enough to hang on a wall. Small size is possible because water has a much higher heat-carrying capacity than air, and the electric elements are immersed directly in the water. This saves space and provides very rapid heating of the water. Nearly all the heat produced by the elements transfers directly to the water.

## TYPES AND SIZES

*Electric-hydronic* systems are much like other electric heating systems, such as electric resistance systems, in both efficiency and operating cost. Wall-mounted types may measure 24 in. high by 30 in. wide by 16 in. deep. Btu per hour (Btuh) ratings range from 12,000 to 300,000. Conventional floor models are rated from 10,000 Btuh to as high as 6,000,000 Btuh.

**289**

The most common systems are:

- Central systems with a boiler and storage facility. They take advantage of off-peak power periods at lower kWh rates.

- Central systems with a boiler that uses multiple electrodes suspended in liquid.

- Central systems with a boiler that uses single or multiple sheathed elements.

There are two basic categories of electric boilers. One category produces hot water or generates steam in a conventional hydronic system. In other words, it is a system that heats and recirculates water. Or, it generates and circulates steam, which returns to the boiler as condensate.

The other group of electric boilers generates steam without any condensate return arrangement. This type of installation is called a *steam humidification* application. The design of this type of boiler must take into account the buildup of solids that occurs when water is boiled off. The solids left behind in the vessel can clog it and reduce heat transfer. The boilers have two features to cope with this problem. One is an automatic *blowdown* feature, which is carried out at regular intervals. The other is the use of a *removable cylinder* as the steam generator. The cylinder is easily removed when solids build up and the boiler becomes inefficient.

This type of boiler has many components and features, including:

- water filter

- pressure regulator and pressure gauge

- water makeup solenoid valve

- water makeup needle valve

- gooseneck tube

- air gap

- fill cup

- stand pipe

- replaceable steam generator cylinder

- electrodes

- steam orifice

- steam hose

- steam distributor pipe

- condensate return line

- continuous cycle timer

- microswitch

- blowdown drain valve.

Each electric-hydronic boiler has its own characteristics. However, all have some common basic components:

- electric *elements* or *electrodes* that produce heat

- the boiler *casting*, or *vessel*

- water for carrying and distributing heat

- circulating pump (hot water system) or condensate pump (steam system)

- electrical controls to operate the heating elements and pump used

- various safety controls for the hydronic and electrical system. The hydronic system has a limit control, vent, and relief valve. The electrical system has a step or sequence controller, relays or contactors, and fuses or circuit breakers.

Heat distribution is the same as for any hydronic system. Any existing type of hydronic radiation device may be used as a terminal unit.

## ELECTRIC VERSUS CONVENTIONAL BOILERS

Figure 15-1 on the next page shows a typical packaged electric-hydronic boiler. The schematic drawing points out some differences between electric-hydronic boilers and those that use other fuels. A major difference is the absence of a *stack* or *vent* to discharge combustion gases. A vent is not needed, since such gases do not exist. Because venting is not a concern, an electric-hydronic boiler may be located anywhere in a building.

In addition, there are no carbon deposits or other products of combustion. Thus, there is no fallout inside a building. Periodic cleanup is not needed. Another plus for the electric-hydronic system is that you can easily increase or decrease Btuh output in the same boiler. It can be done without regard for primary or secondary air amounts, combustion chamber changes, baffling, or sufficient draft. You must consider these factors to take such action (output change) with other fuels. In an electric system, you simply remove or add electric elements, or change the capacity of the existing elements. An extreme increase in output could require an increase in electrical conductor, fusing, and/or switching component (relay or contactor).

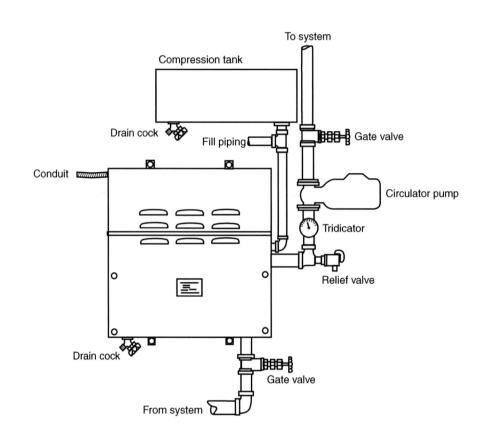

**FIGURE 15-1.** *Packaged electric-hydronic boiler*

The direct transfer of heat to water without flue losses results in high efficiency. Actual heat loss in an electric-hydronic boiler is about 4 to 5%. (It is about 14 to 16% for a forced-draft, cast iron boiler fired with gas or oil.)

## THREE IMPORTANT DESIGN FACTORS

### Electric heating elements

The heart of the electric-hydronic system is the electric heating element. Watt density, configuration, and size of elements are the most important factors in boiler design. The capacity of the elements determines Btuh output and, to a great extent, boiler efficiency.

*Electrode* and *cartridge* elements are available. However, the *sheathed* element is the most widely used. One reason is its low watt density. It produces about 100 watts of output for each square inch of element surface. This characteristic results in low surface temperatures, and contributes to a longer element life.

The sheathed unit is made in several configurations. They include:

- straight return-bend

- tubular

- hairpin

- three-leg

- spiral.

It is important that elements be accessible for inspection or replacement. An element will last for years in water, but can burn out in seconds if energized in the atmosphere.

### Boiler castings or vessels

The *vessel* is second in importance to the heating element. (It is called a *casting* when referring to the more common cast iron boilers.) Most residential electric-hydronic boilers hold between one and two gallons of water. Commercial and industrial types hold much more. All are fast-recovery units. The boiler needs to contain only a small percentage of the system's water, since the circulator moves the water continuously when the system calls for heat. Boiler size and shape depend largely on the number and capacity of the electric heating elements. The water needs room to move freely about each element. There can be no restricted areas, because they could overheat. The shape must permit free flow of water from the inlet, around corners and elements, to the outlet.

### Water

Next in importance is water, the heat carrier. There must always be enough water in the boiler to prevent overheating. Water should flow through the boiler at a rate that gives an even transfer of heat from the elements. This eliminates hot spots.

As in a conventional hydronic system, the circulator in an electric-hydronic system should be able to handle the required flow rate through boiler and piping at an established head.

## ELECTRICAL SYSTEM CONTROLS

There are usually several elements in an electric-hydronic boiler. Each is switched on or off separately, usually by components in a *step* or *sequencing* control. These controls are analyzed in another Lesson of this book. They energize the elements, one at a time, at set intervals. This avoids boiling or *flashing* because of too much energy being used in a short time. When the demand for heat is satisfied, elements are de-energized. This also is done one at a time, in reverse order.

It is important for the electric controls to energize the circulating pump before any of the heating elements are energized. They must continue pump operation until all of the heating elements are de-energized. Element controls (either step or sequence) operate on the *proportional* or *modulating* principle. They energize only the number of heating elements required to satisfy the temperature control. Closer control is sometimes achieved by using both an indoor and outdoor thermostat.

There are different ways to control the time lag between element switching. It can be done by mechanical means, such as cam-operated switches—or thermal time delay relays or contactors can be energized by a time delay relay. Now there are more sophisticated controls because of new developments in the electronics field. They include solid-state devices with semi-conductors and other electronic components. These are not yet as widely used as mechanical types. They are much more expensive.

Operating controls, thermostat, circulating pump, and heating elements are electrically interconnected to respond to demands for heat. A high-limit water temperature control is used as a backup safety device. It is usually set at 220°F, or 20° higher than the operating control setting. In a steam system, boiler and heating elements are controlled and protected by electrical operating and safety controls that are steam pressure-activated. In either case, electrical safety controls are one of two types. In one, each element is fused separately. In the other, a circuit breaker panel at the head of the system protects the entire electrical system against overload.

## HYDRONIC SIDE CONTROLS

Normal hydronic safety controls include:

- pressure relief valves

- operating controls

- temperature controls

- air eliminators.

As with any hydronic system, air eliminators may have either a manual or automatic vent.

As with all hydronic systems, electric-hydronic boilers can be used for *zoned* heating. Figure 15-2 shows the most practical method. It has separate valves that control water flow in response to each zone's thermostat. If zone controls are used, make sure to use 1,750-rpm pumps. The smaller 3,500-rpm pumps increase water hammer and its resulting noise. Another method uses separate circulating pumps for each zone. This is obviously more expensive. It is used from necessity rather than choice.

In a large building, it is feasible to size and install a separate boiler for each zone. This takes advantage of the compactness of the electric-hydronic boiler. While relatively new, electric-hydronic boilers are fast becoming performance proven. They are especially useful when the owner wants electric fuel and the benefits of hydronic heating. They also are uniquely qualified to meet the requirements for self-contained generators for steam humidification. Such a product is widely used where no source of steam exists, or where a central source is remote from the area that needs humidification.

Steam humidification can cause problems with the main steam boiler used for heat. It can make water treatment much more difficult. If boiler water treatment

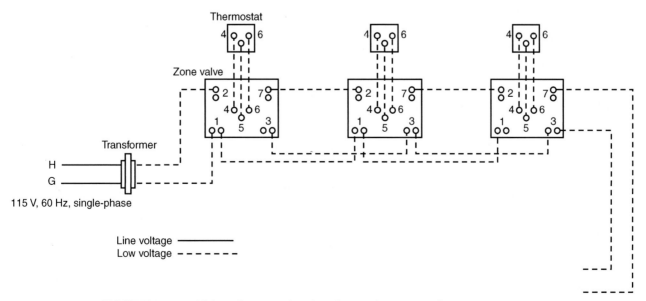

**FIGURE 15-2.** *Wiring diagram showing three-wire zone valves*

is not being performed, the boiler will likely fail prematurely. Adding a boiler designed for steam humidification can prevent many problems.

The Carnes Lumatic® steam humidification system is a good example of the electric-hydronic steam boiler put to one of the uses for which it is especially suited. It is a truly unique, all-electric, automatic steam-generating humidification system. The heart of the Lumatic system is the boiler or steam generator cylinder. Since no combustion is involved in this design, this vessel does not need to be made of metal. In this case, it is a high-temperature polypropylene cylinder with built-in lattice electrodes. The usual problems with mineral solids, etc., are virtually eliminated. The generator cylinder, with electrodes, can be removed and replaced in minutes if there are signs of excessive solids being formed.

A unit may house one, two, or three separate generator circuits. Total steam output can be up to 86.2 lb/hr. A typical electric-hydronic boiler system used for steam humidification includes the following components:

- electrical section (pre-wired)

- high-voltage block and grounding lug

- contactor and thermal overload relay

- 30-A ammeter (one for each steam generator circuit)

- built-in transformer (24-V secondary)

- control circuit fuse (8 A, wire in glass)

- 24-V terminal strip

- continuous cycling timer

- manual ON/DRAIN switch (one for each steam generator circuit)

- steam generator cylinder section (pre-piped and pre-wired)

- replaceable cartridge water filter

- pressure-reducing valve and gauge

- makeup water solenoid valve (one for each generator circuit)

- adjustable needle valve to regulate makeup water flow

- gooseneck tube, keeping the makeup water solenoid valve and the adjustable needle valve always under water, preventing scale buildup

- makeup water fill cup

- stand pipe

- overflow pipe (one from each fill cup)

- tap water boiled in the steam generator cylinder

- lattice electrodes (an integral part of the steam cylinder)

- drain solenoid valve (continuously under water to prevent scale buildup)

- flexible steam hose

- adjustable steam orifice to regulate output

- steam distributor pipe

- condensate return line (copper tubing, compression fittings)

- system component cabinet

- knockouts for power and control wiring

- drain connection (cabinet bottom forms drain pan)

- air gap waste fitting tailpiece

- ammeter (one for each steam generator circuit)

- indicator light (one for each steam generator circuit),

## OPERATING CYCLE

### Tap water flow

Tap water is piped into the water filter. The filter removes any foreign matter particles over 50 microns in size. From the filter, water flows to the pressure regulator. Pressure is reduced to 10 psi, regardless of fluctuations in the water supply to the unit. As sediment builds up on the filter cartridge, you may have to adjust the pressure regulator to maintain 10 psi.

From the pressure regulator, tap water flows to the makeup water solenoid valve. On a call for humidity, this valve opens. Water flows to the makeup water adjustable needle valve, up the gooseneck tube, across the air gap, and into the fill cup on the standpipe. The air gap is a contamination safeguard. It is required by some plumbing codes.

Makeup water then flows into the bottom of the steam generator cylinder. The water is used as the *resistance*. When it rises to touch the electrodes, it completes the circuit. Current begins to flow as registered on the ammeter in the circuit for that cylinder.

Within the capacity of the steam generator cylinder, two factors determine the actual steam output of each generator circuit. One is the opening of the adjustable steam orifice at the entrance of the steam distributor pipe. The other is the pressure that is the difference between the water levels in the standpipe and the cylinder.

Water fills the generator cylinder and begins to cover the lattice electrode. It covers it as much as needed to generate all the steam that can be pushed across the steam orifice opening. If water covers too much of the electrode, steam will generate at a greater rate than can pass through the orifice. *Back pressure* will build up in the cylinder. This in turn depresses the water level in the cylinder. The standpipe provides a head of approximately 13 in. w.g. If water in the generator does not cover enough of the electrode, equilibrium back pressure will not be reached. More water will be pushed into the cylinder until it covers enough of the electrode to generate as much steam as can be pushed across the steam orifice opening. Thus, the water in the generator cylinder continuously and automatically seeks the proper level.

Makeup water boiling in the steam generator leaves behind mineral solids. They are drained away or trapped in the disposable generator cylinder. This means that nearly pure water vapor is injected into the air stream.

Condensate that forms in the steam hose falls back into the steam generator for re-evaporation. A small amount of steam condenses in the distributor pipe. It returns to the standpipe via the condensate return line. Because of the short run of steam hose, generator cylinder construction, adjustable steam orifice, and steam distributor pipe, dry steam is injected into the air stream. A drip pan or tray under the steam distributor pipe is not needed.

### Drain cycle

The continuous cycle timer automatically actuates a microswitch. It, in turn, energizes the drain solenoid valve. The drain valve is kept open long enough to drain away some of the mineral sludge and mineral enriched water. During the drain cycle, makeup water continues to flow into the standpipe. This provides a flushing action for the drain line and drain solenoid valve. It also reduces the temperature of the waste water.

### Balancing the system

On start-up, set the *adjustable steam orifice* so that the proper amperage draw is observed for the desired output. Calculate correct values from the graphs shown in Figures 15-3 and 15-4. Figure 15-3 is for the single-phase units listed. Figure 15-4 on the next page is for the three-phase units listed. Note that amperage draw depends on pounds of steam per hour required, and on power supply voltage. When the proper ampere draw is achieved, the *adjustable makeup water needle valve* should be set. It should allow makeup water flowing

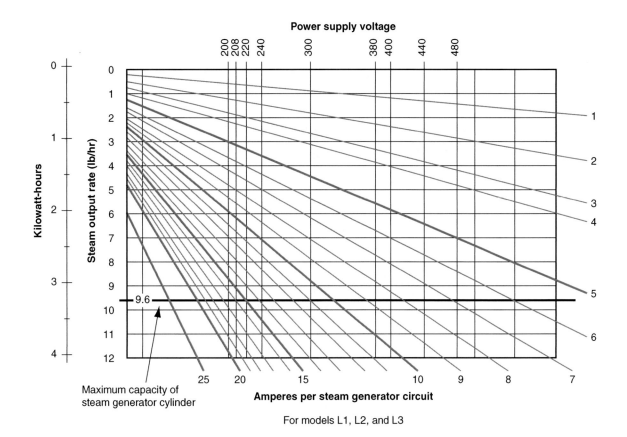

For models L1, L2, and L3

**FIGURE 15-3.** *For each "A" or "AX" steam generator cylinder circuit (single-phase cylinder, two lattice electrodes)*

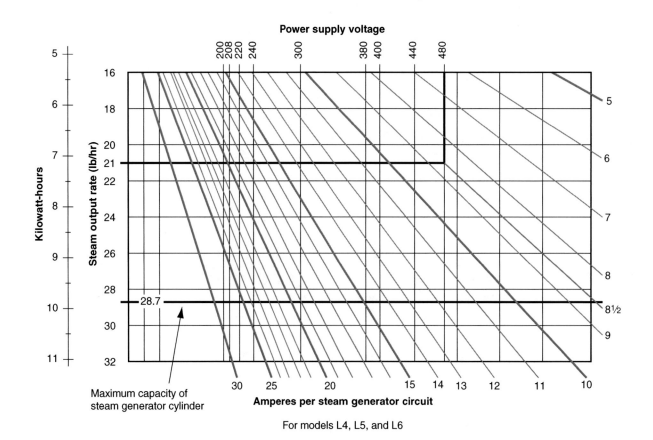

FIGURE 15-4. *For each "B" steam generator cylinder circuit (three-phase cylinder, three lattice electrodes)*

into the standpipe to compensate for water being converted into steam in the generator cylinder. As long as a supply of makeup water is visible in the fill cup, the steam generator cylinder is not being starved of makeup water.

Once these adjustments are made, there should be no need to readjust either the steam orifice or the makeup water needle valve. When there is no call for humidity, power is off to the steam generator and the makeup water solenoid valve is closed. Control action is either ON or OFF. On a call for humidity, steam is generated at the rate determined by the adjustable steam orifice opening. The makeup water solenoid valve opens to admit makeup water at the same approximate rate.

## Safety provisions

The standpipe provides a water column head of approximately 13 in. w.g. This is enough to overcome resistance in the steam hose and distributor pipe and duct static pressure. Yet, pressure in the steam generator cylinder is so low that the cylinder is not classified as a pressure vessel.

The fill cup on top of the standpipe is open to the atmosphere. Also, the adjustable steam orifice is designed so that a minimum opening remains when it is closed down. Therefore, the cylinder is always open to the atmosphere at both ends. Because of this construction, and the use of water in the cylinder as the electrical resistance, this system has several inherent fail-safe features.

For example, assume that the makeup water supply to the cylinder is accidentally shut off, but there is still a call for humidity. In this case, the water in the cylinder would boil off until its level reached the bottom of the lattice electrode. At this time the element circuit would open, current flow would cease, and the unit would cool down. Or, assume that the steam hose is accidentally pinched shut. On a call for humidity, steam would be generated and back pressure would build up in the steam generator. This, in turn, would depress the water level. The level would drop to the bottom of the electrodes. This would cut off the electric circuit to the elements, just as it would with a makeup water shortage.

There is another important safety feature. It ensures that the boiler will not generate steam indefinitely should the contactor contacts fuse together in the closed position, or the armature hang up in this position for any reason. Once the humidistat in the 24-V control circuit is satisfied, the makeup water solenoid valve in the same circuit closes. Water remaining in the steam generator cylinder would boil off until it reached the bottom of the electrodes. Then the high-voltage circuit would be de-energized at that point in the electrical system.

### Routine maintenance

Routine maintenance for this type of electric-hydronic boiler includes replacing the disposable steam generator cylinder with lattice electrodes. Complete change-out takes about five minutes for each cylinder. Frequency of change-out depends on the mineral content of the tap water used, and the type of application.

The water filter cartridge needs to be cleaned or replaced when it is not possible to maintain 10 psi downstream from the pressure regulator. The frequency of cleaning or replacement depends on the turbidity of the local tap water. From time to time, the drain solenoid valve and drain lines may need cleaning. Check to see if cleaning is needed by putting the manual ON/DRAIN for each circuit in the "drain" position. Observe the air gap waste. It will show if drain lines and drain solenoid are sufficiently clear.

Long shutdown periods may take place, such as during the summer cooling cycle in a comfort application. If so, each steam generator cylinder should be drained completely using the ON/DRAIN manual switch. Do this before switching off all power to boiler components and closing the water supply valve.

1. What is the water capacity of a residential-type electric-hydronic boiler?

2. Where are the electric heaters located in electric-hydronic systems?

3. What is the variation in Btu output for electric-hydronic systems?

4. What are the two categories into which electric boilers may be divided?

5. What is the effect of the buildup of solids in a boiler?

6. What components prevent the buildup of solids?

7. What item generally found on conventional boilers is not a part of electric boilers?

8. What advantage does an electric boiler have over a conventional boiler regarding location?

9. Why is it not necessary to perform periodic cleanup on electric boilers?

10. What else may have to be changed when electric element size is increased?

11. What is the approximate heat loss in an electric-hydronic boiler?

12. What is the approximate heat loss in a forced-draft cast iron boiler?

13. What are the most important factors in the design of electric-hydronic boilers?

14. What determines Btuh output and boiler efficiency?

15. What type of elements are generally used?

16. What is the approximate output per square inch of element?

17. What will happen if the element is energized in the atmosphere?

18. What is the function of the circulator when the system calls for heat?

19. What must controls do before energizing the heaters?

20. What is done to obtain closer control of elements?

21. In what ways can time lag element switching be established?

22. What is used as a backup safety device in a hot water boiler?

23. How are boiler and heating elements controlled and protected in a steam heating system?

24. What are the two types of electrical safety controls?

25. What do normal hydronic safety controls include?

26.     Name two ways in which zoned heating is accomplished.

27.     Where may self-contained electric-hydronic generators for steam humidification be used?

28.     Since no combustion is involved in electric-hydronic steam generation for humidification, the boiler may be constructed of _____.

29.     What happens when the Carnes Lumatic system is operating and steam is generated faster than it can be passed through the orifice opening?

RSES

# Electric Heating
## Student Supplement

**RSES®**
The HVACR Training Authority

Congratulations on your decision to further your education and career by taking part in an RSES study course! The accompanying book is your primary learning tool, and should serve you well as a source of reference in the future. Feel free to write in your book, and make notes as needed in the page margins. The answers to the Lesson Review Questions can be found on the pages that follow.

If you are attending classes led by an instructor, you may ignore the instructions below, which are intended for participants in the self-study program.

**RSES SELF-STUDY TRAINING COURSE INSTRUCTIONS**

Your first step in furthering your education was purchasing the accompanying book. You may wish to demonstrate the skills and knowledge that you obtain through your studies by participating in the Final Examination and earning a Certificate of Completion for the course. Participation in the Final Examination is optional (and does require an additional fee).

After you have studied all of the Lessons in the book, completed all of the Lesson Review Questions, and feel that you understand the material thoroughly, you may apply to take the Final Examination. A form for ordering a Final Examination is included in this booklet.

Final Examinations are not sent out directly to participants. You will need to arrange for a proctor who can conduct the exam for you. A Chapter Officer, Chapter CM Monitor, Regional Director, Deputy Director, or E&E Board Member may serve as a proctor. If none of the aforementioned individuals is available to administer the exam for you, other arrangements can be made. In many instances, local libraries are willing to administer exams (upon request). A manager or supervisor at your place of employment, a clergyperson, etc., also may be approved to administer the Final Examination.

All proctors will be contacted prior to Final Examinations being sent out. RSES reserves the right to approve or deny the exam request and/or the individual requested to serve as proctor.

Once a proctor has been selected and tentative arrangements have been made, complete the RSES Self-Study Program Final Examination Request form and mail or fax this information along with your payment of $50 to:

RSES
Self-Study Program
1911 Rohlwing Road, Suite A
Rolling Meadows, IL 60008
Fax: (847) 297-5038

The Final Examination consists of 100 multiple-choice questions. The Final Examination will be shipped to the proctor and must be taken in the presence of the proctor. The finished Final Examination should be sent to RSES Headquarters for processing via a trackable shipping method by the proctor no later than 72 hours after completion.

The Final Examination is a closed-book test. You will be allowed 3 hours to complete the exam. You must achieve a score of 70% or better to receive a Certificate of Completion.

Good luck and best wishes for your continued success in the HVACR industry!

## Lesson 1
## Heating with Electricity

1. *Resistance heating and heat pumps.*
   **Ref: 1/1**
2. *All energy is converted into heat. (There is no waste).*
   **Ref: 3/2**
3. *No.*
   **Ref: 3/4**
4. *The movement or "flow" of electrons in an electrical conductor.*
   **Ref: 4/5**
5. *Resistance.*
   **Ref: 4/5**
6. $E = I \times R$, or $I = E \div R$, or $R = E \div I$
   **Ref: 5/3**
7. *3%*
   **Ref: 6/2**
8. *Heat is produced.*
   **Ref: 6/3**
9. *Watts.*
   **Ref: 6/5**
10. *4,800 W*
    **Ref: 7/1**
11. *3.413 Btuh*
    **Ref: 7/1, 2**
12. *16,382.4 Btuh*
    **Ref: 7/1, 2**
13. *Alloys of iron, nickel, chromium, and manganese.*
    **Ref: 8/5**
14. *Vary the current, vary the resistance of the heating element, or vary the applied voltage.*
    **Ref: 10/3**
15. *A system that switches from 120 to 240 V when heating demand increases.*
    **Ref: 10/7**
16. *By operating an intermediate switching relay.*
    **Ref: 12/1**
17. *Positive charges, negative charges.*
    **Ref: 12/2, 3**
18. *Voltage, or potential difference.*
    **Ref: 13/2**
19. *It increases. The conductor becomes a superconductor at temperatures near absolute zero.*
    **Ref: 14/5**
20. *33,000 ft-lb/min*
    **Ref: 16/1**
21. *0.25 Ω*
    **Ref: 17/2**
22. *Yes.*
    **Ref: 17/4**
23. *Because neither of the lines in a 208 or 240-V single-phase circuit is grounded.*
    **Ref: 17/5**
24. *Because it is more efficient to generate and use.*
    **Ref: 18/1**
25. *Three.*
    **Ref: 18/3**
26. *Because none of the three conductors in the three-phase circuit is grounded.*
    **Ref: 19/3**
27. *30 V or less.*
    **Ref: 19/5**
28. *Transformers.*
    **Ref: 19/6**

## Lesson 2
## Resistance Heating

1. *The amount of resistance in the conductor, the applied voltage, and the current flow.*
   **Ref: 25/1**
2. *Conduction, convection, and radiation.*
   **Ref: 25/2**
3. *Yes.*
   **Ref: 26/2**
4. *In stoves, radiant and convective heaters, and electric water heaters.*
   **Ref: 26/3**
5. *The ability to travel through air without losing much heat to the air.*
   **Ref: 27/2**
6. *Portable, wall-mounted, ceiling, baseboard, floor-inserted, and slab heaters.*
   **Ref: 27/4**
7. *They take more time to heat up than other types of heaters.*
   **Ref: 28/4**
8. *In bathrooms, entryways, and other areas where quick warmth is desired.*
   **Ref: 29/3**

9. *More positive air circulation and more rapid heat distribution.*
**Ref: 29/4**

10. *Embedded cable radiant heaters, radiant panels, and combination heating and lighting units.*
**Ref: 30/2**

11. *Usually during construction.*
**Ref: 30/3**

12. *They do not interfere with furniture or drapery location, and they provide uniform heat.*
**Ref: 30/4–31/1**

13. *In residences and commercial buildings.*
**Ref: 32/1**

14. *Baseboard heaters take up minimum space in a room, and deliver heat along a broad area at the outer perimeter of the room, where it is most needed.*
**Ref: 32/2**

15. *Electric hydronic baseboard heaters are filled with fluid, which is heated by an immersion-type element built into the baseboard section.*
**Ref: 32/4**

16. *By ducts or pipes.*
**Ref: 33/2**

17. *Electric furnace, electric boiler, electric heat pump, and central fan with duct or register heaters.*
**Ref: 33/4**

18. *Temperature limit controls.*
**Ref: 34/2**

19. *Yes.*
**Ref: 34/3**

20. *Directly in the water being heated.*
**Ref: 34/4**

21. *Outdoor air or water.*
**Ref: 35/3**

22. *Cooling load.*
**Ref: 35/4**

23. *In the duct or diffusing register.*
**Ref: 35/6**

24. *Duct and register heaters.*
**Ref: 36/1**

25. *Yes.*
**Ref: 36/3**

26. *Suspend it from the ceiling, or mount it high on a convenient post or pillar.*
**Ref: 36/3**

27. *In high-velocity ducts, where it is necessary to raise the air temperature very rapidly.*
**Ref: 37/4**

28. *To replace air that is exhausted by exhaust fans.*
**Ref: 38/3**

29. *Divide Btuh by 3,412.*
**Ref: 39/2**

30. *27*
**Ref: 39/6**

**Lesson 3**
**Heat Pumps**

1. *That outside air is both the heat source and the heat sink.*
**Ref: 45/2**

2. *By compression.*
**Ref: 46/5**

3. *Reversed.*
**Ref: 46/7**

4. *Heat during the cool part of the day, and cool during the warm part of the day.*
**Ref: 46/8–47/1**

5. *Heat and cool one or two rooms.*
**Ref: 48/2**

6. *Heat and cool a number of rooms or the whole house.*
**Ref: 48/3**

7. *Packaged units contain all the components in one package.*
**Ref: 48/4**

8. *Two sections, an indoor section and an outdoor section.*
**Ref: 48/5**

9. *Heating, cooling.*
**Ref: 48/7**

10. *Water.*
**Ref: 49/3**

11. *One that uses water for the heat source and has the indoor coil located in the air stream.*
**Ref: 50/4**

12. *Because it could be either, depending on whether the heat pump is heating or cooling.*
**Ref: 51/3**

13. *The evaporator must be at a lower temperature than the outdoor temperature.*
**Ref: 52/6–53/1**

14. *Less.*
    **Ref: 53/3**
15. *Higher.*
    **Ref: 53/3**
16. *1.5 to 6*
    **Ref: 53/4**
17. *A four-way or reversing valve.*
    **Ref: 54/5**
18. *It protects the compressor against slop-over of liquid refrigerant during a change in cycle.*
    **Ref: 55/1**
19. *To the single-inlet side of the main valve cylinder.*
    **Ref: 57/2**
20. *Through bleed holes.*
    **Ref: 57/3**
21. *When heating is called for.*
    **Ref: 57/6**
22. *By the amount of heat required over and above that which the heat pump can supply. In colder climates, 100% of the heating load is often used.*
    **Ref: 58/5–59/1**
23. *A two-step room thermostat is used to turn on the strip or resistance heaters, and outside thermostats are used to determine how many strip or resistance heaters are used.*
    **Ref: 59/3, 4**
24. *Only when the compressor alone is incapable of meeting the heating requirements.*
    **Ref: 59/3**
25. *Starts the heat pump compressor.*
    **Ref: 59/4**
26. *1½ to 2°F*
    **Ref: 59/5**

**Lesson 4**
**Radiant Heating Systems**

1. *It is made of a resistor embedded in an electrical insulating refractory within a metal tube.*
   **Ref: 66/5**
2. *They are rugged and can stand up well against impact, vibration, and splashing. They can be mounted horizontally, vertically, or at any angle in between.*
   **Ref: 66/5–67/1**

3. *They are easy to match to exact heat, voltage, and length requirements. They also have a quicker response time than metal sheath heaters.*
   **Ref: 67/5**
4. *Energy output, energy input.*
   **Ref: 68/3**
5. *The higher the element temperature, the higher the radiant efficiency.*
   **Ref: 68/3**
6. *Light colored objects generally absorb less radiant heat.*
   **Ref: 69/1**
7. *Fixtures with narrow beam patterns that largely confine radiant energy to the target area.*
   **Ref: 69/2**
8. *In a row, parallel to the longest dimension of the area.*
   **Ref: 70/1**
9. *Multiply the commonly used snow-melting watt densities shown in Table 4-2 by the target area in square feet, then multiply the resulting product by a correction factor of 1.6.*
   **Ref: 70/6–71/1**
10. *A point-by-point method, which involves dividing the target area into a grid pattern of $1\text{-}ft^2$ squares and calculating the watts per square foot of radiant energy that a fixture will radiate on each square foot of grid.*
    **Ref: 71/2**
11. *20 to 30 minutes, unless the air temperature is well below 20°F or high winds prevail.*
    **Ref: 71/3–72/1**
12. *The equipment does not have to be turned on until snow actually begins to fall.*
    **Ref: 72/1**
13. *Either manually, or automatically with a snow detector.*
    **Ref: 72/1**
14. *Reflectors should be cleaned at least once a year, preferably at the beginning of winter.*
    **Ref: 72/3**
15. *An outdoor thermostat, which will turn the system off when the outdoor ambient temperature exceeds 35°F, should be incorporated in the control system.*
    **Ref: 72/4**

16. *High-velocity air circulation, which can create uncomfortable conditions, is not required in the case of radiant heating because of relatively low air temperatures.*
   **Ref: 74/1**

17. *It absorbs radiation, almost like any black object.*
   **Ref: 74/3**

18. *The ability of an infrared system to create comfortable conditions at lower ambient temperatures, and the lack of convection air currents.*
   **Ref: 75/2**

19. *Standard heat load calculations are performed using data from ASHRAE or from ACCA's Manual N, and the heat load then is adjusted (multiply the heat load by 85%). The input Btu based on electric usage per unit is determined. This figure is divided into the heat load (after it has been adjusted) to determine the number of units needed.*
   **Ref: 77/2**

20. *Infrared energy will be absorbed or reflected, and will not reach the subject.*
   **Ref: 87/1**

21. *Aluminum sheets.*
   **Ref: 87/1**

22. *Coupling alternate heaters to separate thermostats permits heaters to be cut off in stages.*
   **Ref: 88/2**

23. *On walls or building columns approximately 5 ft from the floor, and shielded from direct radiation.*
   **Ref: 88/4**

24. *In areas where occupant density is low and work stations relatively static, or in areas with an extremely high infiltration rate and limited work stations.*
   **Ref: 88/5**

25. *Control each heater with a manually operated switch.*
   **Ref: 96/4**

**Lesson 5**
**Duct Heaters and Furnaces**

1. *They are used as primary heat sources, as supplemental heaters, and for preheating or reheating.*
   **Ref: 103/1**

2. *120, 550*
   **Ref: 103/1**

3. *Automatic reset and manual reset.*
   **Ref: 104/1**

4. *Steel coated with aluminum for corrosion resistance.*
   **Ref: 104/6**

5. *3,413*
   **Ref: 105/1**

6. *It prevents the duct heater from operating unless the fan is on.*
   **Ref: 105/5**

7. *A way of providing power in stages to meet the demand.*
   **Ref: 106/4**

8. *Increasing or reducing the size of a duct to accommodate the duct heater.*
   **Ref: 106/9**

9. *The amount of electric heat (in watts) produced within a given area.*
   **Ref: 107/1**

10. *In kilowatts per square foot of face area.*
   **Ref: 107/1**

11. *Only from the sides of the duct—never from the bottom or top of the duct.*
   **Ref: 108/6**

12. *4 ft*
   **Ref: 109/1**

13. *At least 18 in.*
   **Ref: 109/1**

14. *A fan relay, to prevent the heater from operating unless the fan is on.*
   **Ref: 110/1**

15. *22.5 kW*
   **Ref: 114/5**

16. *60 watts per square inch.*
   **Ref: 114/5**

17. *Type RH or its equivalent, suitable for 75°C.*
   **Ref: 114/6**

18. *Air failure protection.*
   **Ref: 123/4**

19. To limit the kilowatts switched on at one time, thus eliminating light dimming.
    **Ref: 124/3**

20. Add 50% to the total requirement for contactor in-rush current.
    **Ref: 125/2**

21. $$\text{Temperature rise} = \frac{kW \times 3,081}{cfm}$$
    **Ref: 125/6**

22. 20%
    **Ref: 127/4**

23. 4.5 to 6 kW
    **Ref: 127/5**

24. Low-wattage furnaces.
    **Ref: 128/6**

25. It prevents total heating until the outdoor temperature has dropped below a given setting (usually between 0 and 30°F).
    **Ref: 129/4**

26. Velocities below 900 ft/min on supply ductwork, and below 700 ft/min on return air ductwork.
    **Ref: 131/4**

27. Friction, turbulence in straight ductwork, and eddy flow in elbows and bends.
    **Ref: 132/1**

28. In publications of NESCA, SMACNA, ACCA, AMCA, ASHRAE, and other trade publications.
    **Ref: 132/1**

. . . . . . . . . . . . . . . . . . . . . . . . . . . . . . . . . . . . . .

**Lesson 6**
**Baseboard and Unit Heaters**
. . . . . . . . . . . . . . . . . . . . . . . . . . . . . . . . . . . . . .

1. A sensitive thermal cut-out, which reacts to overheated conditions.
   **Ref: 137/2**

2. Standard-wattage and high-wattage.
   **Ref: 137/3**

3. Heaters should be centered on an outside wall under a window to counteract the downward flow of cool air caused by heat loss through glass or wall.
   **Ref: 138/1**

4. Through the wall or through the floor.
   **Ref: 138/5**

5. Heaters can be mounted against plaster wall, semi-recessed by mounting directly to wall studs, or mounted to insulation board used in solid masonry construction.
   **Ref: 140/1**

6. Wires are run in the raceway.
   **Ref: 140/5**

7. To prevent warping, it is essential to fasten only at those locations where the panel comes in direct contact with the wall.
   **Ref: 141/2**

8. Use horizontal wood headers to frame the steel wall box.
   **Ref: 142/5**

9. 24 in.
   **Ref: 142/5**

10. Heat loss of the glass area.
    **Ref: 143/4**

11. 5 ft
    **Ref: 143/4**

12. Bathrooms, or areas where water may saturate the heater.
    **Ref: 144/1**

13. At least 1 in. from the nearest fold of the drapes.
    **Ref: 144/2**

14. The end of the heater should be no closer than 3 ft from the wall.
    **Ref: 144/2**

15. Make certain that all foreign material is removed from the inside of the heater.
    **Ref: 145/4**

16. Newer ceiling heaters have an automatic reset protector. Some older ceiling heaters have a fusible link.
    **Ref: 146/5**

17. Unit heaters should be located in such a way that they discharge air parallel to exposed walls.
    **Ref: 147/1**

18. The units should be arranged in such a way that each supports the air stream of the next, thus creating circulatory air movement in the area.
    **Ref: 147/1**

19. Toward the windward side of a building exposed to prevailing winds.
    **Ref: 147/1**

20. *One or more units should be installed to discharge warm air across the opening, not toward it.*
    **Ref: 147/1**

21. *To prevent the discharge from one unit from being directed into the inlet of another.*
    **Ref: 147/2**

22. *To provide ample air supply, proper fan operation, and adequate service access.*
    **Ref: 147/2**

23. *A minimum of 7 ft, and not exceeding the maximum recommended mounting height.*
    **Ref: 147/2**

24. *On an inside wall approximately 5 ft above the floor, where it will not be affected by direct heat from the unit or other sources, or by drafts from frequently opened doors or windows.*
    **Ref: 148/4**

25. *No. 14 AWG*
    **Ref: 149/2**

26. *Once a year, before the heating season.*
    **Ref: 152/3**

## Lesson 7
## Radiant Heat Installation

1. *Basements, workshops, garages, bowling alleys, patios, loading docks, swimming pools, etc.*
   **Ref: 157/1**

2. *For small areas where natural convection is sufficient to maintain an even temperature.*
   **Ref: 159/4**

3. *Near cold air inlets.*
   **Ref: 159/5**

4. *To provide auxiliary heating for areas of greatest heat loss.*
   **Ref: 160/2**

5. *52 to 60 in. above the floor.*
   **Ref: 161/3**

6. *1¼*
   **Ref: 162/2**

7. *13*
   **Ref: 162/5**

8. *3.414*
   **Ref: 163/3**

9. *One with a low R value.*
   **Ref: 164/1**

10. *85°F*
    **Ref: 164/2**

11. *2.0*
    **Ref: Figure 7-7**

12. *2½ in.*
    **Ref: 165/2**

13. *Approximately 300 ft.*
    **Ref: Figure 7-8**

14. *Two.*
    **Ref: 165/4, 5**

15. *Parallel.*
    **Ref: 167/2**

16. *Low-voltage.*
    **Ref: 167/4**

17. *140°F*
    **Ref: 169/5**

18. *National Electrical Code.*
    **Ref: 170/4**

## Lesson 8
## System Control Devices

1. *Ductwork or piping.*
   **Ref: 175/2**

2. *5,000 W (5 kW)*
   **Ref: 176/3**

3. *The low-voltage thermostat.*
   **Ref: 176/3**

4. *By using one or more switching relays.*
   **Ref: 177/1**

5. *24 V*
   **Ref: 177/3**

6. *High-voltage.*
   **Ref: 177/3**

7. *5 ft*
   **Ref: 177/4**

8. *On an inside wall.*
   **Ref: 177/4**

9. *So that the adjustable anticipation heater can be matched to the current draw through the thermostat.*
   **Ref: 178/2**

10. *It increases the cycling rate.*
    **Ref: 178/3**

11. *Ammeter.*
    **Ref: 178/5–179/3**

12. *Adjust the setting to 0.45.*
    **Ref: 180/3**

13. *Yes.*
    **Ref: 181/2**
14. *Stages.*
    **Ref: 182/3**
15. *By eliminating the need for line-voltage wiring.*
    **Ref: 183/1**
16. *Approximately 75 seconds (from a cold start).*
    **Ref: 186/3**
17. *An understanding of the function, operation, and electrical circuitry of heating load relays.*
    **Ref: 186/4**
18. *Overcurrent protection and high-temperature protection.*
    **Ref: 187/2**
19. *Overheating.*
    **Ref: 188/1**
20. *A disk-type limit switch for each heater element.*
    **Ref: 188/2**
21. *Yes.*
    **Ref: 190/1**
22. *Heater No. 3 will be de-energized.*
    **Ref: Figure 8-13**
23. *Nothing.*
    **Ref: Figure 8-15**
24. *Heater No. 2.*
    **Ref: Figure 8-17**
25. *Operation will continue until the fan is sequenced off through the second control switch.*
    **Ref: Figure 8-17**
26. *Heaters 1, 2, and 3.*
    **Ref: Figure 8-23**
27. *Heaters 4, 5, and 6 will operate if the outdoor thermostat contacts are closed.*
    **Ref: Figure 8-24**
28. *Yes.*
    **Ref: Figure 8-24**

**Lesson 9**
**Electric Furnaces**

1. *The heating effect of an integral heater (warp switch).*
   **Ref: 203/2**
2. *An automatic reset limit switch and, in addition, a fusible link.*
   **Ref: 203/3**
3. *About 18 seconds.*
   **Ref: 204/1, Figure 9-1**

4. *Generally, about 90 seconds.*
   **Ref: 205/4**
5. *Closed.*
   **Ref: Figure 9-4**
6. *Measure the current draw and voltage to see if the coil is pulling the correct amount of watts.*
   **Ref: 206/3**
7. *1.73*
   **Ref: 206/3–208/1**
8. *All of them.*
   **Ref: 208/1**
9. *Yes.*
   **Ref: 208/2**
10. *Be sure that the power is off and remove the power wires from both heating element terminals.*
    **Ref: 208/1**
11. *10 to 12 ohms of resistance.*
    **Ref: 208/3**

**Lesson 10**
**Duct Heaters**

1. *A test using very high voltage to ensure that equipment will not short under extreme conditions.*
   **Ref: 212/5**
2. *Heating elements that have the helical coiled resistance wire exposed to the flow of air through the heater.*
   **Ref: 212/9**
3. *A circuit that includes the holding coil of the secondary contactor and the manual reset control device.*
   **Ref: 212/11**
4. *4 ft*
   **Ref: 213/7**
5. *18 in.*
   **Ref: 213/7**
6. *From either side, but never from the top or bottom.*
   **Ref: 213/7**
7. *Air velocity and heater thickness.*
   **Ref: 215/1**
8. *To reduce current inrush as the heaters are energized.*
   **Ref: 215/2**

9. *Standards of the National Fire Protection Association and, in Canada, Canadian Standards.*
   **Ref: 216/1, 2**
10. *Flange type.*
   **Ref: 216/3**
11. *Be certain that the control box is located for easy access.*
   **Ref: 216/3**
12. *Maintain a sufficient minimum air flow.*
   **Ref: 216/4**
13. *Increased.*
   **Ref: 216/4**
14. *Approximately 730 ft/min.*
   **Ref: 217/1**
15. *650 ft/min*
   **Ref: Figure 10-5**
16. *Two.*
   **Ref: Figure 10-6**
17. *One.*
   **Ref: Figure 10-6**
18. *Neutral.*
   **Ref: Figure 10-6**
19. *Factory built-in mercury contactors.*
   **Ref: 219/2**
20. *Upright.*
   **Ref: 219/3**
21. *48 A*
   **Ref: 220/1**
22. *60 A*
   **Ref: 220/1**
23. *34,130 Btu*
   **Ref: Table 10-1**
24. *36.1 A*
   **Ref: Table 10-1**
25. *Air flow, or the absence of air flow.*
   **Ref: 221/1**
26. *Pneumatic and positive static pressure.*
   **Ref: 221/1**
27. *To avoid trouble caused by turbulence.*
   **Ref: 221/2**
28. *At least 15 in.*
   **Ref: 221/2**
29. *Closed.*
   **Ref: 226/3**

**Lesson 11**
**Multi-Step Controllers (Part 1)**

1. *Cams.*
   **Ref: 233/2**
2. *Yes.*
   **Ref: 233/2**
3. *A balancing relay.*
   **Ref: 233/2**
4. *To control a damper motor.*
   **Ref: 234/1**
5. *Single-phase.*
   **Ref: Figure 11-1**
6. *A counterclockwise limit switch.*
   **Ref: Figure 11-1**
7. *Hunting (rapid cycling).*
   **Ref: 236/2**
8. *160°*
   **Ref: 236/2**
9. *Widen the controller throttling range or use a delay timer.*
   **Ref: 236/5**
10. *Only when the timer switch contacts are closed.*
   **Ref: 236/6**
11. *Narrow.*
   **Ref: 236/7**
12. *R to B.*
   **Ref: 237/2**
13. *It slows down cam rotation.*
   **Ref: 238/3**
14. *A fourth snap switch allows the camshaft to return only to its midpoint.*
   **Ref: 240/1**
15. *Air pressure.*
   **Ref: 241/5**
16. *By a pneumatic-electric (PE) switch.*
   **Ref: 241/5**
17. *3 to 15 psi*
   **Ref: 241/5**
18. *Pilot devices.*
   **Ref: 241/6**
19. *Heat added, heat lost.*
   **Ref: 242/3**
20. *Low (less than 10 V).*
   **Ref: 244/2**

**Lesson 12**
**Multi-Step Controllers (Part 2)**

1.  *The SPDT relay controls the electric heat sequencer or contactor.*
    **Ref: 249/2**
2.  *Make sure that the heating and cooling thermostats are set at least 2°F apart.*
    **Ref: 249/2**
3.  *The second modular thermostat has either a 0 to 10-V dc or a 0 to 20-mA output.*
    **Ref: 250/1**
4.  *Up to ten stages.*
    **Ref: 250/2**
5.  *From 1 to 30°F.*
    **Ref: 250/2**
6.  *More, less.*
    **Ref: 250/3**
7.  *When there is a night setback control.*
    **Ref: 251/1**
8.  *The building heats more evenly, and it saves on the electric demand rate if there is a night setback thermostat.*
    **Ref: 251/2**
9.  *A large three-phase controller can handle up to 550 A or more.*
    **Ref: 251/4**
10. *A remote sensor allows the controls to be located in a secure area, which helps prevent tampering and vandalism.*
    **Ref: 251/5**

**Lesson 13**
**Electronic Sequencing Control**

1.  *From 55 to 85°F.*
    **Ref: 256/1**
2.  *From 3 to 30°F.*
    **Ref: 256/1**
3.  *The area of temperature setting for the thermostat in which neither heating nor cooling will be called for.*
    **Ref: 256/1**
4.  *The remote sensor makes it possible to mount the thermostat/controller in the manager's office or control room, while the sensor can be installed in the controlled space.*
    **Ref: 256/1**

5.  *The status panel has six indicator lights that monitor heating, cooling, and fan functions.*
    **Ref: 256/2**
6.  *Any position.*
    **Ref: 256/3**
7.  *−40°F, +150°F*
    **Ref: 257/1**
8.  *Up to six W973 logic panels.*
    **Ref: 257/1**
9.  *The satellite sequencer is used so that up to ten stages of heating and/or cooling can be accommodated.*
    **Ref: 257/1**
10. *The setback module closes the fresh air damper and changes the fan from constant run to intermittent run during night setback. It also allows for the air conditioning to be shut down or set back and the heat to be set back for nighttime operation.*
    **Ref: 257/2**
11. *Four sensors allow for average temperature sensing of a large zone, or a zone with windows on one side.*
    **Ref: 257/3**
12. *The load analyzer responds to the highest heating and cooling demand signal from the zone thermostats and controls heating and cooling.*
    **Ref: 259/1**
13. *Any position.*
    **Ref: 259/1**
14. *−40°F, +150°F*
    **Ref: 259/1**
15. *From 55 to 85°F.*
    **Ref: 259/2**
16. *From 3 to 30°F.*
    **Ref: 259/2**
17. *Up to four remote sensors can be used.*
    **Ref: 260/1**
18. *The limit controller provides for a low limit for the cold deck and a high limit for the hot deck. It also provides economizer and mixed-air low-limit control for the system.*
    **Ref: 260/2**
19. *The electronic heat sequencer allows for up to five ON/OFF stages of electric heat.*
    **Ref: 260/2**

20. *Each zone adder can handle up to 12 additional zones.*
    **Ref: 260/2**

21. *The discharge air temperature controller controls either heating or cooling discharge air temperature.*
    **Ref: 260/3**

22. *To allow for the control and monitoring of many, if not all, of the building's mechanical and electrical parameters.*
    **Ref: 260/5, 6**

••••••••••••••••••••••••••••••••••••••••••••

**Lesson 14**
**Decentralized Electric Heating Systems**

••••••••••••••••••••••••••••••••••••••••••••

1. *No. They receive heat from a central boiler and are considered part of centralized system.*
   **Ref: 263/1**

2. *1) To serve as the primary source of heat for a whole building.*
   *2) To provide supplemental heat.*
   **Ref: 263/2**

3. *Baseboard, ceiling cable, radiant ceiling panel, and unit heaters.*
   **Ref: 264/1**

4. *In radiant or convective heaters, where it is desirable to have relatively high temperatures.*
   **Ref: 264/3**

5. *A radiant heater.*
   **Ref: 264/3**

6. *Plastic.*
   **Ref: 264/4**

7. *Ceramic or metal.*
   **Ref: 264/5**

8. *Heat-dissipating fins are provided.*
   **Ref: 264/5**

9. *Under windows and along outside walls.*
   **Ref: 265/2**

10. *It has a sensing element that runs the entire length of the heater to protect against hot spots.*
    **Ref: 265/3**

11. *A built-in or wall-mounted line-voltage thermostat.*
    **Ref: 265/4**

12. *To prevent the heating elements from affecting the thermostat operation.*
    **Ref: 266/1**

13. *Provide a thermostat that breaks both sides of the circuit.*
    **Ref: 266/3**

14. *They are simpler, and easier to install.*
    **Ref: 266/4**

15. *A low-voltage system.*
    **Ref: 266/4**

16. *A switching relay and a transformer.*
    **Ref: 266/5, Figure 14-4**

17. *They are used with low-voltage controls.*
    **Ref: 267/1**

18. *In the wiring compartment of the heater, or away from the heater.*
    **Ref: 267/3**

19. *Locate the thermostat where it will sense a representative temperature. Avoid hot or cold locations.*
    **Ref: 268/1**

20. *During construction.*
    **Ref: 268/2**

21. *A continuous length of insulated resistance wire with a constant heat output for each foot.*
    **Ref: 268/3**

22. *1) Cable embedded directly in ceiling material.*
    *2) Radiant ceiling panels.*
    **Ref: 268/3–269/4**

23. *It is completely out of the usable room space, and therefore does not interfere with drapery or furniture location. It also provides uniform heat delivery.*
    **Ref: 268/3**

24. *Because of the large mass of the system.*
    **Ref: 268/4**

25. *A line-voltage thermostat.*
    **Ref: 268/5**

26. *Usually faster.*
    **Ref: 269/3**

27. *Bathrooms, entry halls, and places where the heating rays will not be blocked off.*
    **Ref: 270/1**

28. *Mineral-insulated cable.*
    **Ref: 272/1**

29. *In spot heating applications.*
    **Ref: 272/6–273/1**

30. *Quartz tube and metal-clad element heaters.*
    **Ref: 273/2**

**Lesson 15**
**Electric Boilers**

1. *Generally two or three gallons.*
   **Ref: 289/2**
2. *They are immersed directly in water.*
   **Ref: 289/2**
3. *Btu output ranges from 10,000 to 6,000,000 Btu for conventional floor models.*
   **Ref: 289/3**
4. *One is designed for producing hot water or steam in a conventional hydronic system. The other is specially suited for generating steam without any condensate return arrangement.*
   **Ref: 290/2, 3**
5. *They reduce heat transfer.*
   **Ref: 290/3**
6. *An automatic blowdown feature, and a removable steam generator cylinder.*
   **Ref: 290/3**
7. *A stack or vent to discharge combustion gases.*
   **Ref: 292/1**
8. *Since no stack or vent is required, it can be located anywhere.*
   **Ref: 292/1**
9. *There are no carbon deposits or other products of combustion—hence, no fallout inside the building.*
   **Ref: 292/2**
10. *Supply conductors, fusing and switching components.*
    **Ref: 292/2**
11. *4 to 5%.*
    **Ref: 292/3**
12. *Approximately 14 to 16%.*
    **Ref: 292/3**
13. *The watt density and the configuration and size of the electric elements.*
    **Ref: 292/4**
14. *The capacity of the electric element.*
    **Ref: 292/4**
15. *Sheathed electric elements.*
    **Ref: 293/1**
16. *100 W*
    **Ref: 293/1**
17. *It will burn out in seconds.*
    **Ref: 293/3**
18. *To move the water continuously.*
    **Ref: 293/4**
19. *Start the circulating pump before any heating elements are energized and continue operation until all heating elements are de-energized.*
    **Ref: 294/2**
20. *Utilize an indoor and an outdoor thermostat.*
    **Ref: 294/2**
21. *By cam-operated switches, or by thermal time delay relays.*
    **Ref: 294/3**
22. *A high-limit water temperature control.*
    **Ref: 294/4**
23. *By appropriate steam pressure-activated electrical controls.*
    **Ref: 294/4**
24. *One type has each element fused separately. In the other, the entire electrical system is protected by a circuit breaker panel.*
    **Ref: 294/4**
25. *Pressure relief valves, operating controls, temperature controls, and air eliminators.*
    **Ref: 294/5–295/1**
26. *1) Separate water valves responding to thermostat demands for the zone.*
    *2) Separate circulating pumps for each zone.*
    **Ref: 295/3**
27. *Where a source of steam does not exist, or where a central steam source is too remote from the area.*
    **Ref: 295/4**
28. *Polypropylene.*
    **Ref: 296/2**
29. *Back pressure will build up, causing the water in the generator to seek the proper level.*
    **Ref: 298/5**

# SELF-STUDY FINAL EXAMINATION REQUEST FORM

## for *Electric Heating*
## Heating series

1911 Rohlwing Road, Suite A
Rolling Meadows, IL 60008-1397
Phone: 800-297-5660 or 847-297-6464
Fax: 847-297-5038
Web site: www.rses.org

Today's date _____

Test date _____

**Note:** *Please submit this form 14–21 days in advance of test date.*

## ABOUT YOU

Name ❏ Mr. ❏ Ms. _____

Address _____

City _____ State/Province _____ Zip/Postal Code _____

Phone _____ E-mail _____

Are you a member of RSES? ❏ Yes ❏ No Member No. _____ Chapter No. _____

## PROCTOR INFORMATION

Name ❏ Mr. ❏ Ms. _____

Phone _____ E-mail _____

Job title (or RSES Chapter/Regional position) _____

Are you a member of RSES? ❏ Yes ❏ No Member No. _____ Chapter No. _____

**Note:** *The address below is where the Examination(s) will be sent. No PO boxes, please!*

Address _____

City _____ State/Province _____ Zip/Postal Code _____

## PAYMENT OPTIONS

❏ Check or money order enclosed *(make payable to RSES in U.S. dollars)*

Credit card ❏ VISA ❏ MASTERCARD ❏ AMERICAN EXPRESS ❏ DISCOVER

Card No. _____ Expiration date _____

Authorized signature _____

1911 Rohlwing Road, Suite A   Rolling Meadows, IL 60008   800-297-5660   www.rses.org